THE STORY OF PERUGIA

BY

MARGARET SYMONS
& LINA DUFF GORDON

Copyright © 2013 Read Books Ltd.
This book is copyright and may not be
reproduced or copied in any way without
the express permission of the publisher in writing

British Library Cataloguing-in-Publication Data
A catalogue record for this book is available from the
British Library

Contents

Lady Duff Gordon 3

PREFACE 5

CHAPTER I
The earliest Origins of Perugia and growth of the City 11

CHAPTER II
The Condottieri and the Rise of the Nobles 50

CHAPTER III
The Baglioni. Paul III. and last years of the City 80

CHAPTER IV
The City of Perugia. 110

CHAPTER V
Palazzo Pubblico, The Fountain, and the Duomo. 138

CHAPTER VI
Fortress of Paul III.—S. Ercolano—S. Domenico—S. Pietro—S. Costanzo 181

CHAPTER VII
Piazza del Papa, S. Severo, Porta Sole, S. Agostino, and S. Francesco al Monte 213

CHAPTER VIII
Via dei Priori—Perugino's House,—Madonna della
Luce—S. Bernardino and S. Francesco al Prato. 239

CHAPTER IX
Pietro Perugino and the Cambio 257

CHAPTER X
The Pinacoteca 273

CHAPTER XI
The Museum, and Tomb of the Volumnii 312

CHAPTER XII
In Umbria 340

THE STORY OF PERUGIA

by

Margaret Symons
and Lina Duff Gordon
Illustrated by M. Helen James
1901

Perugino.

Lady Duff Gordon

Lucie, Lady Duff Gordon was born in 1821. She contracted tuberculosis at a young age, and at the age of twenty emigrated to South Africa, in the belief that the climate would aid her health. A decade later, she moved once more to Egypt, where she settled in Luxor, learning Arabic and immersing herself in the local culture. Gordon became famous for two works she penned while living abroad; *Letters from the Cape and Letters from Egypt* (1863-1865). Her letters home are celebrated for their humour, her outrage at the ruling Ottomans, and the many personal stories gleaned from the local people she met. Most were written to her husband and mother. Gordon died in 1869.

PREFACE

WHEN but a little while ago we undertook to write a "guide book" to one of the better known towns of Central Italy, we realised perhaps imperfectly how wide and full was the field of work which lay before us. The "story" of Perugia is, like the story of nearly all Italian towns, as full and varied as the story of a nation. Every side-light of history is cast upon it, and nearly every phase of man's policy and art reflected on its monuments. To do justice to so grand a pageant in a narrow space of time and binding was, we may fairly plead, no easy task; and now that the work is done, and the proofs returned to the printer, we are left with an inevitable regret; for it has been impossible for us to retain in shortened sentences and cramped description the charm of all the tales and chronicles which we ourselves found necessary reading for a full knowledge of so wide a subject.

If this small book have any claim to merit it is greatly due to the faithful and ungrudging help rendered to its authors throughout their study, by one true guide; by many old friends; and by the inhabitants of the town whose name it bears for title. We can never adequately express our sense of gratitude to the people of Perugia, to whom we came as utter strangers, but who received us with such great courtesy and kindness as to make our stay and study in their midst a pleasure as well as an education.

Our book is intended for the general traveller rather{viii} than for the student. We have offered no criticism, and have quoted whenever we could from the pages of contemporary chronicles. We have dealt with Perugia as with the heroine of a novel, describing her particular progress, and not confounding it with that of neighbour towns, equally important in their way, and each struggling, as perhaps only the cities of Italy knew how to struggle, towards an individual supremacy in a state lacerated by foreign wars and policies.

In dealing with one of the most vivid points in the history of the town—the Rule of the Nobles—we have, with some diffidence, incorporated into our narrative the words of one who had already drawn his description of the subject straight from the original source, treating it with such a powerful sympathy as it would have been impossible for us to rival. For further knowledge of this terrible period we can but refer the student to the chronicle of Matarazzo. (*Archivio Storico*, vol. xvi. part 2.)

With the art of Umbria we have dealt only shortly, and from the point of view of sentiment rather than that of criticism. For a severe and thorough knowledge of the technique and use of colours employed by the men who lived through such scenes as we have described in chapters II. and III. we must refer the reader to the works of other authors. For our dates, and facts in reference to art, we have relied on Kugler, Crowe and Cavalcaselle, Rio, Vasari and the local writers, Mariotti, Lupatelli, Mezzanotte, etc.

It remains to give a list of the books which we have consulted for the history. Amongst these are the Perugian chronicles contained in the *Archivio Storico d'Italia*; Graziani, Matarazzo, Frolliere, and Bontempi; Fabretti's chronicles of Perugia, and his "*Vita dei Condottieri, etc.*"; and the local histories of Ciatti, Pellini, Bartoli, Mariotti, and Bonazzi. Villani and Sismondi have been consulted; Creighton's "*History of the Papacy during the Reformation,*" and von Ranke's "*History of the Popes.*"

Of the purely local histories mentioned above Bonazzi's is the most important. His two bulky volumes are excellent reading in spite of his sarcastic and often unjust bitterness against the clerical party. A number of local pamphlets, the names of whose authors we cannot here enumerate, have been used for various details, together with other books on a variety of subjects, such as Dennis' "*Etruria,*" Broussole's "*Pélerinages Ombriens,*" Hodgkin's "*Italy and her Invaders,*" etc., etc.

When all is told, by far the most valuable and trustworthy authority on Perugian matters is Annibale Mariotti. A local gossip who combines with his gossiping qualities an exquisite sense of humour, and a real genius for investigation in matters relating to his native town, is the person of all others from whom to learn its actual life and history. Mariotti is an eminent specimen of this class of writers, and no one who is anxious to understand the spirit of Perugia should omit a careful study of his works on the *Popes*, the *People*, and the *Painters* of Perugia.

For personal help received we have the satisfaction of offering in this place our sincere thanks to Cav. Giuseppe Bellucci, professor at the University of Perugia, whose wise and kindly counsel has led us throughout to an understanding of countless points which must, without him, have remained unnoticed or obscure. Our notes on the museum are practically his own. We would mention also with grateful thanks Dr Marzio Romitelli, Arcidiacono of the cathedral of Perugia, who generously opened his library to us, and many of whose suggestions have been of service to us. To Count Vincenzo Ansidei, head of{x} the Perugian library, our sincere thanks are offered here.

We must further acknowledge the help of Signor Novelli of Perugia; of Mrs Ross, Mr Hayllar, and Cav. Bruschi, head of the Marucelliana Library at Florence. Lastly, of Mr Walter Leaf and Mr Sidney Colvin in the revision of proofs.

The comfort of our quarters in the Hotel Brufani needs no description to most Italian travellers, who are already familiar with that delightful house; but we are glad to mention here our appreciation of the care and thoughtful kindness shown to us by our English hostess in the Umbrian town. The courtesy received by us at headquarters from the Prefect of Umbria and Baroness Ferrari his wife, made our stay, from a purely social point of view, both easy and delightful.

To close these prefatory notes we can but say how sincerely we trust that the following pages may serve only as a preparation, in more capable hands, for further and far fuller records of a city whose history is as enthralling to the student of men as its pictures and position must ever be to the lover of what is beautiful in nature and in art.

August 21st, 1897.

Am Hof. Davos.

THE STORY OF PERUGIA

CHAPTER I

The earliest Origins of Perugia and growth of the City

SOMETIMES in a street or in a country road we meet an unknown person who seems to us wonderfully and inexplicably attractive. Perhaps we only catch a passing vision; the face, the figure passes us, oftener than not we never meet again, and even the memory of the vision which seemed so full of life, so strong, and so enduring, passes with the years, and we forget. But had we only tried a little, it would, in almost every instance, have been possible to follow the figure up, to learn what we wanted to know about it, to understand the reason why the face was full of meaning to us, and what it was which went before and gave the mouth its passion, the eyes their pain and sweetness. In nine cases out of ten we can, in this nineteenth century, discover the birth and parentage, the loves and hates, of any human being we may wish to know. But this is not the way with cities, and although they attract us in almost precisely the same fashion as people do, we cannot always trace their earliest origins. There are certain towns we come across in travel, of which we know very well that we want to know more. Perugia is one of these. It at once catches hold of one's imagination. No one can see it and forget it. A breath of the past is in it—of a past which we dimly feel to be prehistoric. Boldly we set to work to learn its history, and at first this seems an easy matter: the later centuries are a full and an enthralling study, for as long as men knew how to write they were certain to write about themselves, and the writers of Perugia had a wide dramatic field to work upon. But then come the records which are not written—which, in fact, are merely hearsay; and further even than hearsay is the period when we know that men existed, but which has no history at all beyond a few stone arrow heads, and bits of jade and flint. Yet, to be fair to a place of such extraordinary antiquity as this early city of the Etruscan league, one is unwilling to leave a single stone unturned, and in the following sketch we have gathered together, as closely as we could, the earliest facts about a city which attracts us, as those unknown people attract us whom we meet, admire, and lose again in the crowd.

"It seems," says Bonazzi, the most modern historian of Perugia, "that in the earlier periods of the world all this land of ours (Umbria) was covered by the sea, and that only the highest tops of the Apennines rose here and there, as islands might, above the waves. Then other hills arose, a new soil was disclosed, and great and horrid animals, whose teeth were sometimes metres long, came forth and trod the terrible waste places. In the silence of these squalid solitudes, no voice of man had yet been heard, and the stars went on their way unnoticed, across the firmament of heaven...."

But Bonazzi's science, though highly picturesque, was not entirely correct, and the following account, written by an inhabitant of Perugia who has studied the history of his town and neighbourhood with faithful precision and from the darkest periods of their existence, may well be inserted here.

"The city of Perugia," Prof. Bellucci writes, "is built upon a piece of land which was formed by a large delta of the primeval Tiber. In very early times (during the period known as pliocene) the Tiber, before running into the sea, formed in the central basin of Umbria an immense lake. The soil of which the actual plain of Umbria is now composed, and the numerous low hills which surround it, are made up either of river deposits such as sand and rubble left behind by the rush of waters, or else by clay deposits which slowly formed themselves in the quiet bosom of the lake. The date of these deposits is shown by the fossil remains which are found in them: elephants, rhinoceros, hippopotamus, stags, antelopes, hyenas, wild dogs, &c., all of which indicate a much warmer climate than that of the present day. In the period following on this, the great lake of Umbria began to empty itself; and as the soil washed gradually away, the waters forced a passage through the mountains below Todi, and from that time onward the Tiber gradually assumed its present course. The characteristic fauna of this second period distinguishes it from the first. Numerous remains found in the primitive gravel deposits of the Tiber prove the existence of man in our neighbourhood during both these periods (namely the paleolithic and neolithic). But the final drying up of the great lake basin or valley of Umbria was a very slow process, and even in Roman times the extent of these stagnant waters was so wide that the present town of Bastia on the road to Assisi was surrounded by them on every side and went by the name of *Insula Romana*. The final drainage of the lake was not completed till some time in 1400, when the river Chiagio burst through the rocky dykes under Torgiano and lowered the level of the water by four metres. Thus central Umbria at last assumed its present aspect. We stand upon the hill-top at Perugia where once thousands of years ago the turbid waters of the Tiber rushed along, and at our feet stretch the green and fertile fields of Umbria, all the fairer for the fertilising waters of that mighty lake which, in the dim and distant past, had covered them completely."

We have no definite date or name for those first men who came to live in this strange marshy wilderness. We have only the relics of their patient industry. An inexhaustible store of arrow-heads and other barbarous stone implements is found in all the hills around Perugia, and splendid hatchet heads of jade upon the shores of Trasimene. No doubt these men lived in holes and caves, perhaps at the foot of this hill where the present city of Perugia stands, or a little to the west of it, but their history is dark and very far away. Dark too and far away, as far as written facts remain, is the history of that almost more mysterious race of men which followed on the prehistoric one, namely, the Etruscans.

This is no place in which to discuss the origin of that extraordinary people whose language and parentage, though they lived and laboured side by side with the most cultivated and inquisitive of European nations, is practically dead to us. It is enough at this point of our history to note that the Etruscans were the first to seal their personality, with the seal of a visible and tangible intelligence, upon this corner of the world, and it is quite probable that they made one of their earliest colonies upon the jutting spur of a line of hills which would have attracted them upon arrival. It is certain that in course of time Perugia became one of the most powerful cities of the Etruscan league. Her museums are full of the pottery, tombs, inscriptions, toys, and coins of the mysterious nation (see Museum, chapter XI.).

Innumerable myths grew up around the foreign people, and individual historians described their advent in individual places and pretty much at random. The earliest chroniclers of Perugia, ignoring the men who had perhaps existed for centuries before this unknown nation landed,—ignoring too, the other settlers,—pounced upon a plum so precious and romantic to stick into the pie of legends that they were concocting; they peeled and stoned the plum to suit their fancy, and having done so, stuck it in with many others to swell the list of dubious tales in their long-winded manuscripts. As these chroniclers were nearly always monks, it was natural enough that they should form their shambling history on the one great history that they possessed, *i.e.*, the Bible. To them the Etruscans were easily and most satisfactorily explained: they descended from the first man, Adam, and they were the sons of Noah. Nay, the monks made an even happier hit, for they declared that Noah in person climbed the Apennines and pitched his tent upon the spur of hill where the present city stands! We can well imagine the old monk Ciatti, one of the earliest historians of Perugia, sitting before his wooden desk upon some dreamy night in May, his Bible propped before him, all Umbria asleep beneath the stars outside his window, and compiling the following entrancing legends concerning the Etruscans and their leader: "Serious writers hold *Janus* to be the same as *Noah*, who alone among men saw and knew all things during the space of six hundred years before the Deluge and three hundred years after the Deluge. The ancient medals which show the two faces of Janus are engraved with a ship, to denote that he was Noah, who, entering an ark in the form of a ship, was saved by divine decree from the universal Deluge."[1] Ciatti next goes on to give a delightful description of the arrival of Noah and his sons; "they penetrated," he says, "into Tuscany,[2] where, fascinated by the loveliness of the country, the agreeable qualities of the soil, the gentle air and the abundance of the earth, they determined to remain; but feeling uncertain where they should fix their dwelling, they were advised by certain augurs to build Perugia on the spot where it now stands." Some say that the name Perugia comes from the Greek word for "abundance." Certainly Ciatti was able to weave this fact into his legendary web: "Whilst, waiting for the Augurs," he writes, "two doves passed by them, flying to their nest, one carrying a branch loaded with olives and the other an ear of corn. Soon after there came a big wild boar carrying on his tusks a bunch of grapes. They took these signs to mean good omens, and they decided to build Perugia on the spot."

*VIA DEL AQUEDOTTO,
SHOWING TOWER OF THE CATHEDRAL*

Ciatti must have been an honest chronicler. Had we been given his early possibilities of making history in our own fashion, we must inevitably have told a credulous public that the ark itself rested upon the spurs of the Apennines and disgorged its contents on the hill where stands the present city of Perugia. But Ciatti withheld his hand from this, and we too must bare our heads before the fact of Ararat, and only hold to that of Noah, in his five-hundredth year or so, wandering unwearied forth to form a mighty nation on the coasts of Italy!

But before leaving Ciatti and his early myths, we must do him the justice to say that he was not utterly ignorant of a dim nation and of dimmer monsters living perhaps before the days of the Deluge. The old monk, like other wise historians, sets to work to hunt up the heraldry of his native city, and thus he explains the origin of the griffin on the city arms. The enthralling hunt described savours surely of something in an even earlier age?

"Now it so happened that, when the people of Perugia and of Narni were at the height of their prosperity, they became consumed by a very warlike spirit, and cultivated freely all military exercises, and on one occasion they challenged each other to a trial of prowess in a celebrated hunt. They agreed to meet in the mountains round about Perugia, which were then the haunt of fierce and terrifying wild beasts, and having come to that mountain which now takes its name from the event (Monte Griffone) they found there a griffin, which the Perugians captured and killed. After some dispute the monster was divided, the skin and claws being best worthy of preservation were taken by the Perugians, whilst the body fell to the people of Narni. In memory of this occurrence the Perugians took for their arms a white griffin—white being the natural colour of that animal—while the people of Narni took a red griffin, corresponding to the part which had fallen to their share, on a white field."[3]

But, to pass from the realms of myth to those of reality, it seems quite certain that the Etruscans—or Rasenae as they are sometimes called—spread themselves over a large part of Italy, building and fortifying their cities, making roads and laws and temples, and casting the light of an older art and civilisation upon the land to which they came as colonists. One of the chief of their cities was Perugia. Fragments of the old walls, built perhaps three thousand years ago, still stand in places, clean-cut, erect, and menacing, around the Umbrian city.

The lives of the Etruscans can only be studied through their art, and Perugia holds an ample store of this in her museums. There, in those rather dreary modern rooms, stone men and women smile upon their tombs, and the sides of these tombs bristle with long inscriptions written in an alphabet that we can partly read, but in a language that we cannot understand. Mirrors, and beautifully painted pots, children's toys and ladies' curling-tongs—the Etruscan dead have left no lack of records of their ways of living. But, strong as was their personality, another and a stronger force had struggled through the soil of Italy. Rome had arisen to shine upon the growing world. It remained for Rome to leave the stamp of veritable history upon the city of Perugia.

Throughout the early history of Rome, we catch dim rumours of an occasional connection or warfare with this corner of Etruria. It is not till 309 B.C. that we have any distinct mention of Perugia in connection with Rome. In that year the Roman Consul, Fabius, fought a battle with the Etruscans under the walls of the town. The Etruscans lost the day, Perugia and other cities of the League sued for a truce with Rome which was granted to them. Fabius entered Perugia "and this was the first time," says Bartoli, "that the banner of foreigners had waved across our city." Perugia bitterly resented the rule of the foreign power, and, breaking her truce, she made several passionate efforts to regain her freedom. But in vain. Her blood, perhaps, was old, and grown corrupt, the blood of Rome was new and palpitating. She was again and again overcome by Fabius. In 206 B.C. we find her, not exactly submitting to Rome, but playing the part of a strong ally, and cutting down her woods to help in the building of a fleet for Scipio. Her history continues dark—overshadowed by that of Rome. We hear a faint rumble of the Roman battles. We catch dull echoes of Hannibal and Trasimene, for Trasimene is very near Perugia. Did some of her citizens creep down perhaps, and get a vision of the fight? Did any of those much-bewigged Etruscan ladies, who we know were very independent in their ways, tuck up their skirts and follow through the woods to have a look at the elephants and shudder at the swarthy African?

We cannot tell. The next clear point in her history is a terrible one for Perugia. She fell, but she fell by a mighty hand, by that of the emperor Augustus. In the year 40 B.C. the Roman Consul, Lucius Antoninus, who, it may be said, was defending the liberty of Rome whilst Mark Antony lay lost in a love-dream upon the banks of Nile, took refuge within the walls of Perugia from the pursuit of Octavius (Augustus) who then laid siege to the town. For seven months the brave little city held out, but she was reduced to such a terrible distress of famine that Lucius at last gave way, and opened her gates to the conqueror. Octavius entered Perugia covered with laurels. The citizens prayed for mercy. He spared most of the men and women, but he excepted three hundred of the elders and saw them singly killed before his eyes. When they prayed for grace he merely tossed his head back and repeated: "They must die." This ordeal over, Octavius decided to postpone the sack of the city until the following day. But one of its citizens, Caius Cestius Macedonicus, hot with all the shame of the thing, got up at night and made a funeral pyre of his house. He set fire to its walls, and as it burned he stabbed himself and died there. The flames spread through the city, and before the morning Perugia was burned to the ground. Nothing remained of all its buildings except the temple of Vulcan, and in memory of this fire the town was afterwards dedicated to Vulcan instead of to Juno to whom it had formerly belonged. Octavius returned to Rome bearing before him the image of Juno, which alone had been saved from the flames. Some years later he agreed to rebuild the city, and hence the letters *Augusta Perusia* over her gates.

* * * * * * *

So laying aside for ever *Perusia Etrusca*, that city of strange beasts, strange people, and strange myths, we face *Perusia Augusta*, or the Perugia of Rome.

For some centuries, strange as it may appear, the powerful old Umbrian hill-town seems to have fallen contentedly asleep under the rule of her great protector. It was, as we know, the policy of Rome to adopt the laws and customs of the people whom she conquered rather than to change them, and indeed the alteration seldom went further than in name. The Etruscan rulers therefore took the titles of Roman governors, they did not really alter, and it is probable that the laws of the very earliest settlement have never really become extinct. The *Lucumo* of the Etruscans was in all probability the descendant of the earliest prehistoric village chief, who developed into the *Diumvir* or representative of the Roman Consul pretty much as the present *Sindaco* succeeded to the position of the *Podestà* of the middle ages.

Rome had always loved and studied the religions of the older people, and Bonazzi infers that Rome "delighted in nursing on the breast of her republic those great masters of Divinity who could be made such powerful political instruments for her service." The Romans must have intermarried freely with the Etruscans; the mixture of names and lettering upon their tombs points to this fact. But the strong fresh blood of the younger race seems to have overcome that of the more corrupt one. Other tribes and other tongues pressed in upon the first inhabitants and gradually the language, yes, and the memory of the strange and fascinating people, died.

Of the Roman occupation little trace can be found in the architecture of the city, beyond the walls and gates and the inscriptions over some of these, together with a sorry fragment of a Roman bath. It must be remembered that the entire city was burned to the ground after the siege—burned with all her wealth of monuments and temples—and it does not seem as though the Romans did much to beautify her with grand buildings. Having no old buildings to use as raw material, they were probably content at this period to build strong walls and houses suitable for a fortified town, thus fostering the warlike character of her inhabitants which was to prove so great a point in following centuries.[4]

Roman rule was a very real piece of history, but it is not possible to say that the period of myth and darkness had wholly passed away. We possess a certain knowledge of the Roman government, but the shadow of the Gothic and Barbarian night closes in upon it like a heavy pall; and the next clear and startling point about Perugia is her recapture by Belisarius followed by the siege of Totila (or Baduila).

During those terrible centuries when Italy was being ravaged by perpetual invasions, her lands devastated by war and plagues and famine, and her cities, as one historian says, "no longer cities, but rather the corpses of cities," we find scant mention of actual harm done to Perugia, for it was the north which suffered first. However, as the Goths pressed southward upon Rome, as Rome herself wavered and sank beneath the weight of the northern hordes, and of her own corruption, we gather that the Umbrian cities too became a prey to the barbarians, and that Perugia suffered the fate of all her neighbours. Her historians seek in vain for stated records of this time where all is darkness, but some dim facts shine out, among them the steady growth of Christianity within the city.

The first important date we find follows nearly six hundred years after her capture by Augustus. It was in 536 A.D., that Justinian, who had conceived the mighty plan of recovering Africa from the Vandals and Italy from the Goths, sent one of his best generals, Constantine (under Belisarius), into Umbria to occupy the cities there. Constantine made Perugia his headquarters and for a while his possession of the town seems not to have been disputed by the Goths. Witigis left her on one side as he passed with his armies down to Rome, and it remained for the indomitable Totila to wrest her (in 545) from the power of the Byzantine Empire. Totila is a most prominent figure in the history of the city, and many are the myths which centre round him. He first attacked Assisi, and having conquered her, he turned his greedy gaze upon the fair hill city opposite and instantly desired to possess her also. But realising the strength of her position, which was largely increased by the occupation of a Byzantine general, he determined to get her by foul means rather than fair, and so he bribed one of her citizens to murder Cyprian, who was then the general in command. The citizens rose in eager revolt against this treachery, and Totila soon found that he had undertaken no light thing when he came to besiege the town. Indeed tradition says that the said siege lasted seven years, and however much this may have been exaggerated, it is certain that it was made a hard one for the Goth. Perugia was taken by storm, but after fearful fighting; she fell, but she was upheld to the last by a new power, namely that of her faith. The story of S. Ercolano, the faithful Bishop of the Perugians, is told in another place. It has been admirably illustrated by Bonfigli, it has been described and hallowed in a hundred ways throughout the city's chronicles, and it is vain for modern historians to tell us, as they are inclined to do, that Totila never set foot in Perugia. Bonfigli's fresco is terribly convincing in itself, as are also the naïve and delightful records of Ciatti and Pellini. Among the people of the town Totila has become one of its most important facts, and they declare that his wife lies buried close to the Ponte Felcino together with her husband's hidden treasure.

LOMBARD ARCH ON THE CHURCH OF S. AGATA

Gothic rule was short. Infinite and hurried changes follow on this period. We next hear of the city in the hands of the Lombards. The Lombard occupation is almost as dark as the Gothic.[5] In 592, Perugia became a Lombard Duchy ruled by the Duke Mauritius, who turned traitor to his trust and delivered the city to the Exarch of Ravenna. The news of the Duke's treachery spread northward. Agilulf, King of the Lombards, came hastening down to recapture the city with a mighty army, and he made Mauritius pay for his treachery with his head. This was in 593. A few years later Perugia was restored to the Empire, but at the beginning of 700, she, like many other cities of Italy, attempted to shake herself free from Byzantine rule. It is probable that she did not really succeed in doing so, but this point is at any rate a great crisis in her history, for it is the first time that we find her at all tangibly connected with the Head of the Christian world—with that power of the Church which was to prove, throughout her future, alternately her safeguard and her scourge.

It was about 727 that Leo the Isaurian, Emperor of the East, terrified by certain evils in his kingdom which he took to be signs of Divine anger, made his famous decree against the worship of images. This proved of course a most unpopular edict in Italy, and the reigning Pope opposed it by every means in his power. Many of the most powerful cities joined him, amongst them Perugia, and Greek rule in Italy, already on the wane, was greatly weakened, but we do not hear of any settled breach with the Empire for many years to come. Perugia was, as we shall see, merely advancing towards her own liberation, but the acquired protection of the Popes proved useful to her in her next great crisis.

In 749 Ratchis, King of the Lombards, laid siege to the city, and her fall seemed inevitable. Then, in the moment of her great need, with the Lombard army beating in her very doors, the reigning Pope, S. Zacharias the Greek, accompanied by all his clergy, and by many of the Roman nobles, arrived at her gates, and in words of extraordinary sweetness pleaded her cause with Ratchis. We do not hear what phrases the old man may have used to check a man on the verge of a great victory. We only hear that the Lombard king knelt down and kissed the feet of the Pope. "Thou hast conquered me," he said, very simply, and then he withdrew from the battle, and S. Zacharias passed into the city, and was received with universal joy by her citizens. And not only did Ratchis abandon the siege of a town which he so greatly coveted, but, his whole soul being moved by this new power, he renounced his kingdom and his crown and retired to the monastery Monte Cassino, where he became a monk, living there until he died.

Thus closes another chapter of Perugian history. Within a space of three hundred years, roughly speaking, she had changed the nationality of her rulers four successive times, whilst she herself may be said never to have changed. Her internal history, her internal government, had all along continued pretty much on the first lines. Her entire future policy proves this. In all the small wars which follow, and which lead to her final supremacy over every other city in Umbria—cities which at the outset had been as strong as herself, and even stronger, we trace this masterful and incontestable personality—the personality of the griffin which the old Etruscan settlers captured thousands of years before upon the hill-tops and chose for their city arms.

* * * * * * *

In all the intense complication of the times which follow it is almost impossible to unravel the exact position of individual towns. At one moment we find Perugia belonging apparently to the Duchy of Spoleto, at another joined to the Tuscan League, at another putting herself under the protection of the Pope, whilst all the time nominally belonging to the Empire. Bonazzi remarks that one result of the perpetual conflict between Emperor and Pope was the liberty left to the citizens; in another place he says that in the scant documents which contain her early history, "Perugia is always mentioned alone, always managing her own affairs." The said management dated back in all probability to that of the very earliest settlement, which was mainly agricultural, and managed by chiefs or a Village Council. As the town grew, so likewise did the numbers of its rulers. In Perugia, as in other places, the original Village Council, which was first held in the public square, was abandoned as politics grew complicated. The Consuls, ten in number, two to each Porta or gate, met in council on the steps of the first Cathedral. The finest architectural building in Perugia is notably the Palazzo Pubblico, but long before the construction of this palace there was another building which served the same purpose close to the Duomo in which the different protectors of the city met. We do not propose to trace the form of government here. Suffice it to say that, in Perugia as elsewhere, we find the usual titles of *Consuli* and *Podestà*, then of the Heads of City Guilds, the *Priori* (a very strong power in Perugia), *Capitano del Popolo* and *Capitano della Parte Guelfa*; all of whom recur again and again in her chronicles, playing important parts as peace-makers or as arbitrators in her turmoils and dissensions.

The historians of Perugia, naturally enough perhaps, tend to speak of her as of an independent Republic, but this she never was. She had her own rulers, she grew powerful and individual, she finally became a great capital, but she was never a free state like Florence or Rome. Something in her extraordinary position, something in the character of her people, warlike and tenacious from the first, proved her final force. Great wandering hordes and armies thought twice before they attacked her walls. Thus she enjoyed long periods of ease, and in her stormy breast she nurtured the ferocious families which were to prove her strength, but equally her bane in later years.

Being utterly cut off from mercantile expansion or commerce of an ordinary sort, she used her concentrated force in subduing neighbouring towns, and thus extending her dominion over Umbria. Her power soon became recognised, and many little towns and hamlets sent envoys to present acts of submission to the growing power. When these were given freely she received them graciously, and when withheld she sometimes showed a power of rapacity and cruelty which is well nigh inconceivable.

Her history is full of wars against Siena, Gubbio, Arezzo, Città di Castello, Todi, Foligno, Spoleto and Assisi, all chronicled at great length by her proud historians. We have collected a few scattered facts relating to these, which cast some light upon the character of the Perugians, who, as their power strengthened, began to show, not only a tyrannous disposition, but an occasional spark of the grimmest humour. Leaving aside other events, such as the encroaching power of the Pope, we may now glance at some of these.

The first act of voluntary submission came from the island of Polvese in 1130, and was received with great solemnity in the Piazza di San Lorenzo and in the presence of all the inhabitants of the city. A little later more than nine hundred of the people of Castiglione del Lago came to place their land on the shores of Trasimene under the protection of Perugia. Città di Castello and Gubbio followed suit, and many of the smaller towns and hamlets. But, if submission was sweet, blows, one surmises, were well nigh sweeter to the fierce and savage owners of Perugia, and horrid were the skirmishes—one can scarcely call them battles—which ensued from time to time when towns resisted or rebelled against them.

Assisi and Perugia were ever an eyesore to one another, and their inhabitants scoured the plain between them like packs of wolves. In one of these savage little contests tradition tells us that a certain Giovanni di Bernadone, a youth of only twenty summers, was taken prisoner by the Perugians and kept a year in the Campo di Battaglia. The Palace of the Capitano del Popolo in the Piazza Sopramuro now covers the place where the youth was chained, and we may look on it with veneration, for he was no other than that sweetest soul of mediæval history, St Francis of Assisi.

When Città della Pieve dared to rebel, the action of Perugia was prompt and effective. "Most gladly did the youth of Perugia—hot with the dignity of their city, and by no means disposed to forgive those who despised or disobeyed her—assemble in arms," says Bartoli. The army thus assembled was instantly sent to the recalcitrant city, but the

Pievese had scarcely caught sight of it hurrying towards their gates, than they sent their *Procuratore*, Peppone d'Alvato, to sue for peace and beg forgiveness for their misdeeds. This was kindly granted, but Peppone, accompanied by some hundred and thirty Pievese, was forced to come to Ripa di Grotto and there listen to the reproaches of the *Podestà* of Perugia, whilst the Bishops of Perugia and of Chiusi, the Provost of S. Mustiola, and the *Arciprete* of Perugia, sitting on high chairs, surrounded by various grandees, were in readiness to enjoy the spectacle. All were dressed in their finest, but we are told that the *Arciprete* of Corciano threw all his neighbours entirely into the shade by the splendour and the brilliancy of his many-coloured garments.[6] Peppone kneeling at the Bishop's feet with his hand on the gospels, swore faith and loyalty to the Perugians, and we hear that the Pievese returned home "rejoicing" at the pardon obtained in this most humiliating fashion. This last fact we may take the liberty to doubt, but it is certain that the Perugians enjoyed the whole episode immensely, neither did they consider the humiliation of their enemies complete. A further punishment had yet to be thought of, and at last a brilliant plan was resolved on. The Piazza of San Lorenzo needed paving, and the Pievese were told that they must provide all the necessary bricks for this purpose, and this "puerile waspishness," as Bonazzi describes it, so delighted the hearts of the Perugians that, as we learn, not even the death of the great foe of the Guelph cause, Frederick II., "was able to give them a keener sense of joy."

Perugia and Foligno had always regarded each other with undisguised dislike, skirmishing about and exchanging insults wherever they happened to meet. Once the people of Foligno had come bare-footed, and with a sword and knife hung round their necks, to implore pardon of Perugia, but they revolted again, and the Perugians continued to attack and to molest them. Three times in a single year (1282) their lands were devastated, and finally the town was taken, and the walls demolished, and imperative orders were issued absolutely forbidding these to be rebuilt on the western side. At last Pope Martin IV., amazed and disgusted by the behaviour of a people to whom he was honestly attached, interfered, but Perugia continued to molest her unhappy neighbour with a quite peculiar animosity, whereupon the Pope, angered beyond measure by their disobedience, excommunicated them. "Into such a passion did the Pope fall with the people of Perugia," says Mariotti, "that he issued a most severe excommunication against them." It was just at the time of the Sicilian Vespers. The Perugians, irritated by their sentence of excommunication, determined to celebrate a kind of mock vespers on their own account. Gregorovius says that this is the first instance recorded in history of this strange form of popular demonstration. "They made a Pope and Cardinals of straw, and dragged them ignominiously through the city and up to a hill, where they burned the effigies in crimson robes, saying, as the flames leapt up, "That is such-and-such, a Cardinal; and this is such-and-such, another."

A strange scene, truly, in a half-civilised city! But political and religious causes came between and put an end to these half childish squabbles. A little later the Pope forgave the Perugians, and they continued their evil ways, and persisted in destroying the peace of the Umbrian towns.

Arezzo had the satisfaction of a victory over Perugia in 1335, and in defiance and derision she hanged her Perugian prisoners with a tabby cat hung beside them, and a string of *lasche* dangling from their braces.[7] But pranks like these were not allowed to pass unnoticed, and Perugia did not fail to grasp her finest banner with the lion of the Guelph all rampant on a field of gules, and hurry out to subdue her insolent neighbours. The people of Arezzo were humbled to the dust, but by means too barbaric to be here described.

Thus one by one the cities of Umbria became sufficiently impressed by this forcible fashion of dealing with insurrection, and they recognised that it would be wise, though it might not be pleasant, to swear allegiance to the imperious city. Gualdo next gave up her keys, together with Nocera, but the latter found it impossible to suppress a few oaths whilst signing the documents, and there was a loud wail over the laws imposed upon them.

" ... e diretro le piange
Per grave giogo Nocera con Gualdo,"

says Dante, referring to the subject in the "Paradiso."

Perugia's culminating success seems to have been at Torrita in 1358, when the Sienese were defeated, and forty-nine banners brought back tied to the horses' tails, and the chains of the Palace of Justice torn away and hung in triumph at the feet of the Perugian griffin. Even the powerful Florence accepted Perugia's help in the Guelph cause, and so early as 1230 arbitrations had been exchanged for the purpose of settling all questions of commerce between the two cities.[8]

All these victories, these repeated successes, tended to increase Perugia's independence of spirit, and she was very careful that no one, not even the Pope, should infringe on her rights, or dispute her authority. Her attitude towards the Church is somewhat difficult to understand. It seems to have mystified Clement IV., for he expresses his "dolorous wonder" that the Perugians, who were such devoted allies of the Holy See, could sometimes behave so wickedly towards the clergy. And, curiously enough, the Perugians, lovers of processions, of patron-saints, miracles, and all the rest, could, and did, make laws to exclude all ecclesiastics from having anything to do with their charitable institutions or donations to Churches.[9]

PALAZZO BALDESCHI

We find them protesting both with menaces and oaths against any usurpation of the clergy, "In the names of Christ, the Virgin, S. Ercolano, and S. Costanzo." Even the Pope was taught a lesson, for when John XXI. in 1277 asked for some *lasche* from the Lake of Trasimene, the Perugians called a general council in which it was resolved that the said *lasche* should be sent to His Holiness, but accompanied by the syndicate in order to show the Pope that the fish was the property of the city, and a gift from its citizens merely *given* to him for his Good Friday dinner!

These somewhat petty hostilities did not, however, materially affect the relations between the Papacy and the citizens of Perugia, and all through the twelfth and thirteenth centuries they remained on very friendly terms with one another.

We have thought it best to give a general sketch of the growth of the city, its customs and its wars, before touching on one of the chief characteristics of its history, namely, its close connection with the Papacy. It will, therefore, be necessary to glance back over some centuries, in order to follow the steps by which the power of the Popes arose in Perugia.

At first Papal authority was purely nominal. To the small towns of Italy, living each their concentrated and oftentimes tempestuous lives apart, the great Emperors who passed down to Rome in search of crowns from the hands of Popes, must have appeared as ghosts, their documents as unsubstantial as themselves. The fact that one of these, Pepin, conceded large grants of land in Umbria, including Perugia, to a Pope who never came to look at them, must have seemed to the

Perugians as little beyond a phantom transaction after all. We next hear of Charlemagne in 800 confirming an act by which Perugia, together with a number of other towns and territories, was placed under the *alto dominio* of the Holy See. In 962, Otto I. again confirmed the donation, but the iron hand of Papal power was not felt for many centuries in the rising town; and indeed, however deep the designs of the Church may have been from the very beginning, they were well concealed, and the first Popes who visited Perugia did so in the fashion of people starting on a summer excursion, and not at all in the character of conquerors. They would come to the city with all their suite of Cardinals and favourites, and take up their abode in the cool and spacious rooms of the Canonica, which, as Bonazzi with imperial pride declares, "became the Vatican of Perugia."

Yet it is certain that the policy of the Holy See was deep, and that the growing capital of Umbria appeared no plaything in its eyes. The geographical position of the city—perched as it is on a hill which commands the Tiber and overlooks the two great highways from the Eternal City to the North and to the Eastern Sea—made it a most desirable possession for the Popes, and it was inevitable that Perugia should, sooner or later, submit to, or come into direct conflict with, the power of Papal rule. The open acknowledgment of such a situation was merely a question of time.

Innocent III., who has been called the founder of the States of the Church, was the first Pope who came into direct personal contact with the Perugians. He accepted from them an offer to be their *Padrone*, and to exercise temporal power among them. Half playfully, though with what deep and powerful designs we may divine, he called the citizens his "vassals," and to a certain extent they were willing to submit to his authority; but in so doing they were careful to wring from their "*Padrone*" a promise that their rights and privileges should be respected. Thus for the time they steered clear of the danger of subjection, continued to govern themselves, and preserved that free and independent spirit which hitherto, and in spite of every obstacle, had marked them as a race. Innocent was beloved by the citizens. He came amongst them at a time of much civil discord, when the nobles and the people were preparing for open strife. "He was a peace-maker," says Bartoli, "and he kept his eye on all things; and on this city he looked with a peculiar partiality." The Pope was anxious to promote the Crusades, and was on his way to Pisa to try to make a peace between the Genoese and the Venetians, whose quarrels interfered with his schemes, when he fell ill at Perugia, and died there in 1216.[10]

No sooner had he breathed his last than all his Cardinals hurried into the Canonica to elect his successor, and such was the impatience of the citizens that they even set a guard over these princes of the Church, and kept them short of food in order to hurry their decision. We are not therefore surprised to read that the Papal Throne remained vacant for the space of one day only, and that in consequence of this event the Perugians claim the privilege of having invented the Conclave.

Honorius III. succeeded Innocent, and he attempted, but without success, to heal the ever-widening breach between the nobles and the people. We have described something of the wars outside, but Perugia herself within her walls was a veritable wasp's nest during this period of her steady rise. Her inhabitants became more restless and unmanageable every year. In their perpetual broils the nobles fought beneath their emblem of the Falcon, and the *popolo minuto* (common folk), who sided with them, received the unamiable title of *Beccherini*.[11] The two extremes in the social scale joined hands in a perpetual opposition to the *popolo grasso* (well-to-do burghers), who were called *Raspanti* (*raspare*, to claw), a name probably suggested by their emblem of the Cat.

Honorius in his plan of dealing with the complicated situation can scarcely be described as disinterested; whilst apparently patching up peace, he really attempted to force an acknowledgment of papal power. His policy however, was fruitless, and the nobles resorted to the usual expedient of retiring to their country castles, for, as Bonazzi says, they "preferred to tyrannise alone in the silence of their isolated strongholds rather than to divide their forces in the capital of a powerful federation." But the situation threatened to become intolerable, and we read that through the years from 1223 to 1228 a "perfect pandemonium reigned in and about the city." Cardinal Colonna was sent to try and restore the balance between the rival factions, but, finally, Gregory IX. was forced to come in person, and through his influence the banished nobles were recalled from exile, and a certain degree of peace restored.

Gregory paid many visits to Perugia, much to the annoyance of the Romans, who expressed their wonder that the little hill-town with nothing but its brown walls, towers, and landscape to recommend it, should be preferred by him to the plains and palaces of the Eternal City. This fact is recorded about the year 1228, when Gregory IX. was making an unusually long stay in his excellent and quiet quarters in the Canonica (at S. Lorenzo). The Romans were well aware, Bartoli says, that it was because of their ill-behaviour that he had retired into private life far away in the Umbrian city, and they even accepted as a judgment on their evil ways a certain most horrible inundation of the Tiber which befell them at that period. Deputies hurried across the land from Rome with supplications to the Pope to return to his people, and Gregory went, but he quickly returned to Perugia. The fame of S. Francis of Assisi was then at its height. Gregory felt inquisitive, but not altogether certain of the truth of the tales which were spread abroad concerning this wonderful man. He made numerous enquiries and sent his Cardinals to Assisi to gather all the information they were able to collect about the Saint. But the final manner of the doubting Pope's conversion is described with such marvellous and touching piety in the "Fioretti" that we have inserted it at length in our description of the place where it occurred.[12] In the same year and place Gregory canonized S. Francis, "to the splendour of religion," says one historian. He also canonized S. Dominic and Queen Elizabeth of Hungary, he sent missions into the land of the unfaithful, and gave indulgences of a year and forty days to all who would give money to the building of S. Domenico. So we may fairly say that he did not waste his time, but that he managed to get through a large amount of business during the time that he spent in Perugia.

* * * * * * *

It is difficult to define the exact mutual relations of Pope and city in any corner of Italy, but it is certain that Perugia found Papal power useful to her in many ways, and that on whatever side she happened to have a quarrel on hand, she always turned to the Papal See for help and arbitration. In spirit she was always Guelph, fighting under the emblem of the Guelph lion, and full of Guelph interests. Yet, although openly exercising self-government, almost in the manner of a free republic, under the protection and nominal rule of the popes, she was at the same time patronised by the emperors. In 1355 we read that her ancient privileges were confirmed and new ones granted by the Emperor Charles IV., who seems to have considered it worth his while to gain the friendship of her citizens.

Up to this period we have only had to deal with pleasant passing visits of the popes who sojourned in the city for a while. The time came, however, when the noose which Innocent had so lightly cast about their necks began to pull and tighten. The Perugians revolted hotly against the Popes of Avignon, who, incensed at their rebellion, attempted to check it by every means in their power. To understand the painful struggles which follow, it is necessary to remember that the end of the fourteenth and the whole of the fifteenth centuries were the most prosperous period in Perugia's history. She had grown steadily and uninterruptedly both in power and riches, and in spite of terrible obstacles, ever since the day when the Romans rebuilt her walls more than fifteen hundred years before. In these two centuries she erected her public buildings, extended and settled her government, coined money, started her university, settled with her habitual promptitude all suspicion of rebellion, became one of the *Tre Communi* of Florence, Siena and Perugia, and whilst achieving all these things she continued to foster the passionate feuds and hopeless enmities between the different factions which we have described above. Having grown strong and prosperous it was natural that she should resent any open attempt of a foreign power to subject her, and such an attempt came in the middle of the fourteenth century from the Papal See.

In 1367 the Spanish Cardinal Albornoz was busily employed in recovering the States of the Church. Perugia was at that time faithful to the Pope, and she received the Cardinal with due honours and gave him valuable help, especially in an expedition against Galeotto Malatesta of Rimini. Her goodwill however was of short duration, for the citizens saw themselves despoiled of Città di Castello and of Assisi during the Cardinal's campaigns, and this they would not brook. They therefore sent a strong army at once towards Viterbo, but it was beaten back with heavy loss, and Urban V.'s authority was again firmly rooted at Perugia. He sent his brother, Cardinal Angelico, Bishop of Albano, as Vicar General to represent him in the city. Thus the authority of the popes crept in upon the town, and authority of some kind became every year more necessary as the voice of the people grew and strengthened and as the exiled nobles quarrelled outside the walls. Papal authority was finally represented in 1375 by an imperious French abbot, known in Perugian annals as Mommaggiore, whose doings and buildings have been described in another place. The yoke that Mommaggiore—"that French Vandal, that most iniquitous Nero," as the chroniclers call him,—put upon the neck of Perugia, proved unbearable to every party, and all the different factions for once joined together to break it. Florence and other cities, castles, and fortresses which had "unfurled the banner of liberty," joined in the revolt, and in 1375 the abbot was driven in a very undignified fashion from the city. A republic was then declared and the whole town rejoiced at having broken away from the thraldom of the Popes of Avignon. In vain did Gregory XI. call the people of Perugia "sons of iniquity"; in vain did he hurl the most terrible excommunications against them;[13] the feud between the city and the Pope was only laid to rest when the latter died. It had lasted long, and had produced something worse even than the struggle of two strong powers, for it had served to increase the terrible civil discord within the town. With the accession of Urban VI. a treaty was concluded, and Perugia acknowledged his right of dominion. In 1387 Urban arrived in the city, and as he entered the gates a white dove rested on his hat and refused to be removed by the servants who ran forward to deliver His Holiness from the unexpected visitor. It answered the Pope's touch however, and was handed to his chaplain, and everyone accepted the event as an excellent omen. We will not linger to judge of its excellence, we can only say that the bird heralded an entirely new chapter in the history of the town, which hitherto had developed under general influences and many different hands. Her coming history is that of single influences, of personalities, or, in other words, of despots. The time had come when Perugia was to show the fruit of her stern ambitious character in the individual men whom she had reared. The names of Michelotti, Braccio Fortebraccio, Piccinino and of the noble families of Oddi and of Baglioni are familiar to all who have merely turned the pages of her history. Perugia, like other towns of Italy, had at the end of the fourteenth century reached a point of internal strife from which strong personalities could easily rise up to dispute or to control the existing government. Why it was exactly that the Popes did not from the first forcibly interfere with the turbulent doings of these men, it is difficult to tell. They were constantly coming to the city, constantly appealed to by the citizens and nobles, for ever interfering both by menaces and arms, but it was not till more than a century of blood and tyranny had passed, not till the glory of the town was already on the wane, that the power of the Church came down to crush Perugia like a sledge-hammer.

Strangely enough it was a Pope who first gave the city away into the hands of a private person or Protector.

ARMS OF PERUGIA

CHAPTER II

The Condottieri and the Rise of the Nobles

"The confusion, exhaustion, and demoralisation engendered by these conflicts determined the advent of Despots.... The Despot delivered the industrial classes from the tyranny and anarchy of faction, substituting a reign of personal terrorism that weighed more heavily upon the nobles than upon the artizans and peasants.... He accumulated in his despotic individuality the privileges previously acquired by centuries of consuls, *podestàs*, and captains of the people."— See "Age of the Despots," J. A. Symonds.

DEEP gloom closed in upon Perugia towards the end of the fourteenth century. The breach between the nobles and the people continued to widen. Sometimes one party was driven out of the city, sometimes another. Now and again both parties were recalled, and a compact of peace arranged by an arbitrary person from outside. But this last arrangement produced an even more terrible state of affairs, and crime and bloodshed were the inevitable result. We read of deaths by hundreds and not tens—cruel and indescribable deaths, which make one shudder—and already in the thick of the strife the names of Oddi and of Baglioni are stamped upon the records.

One of the strangest points in the history of the city at this time was the fashion in which these feuds between the rival factions were met by them. Whichever party was weakest retired for the time to the country, leaving the city to their rival till time should favour their own cause.[14]

Bonazzi gives an almost extravagant account of the boorish manner of the exiled nobles' lives. Down in the open country they hunted the abundant wild boar and devoured his flesh when they came home at night. They slept in dark and cavernous halls, and were out at dawn across the fields and forests, killing, hunting, fighting, according to the order of the day. Yet, although they were banished from the walls of their native town, they continued to molest and to disturb the citizens, and whenever the opportunity occurred, in they came again, sometimes openly, sometimes after the manner of thieves. We read of their entering the city at night across the roofs, robbing the cellars and granaries, and murdering such citizens as ventured to interfere.

Sometimes the order was reversed: the nobles got possession of the town, and the people were forced into the country. The terrible unrest of such a state of things may easily be imagined, and, added to these great evils, or, probably, produced by them, came the devastating plagues which ravaged the cities of Italy at the end of the fourteenth century, and the almost equal scourge of mercenary soldiers and private bands of foreign adventurers, who roamed through the rich, ill-governed towns and villages fighting for one family or another, or else engaged in pillaging upon their own account.[15]

In all these quarrels, in all this turmoil and confusion, whichever party happened to be uppermost, the person to appeal to was the Pope, and endless were the messages sent down from Rome. At last, in 1392, both sides seemed to have wearied for the moment of the incessant strife (the nobles at this time were masters of the city, the *Raspanti* were away in exile), and when the Pope, Boniface IX., appeared in person, he was received with enthusiasm. We hear that the *Priori* and the treasurers of the city robed themselves in beautiful new scarlet mantles, the "companies" of the different gates danced through the streets with unmitigated joy, and the people went forth in crowds to meet him. But the breach between the factions was too wide, the situation too complicated for a Pope, who arrived merely in the character of a peacemaker, to grapple with successfully. The presence of Boniface brought no peace, and he retired into the monastery of S. Pietro, which he hastily converted into a fortress, demolishing its tower in his eagerness to secure his own personal safety; and there, as he nervously wondered what next he had better do, he heard the cries of "Down with the *Raspanti*!" answered by "Death to the nobles!" borne in upon the breeze.

Finally, in a manner peculiar to the Perugians, they met together in council to dictate the action of the person they had called in to act for them, and it was settled that the Pope should have full power as arbitrator of peace between themselves and the *Raspanti*. The Pope did exactly as he was asked. He recalled the *Raspanti*, and they entered the city on the 17th October 1393, not merely as a body, but headed by a powerful personality—Biordo Michelotti, one of Perugia's greatest citizens, and the first of the *condottieri* who ever got rule in the city.

Exiled in early youth from his native town, Biordo Michelotti had chosen the career of a *condottiere*, and roamed through the length and breadth of Italy, fighting the battles of different princes. Some say he had fought for the French king against the English. He was essentially a captain of adventure. His manner was kindly, he was brave, honest, frank, and popular among the people wherever he happened to go. Beloved all over Umbria, many of the towns which directly opposed Perugia's tyrannical rule had submitted to that of Biordo. All these successes did not, however, satisfy the man in him, for the ruling ambition of his life was to get the dominion over his native city, and events were now combining to procure for him his heart's desire. The *Raspanti* rallied round him in their exile, and he became their leader, and the champion of their liberty. The nobles, seeing the power of his popularity, offered him bribes to keep out of their way. But Biordo lay low in his fortress at Deruta, and when the Pope's offers of peace arrived he hailed them with delight. A month later he entered Perugia at the head of about 2000 *Raspanti*, who had been exiled from their homes for years. They at once visited the Pope in token of homage and gratitude, and their new lease of power within the city was opened by the re-election of the priors, who were chosen half from the burgher faction and half from the nobility. By this means it was hoped that a lasting reconciliation might be made and an evenly balanced government established. Yet such seemed impossible. Peace endured for the space of one short month, and at the very first opportunity—on the occasion of Biordo's absence from the city—the smouldering fires of party feuds burst out in flames as rampant as before. One of the *Raspanti* was murdered by the nobles, and, just as the *Podestà* was preparing to pass sentence on the assassin, Pandolfo dei Baglioni, "that Perugian Satan," as Bonazzi calls him, interfered on behalf of the criminal.[16] Whereupon the *Raspanti* vowed vengeance, assassinated Pandolfo and Pellini Baglioni on their own threshold, and murdered sixty of their clan. The Ranieri, another noble family, with their friends, took refuge in the strong Ranieri tower, where they were forced to go without food for three days. At last the people dragged them before the *Podestà*, but as he refused to execute them, the unhappy noblemen were conveyed back to their tower, where they were finally butchered, and their bodies thrown out of the windows.

Horrified by these fresh atrocities, and again in search of peace, the Pope loaded his mules and retired with his Cardinals to Assisi. The tumults were just subsiding when Biordo Michelotti returned, and this time he took absolute possession of the city. He met with no sort of opposition. The ring-leader of the nobles, Pandolfo Baglioni, was dead, and the Pope for the minute encouraged the attempt towards peace. Biordo used his power well, and every year his fame and honours increased. To the delight of the Perugians, he succeeded to the command of Sir John Hawkwood over the Florentine forces, and everywhere he pushed the interests of the town, wisely concluding a treaty with Gian Galeazzo Visconti, the powerful lord of Milan (1395).

The Pope, in the meantime, began to regret the encouragement he had given to this very popular hero. His jealousy was roused, and he hired a *condottiere* for a month, in order to fight the Perugians. The hostilities, however, ended with the month, and nothing was accomplished beyond a demonstration of the Pontiff's jealousy. But there was someone else beside the Pope who witnessed the honours paid to Biordo with a jealous hatred, and this was the Abbot of S. Pietro. "The wicked Abbot," as the people called him, belonged to the noble family of the Guidalotti, and he probably felt that the power of his family was too much overshadowed by Michelotti. He had fresh cause to murmur, therefore, when Biordo married Bertolda Orsini of Rome, and the Lords of Urbino, Camerino, San Severo, Gubbio, and other towns came up to offer the happy pair rich presents, and to wish the bride-groom well. Biordo's marriage was a splendid pageant. The city decked herself magnificently to do him honour, and all the people of the country round sent offerings of grain, and wine, and eggs, and cheese, everything which their small farms produced, to show their leader how they loved him.

The Abbot sat at his window, and with no kindly eye he watched the entry of the young bride, close by the monastery walls. Madonna Contessa Orsini came in escorted by the Florentine and Venetian ambassadors. Her dress was made of cloth of gold, she wore a garland of wild asparagus around her head, and jewels sparkled in her hair. The Abbot noted all these things, he saw the women of Perugia running out to meet her, he saw them throw flowers in her path, and then he returned to his cell to brood upon his horrid plans of vengeance. For he had determined to place the town once more beneath the sway of the Church, and in this way to gain for himself a Cardinal's hat, as it was probably the Pope himself who urged him to the deed.

VIA DELLE STALLE

On Sunday, in the month of March 1398, while the citizens were attending a sermon at S. Lorenzo, the Abbot arrived on horseback at the Guidalotti palace on Colle

Landone, to collect his fellow-conspirators, and some twenty of them proceeded to Biordo's house on Porta Sole. Word was sent up to Michelotti that there was important news for him, and he, suspecting nothing, hurried down to meet the Abbot with a courteous greeting. The Abbot stepped forward, took his hand, and kissed Biordo, at which sign the rest of the conspirators fell upon their victim and stabbed him with their poisoned daggers, hitting him such grievous blows that soon he lay weltering in a pool of blood. The conspirators had first intended openly to announce the deed in the piazza, but their courage failed them and the Abbot merely muttered the news to the passers-by as he slunk away to S. Pietro with a few companions. Two of the braver of the assassins, however, stayed behind and, coming into the piazza, cried: "We have slain the tyrant." The citizens, who were at mass, rose with one accord from their devotions, to avenge the death of their beloved leader, and leaving the preacher to continue his sermon to an empty church, they hurried to arms. The Abbot meanwhile hastened from his monastery at S. Pietro to a still safer refuge at Casalina. As he fled he looked back upon the city whose hero he had murdered, and he saw the flames and smoke break out from the palace of those same Guidalotti he had hoped to benefit, whilst the news of the death of his old father and many of his family in the carnage of that day was brought to him as a sorry consolation for his crime.

Biordo's blood was gathered together by the citizens and put into a little silver basin, and above it they placed the banner of Perugia with the white griffin upon a crimson field; and as one chronicler informs us, a heart of stone must have melted at the sight of it.

Thus perished the first of that extraordinary series of men who took upon themselves the terrible task of governing single-handed the city of Perugia. Nearly all died by violence, but the violence done to Biordo was a cruel wrong. A short interval follows, and then the greatest name, perhaps, of all the city's chronicles comes up upon the scene, namely, that of Braccio Fortebraccio di Montone.

The Perugians suspected the ungracious part that the Pope had played in the murder of their leader, and the suspicion made them restless and dissatisfied. It was probably owing to this that they fell a prey to the cunning wiles of the Duke of Milan.

Gian Galeazzo had ingratiated himself with the citizens some time previously by giving them grain during a time of famine, and he now came forward to reap the benefit of his charity by getting himself accepted as Lord of Perugia, which would facilitate his designs on Tuscany. Perugia's connection with Milan, however, only lasted four years. On Gian Galeazzo's death, in 1402, the Duchess of Milan made peace with Boniface IX., and restored Bologna, Perugia, and Assisi to the Church. The Perugians submitted to the Pope (they seem not to have been consulted in the matter of the donation), but with the strict understanding that the exiled nobles should keep at least twenty miles distant from the city. Boniface agreed to this arrangement. Other popes before him had tried to patch up peace between the parties, but he had not the courage to attempt such difficult experiments. It remained for Braccio Fortebraccio to tear through the tangled network of Perugian politics, to unite within himself the powers of both parties, and as the city's despot to raise it to "unprecedented glory."

Braccio Fortebraccio was born at Montone in 1368. He was the son of Oddo Fortebraccio, Lord of Montone, and of Jacoma Montemelini, his wife, of a noble Perugian family. During his youth the *Raspanti* were dominant in the city, and the boy grew up as an exile. He had only his sword and an immense ambition with which to force his way to future power. It was at that time the fashion for young noblemen to win fame for themselves by the life or trade of the *condottieri*. Braccio therefore joined the famous Italian company of S. George, led by Alberigo di Barbiano, whose advent crushed the foreign captains of adventure whose lawless mercenaries had sent terror throughout the rich plains and villages of Italy during the fourteenth century.

In the tents of Alberigo, Braccio di Montone and Sforza Attendolo[17] learned together the science of warfare.

Thence they two went forth to fight the battles of princes, kings, and popes; to create two separate methods of combat, and to fill all Italy with tales of their great valour and their rivalry. Braccio's ambition grew with his success, and he soon aspired to acquiring the whole of Italy. His first step towards this very large design was the capture of his native city of Perugia. But as he represented the party of the nobles, the *Raspanti* manfully resisted any efforts he made to approach them. "It is better even to submit to foreign rule than to make peace with the nobles," they said; and thus it came about that they gave themselves over to Ladislaus, King of Naples, and remained for some six years in connection with the kingdom of Naples. When Ladislaus died in 1414, the Perugians were seized with terror, but the nobles saw their opportunity, and all things seemed to favour the scheme of Fortebraccio.

Braccio had joined the service of Pope John XXIII., and by him had been made governor of Bologna; but when the Pope was deposed by the Council of Constance, Braccio's allegiance ended, and he at once sold the Bolognese their liberty, and with the 82,000 florins which he gained by this transaction he collected a strong army, the exiled nobles flocked to his standard, and they marched at once upon Perugia.

At the news of Braccio's approach terror and consternation spread through the city. The gateways were built up, and the magistrates forbade anyone to leave the town. But the Perugians, "being the most warlike of the people of Italy," as Sismondi says, could not resist so grand a chance of fighting, and seeing Braccio's men clustering around the city's walls, they jumped down from the ramparts into their midst, and took the soldiers unawares by the suddenness of their attack. This was no real battle, but tumults of the sort were the order of the day. In the dead of night men would rush in panic into the piazza, not knowing what had brought them there, and only conscious of one fact: their desire to make a fierce stand for their liberty. Braccio made a fruitless effort to penetrate into the heart of the city, and was driven back ignominiously. The women threw down stones and boiling water on the assailants, whilst they goaded their own men to fight, crying aloud, "Now is your time to wound the enemy,—at him with your swords your teeth and nails!"

At last the Perugians called in the help of Carlo Malatesta, Lord of Rimini, and on the 15th of July 1416, the two armies met between the Tiber and Sant' Egideo on the road to Assisi. The greatest generals of Italy and her best soldiers, says Sismondi, took part in the fierce fighting of that day. The parties closed in deadly conflict; for seven hours they fought beneath the burning sun, and the heat was increased by the dense dust that filled the air. "Most dolorous were the sighs which were heard to issue from the helmets," says Fabretti. Braccio was a wise general. He had carefully prepared beforehand countless jars of water for the refreshment of his men and horses after each skirmish, and this in the end was the cause of his victory. The Tiber was flowing five hundred paces from Malatesta's soldiers, and they finally could bear the terrible thirst no longer but hurried down to drink. Braccio seized upon this moment in which to swoop upon the enemy with all his force. The day was won. Carlo Malatesta and his young nephew Galeazzo Malatesta, were taken prisoners, and it "was strange to note that the humblest of Braccio's soldiers were driving prisoners before them like a herd of cattle."[18]

When the Perugians heard of the defeat they immediately sent ambassadors to offer the government of their city to Braccio. They seem after all their previous fighting, to have at once submitted to their fate, which as it turned out, was an excellent piece of good fortune for them. They made preparations to welcome their new despot in a manner worthy of the man. Fine carpets, brocades, and long gold chains, were hung from the palace windows, flowers lay thick upon the pavement from S. Pietro to S. Lorenzo, whilst elegant gold and silver vases were placed in the windows of the Palazzo Pubblico. "Evviva Braccio, Signore di Perugia," they shouted as he entered, and thus the die was cast.

Anxious to conciliate both parties in the city, Braccio assumed the attitude of Father of his Country and succeeded in inspiring the people with an unusual sense of admiration. Master of all Umbria and Prince of Capua, many towns acknowledged his dominion, and even Rome was forced to accept him at one period as her lord. It is, therefore, scarcely to be wondered at that Perugians have never ceased to lament that Braccio died before accomplishing his vast designs for conquering all Italy, for they feel that they only just missed the chance of rivalling the glory of imperial Rome.

There are infinite records concerning the personality of this extraordinary man.

"He was of medium stature," says Campano, "with a long face and highly coloured, which imparted great majesty to his appearance. His eyes were not black, but very brilliant; they sparkled with fun, yet with a certain gravity. His figure was partly deformed and scarred by wounds. Whether grave or gay he was always high bred, so that his very enemies confessed that among any number of persons he would always be recognised as leader and chief."

In the following lines Campano sums up his character:—

"Braccio was grave and kindly of speech, without artifice or trickery, a gift of nature rather than acquired, though improved by some study. None could soothe an angry person with more grace than Braccio, none could exhort and inflame his followers with more vehemence and ardour to the combat. He was beloved by his soldiers, being neither haughty nor rough spoken, and he united military severity with a certain civil modesty and a courtier-like manner."

One of the most delightful traits of Braccio's character was an intense hatred of idleness, and city-loafers he nicknamed "*I consumatori della piazza*" (wearers out of the pavement of the public square). He encouraged the Perugians to play as well as fight, and it was he who revived the ancient game of the "Battle of the Stones." His soldiers would often join in the sport, and great was the joy of the citizens when the latter were vanquished. Braccio himself was not allowed to play; he would watch the game from an upper window, and much as he often desired to join, his companions prevented him, for it seldom happened that less than twelve men lay killed or wounded at the end of the day. This extraordinary and barbarous game deserves an account in any history of Perugia. It dates back to Roman times, and the credit of playing the "fiercest game in Italy" belonged to Perugia alone, and was believed to be the reason why her people were "of such commanding mould both in spirit and in body." Even the children joined during the first two hours, so as to make them strong and warlike from their infancy.

On the Sundays and feast-days of March, April, and May, and into the middle of June, the citizens met in the Campo di Battaglia, on the road to Monte Luce, and there formed themselves into two parties, one remaining on the level of the square, the other just below. Till nightfall each party fought to drive the other off the ground, and whichever side managed to gain the middle of the square, carried off the palm of victory. This wonderful "game" must have looked like a miniature battle of a somewhat prehistoric kind; for the combatants were all swathed about the neck, their legs encased in thick leather stockings, stuffed with deer's hair and protected by greaves; thickly padded round the body under their cuirasses, their feet in shoes of linen cloth wrapped three times round and stuffed again with the hair of deer. The warlike youths and men wore on the top of everything else a helmet which projected forward in the shape of a sparrow-hawk's head, and thus protected, they were able to watch the stones flying about their heads without being blinded. They were called the "*Armati*," and were led to combat by "Hurlers" (*lanciatori*), who wore a lighter apparel, and threw the stones with extraordinary ability, thereby exciting the citizens to combat. Old men sat at their windows watching the fight with breathless interest. If they saw that their side was losing, they would sometimes tear off coat and mantle, hurry downstairs, and utterly regardless of their age, fling themselves into the thick of the fight. "It was a very beautiful spectacle," exclaims Campano, "to witness the fall, first of this one, then of that, as they were wounded and tumbled to the ground, whilst others, protected by a shield, hurled themselves upon their adversaries with the weight of their entire bodies, diving in and out among the crowd and dealing blows upon their eyes and faces with shield and sword and buckler."

To us it seems strange that at a time when the feuds of centuries lay smouldering and ready to burst out at the smallest provocation, no rancour, no ill-will, seemed to be harboured by the relations of the men who fell dead or wounded in one of these terrible "games."

Besides encouraging sports, fighting wars, and arranging civil matters, Braccio had a passion for building. He rebuilt the city walls in many places. He added the loggia to the front of the Cathedral, that the citizens might have a pleasant shelter in the square in which to discuss and settle their affairs, and it was he who conceived a rather novel and practical piece of engineering by bolstering up the houses of the Piazza Sopramuro with strong walls from beneath.[19] The vanity of the Perugians was immensely flattered by all the great doings of their new leader, and their pride knew no bounds when, on the Feast of S. Ercolano, the neighbouring towns sent in their banners with extraordinary pomp in token of their absolute subjection to the city's rule. So delighted indeed were the people, that they at once sent a message to the Pope to ask him to confirm Braccio's dominion in Perugia. The request was met in stony silence. The Papal See was jealous of Braccio Fortebraccio, yet it could not do without him, and so, for the time, it smothered its wrath and mortification. Martin V. was in need of Braccio's sword to help in regaining the lost possessions of the Church, and he sent for him to Florence to sign the necessary agreements. The visit was disastrous, for even the Florentine street boys exulted in the popularity of the hero:

"Braccio valente
Vince ogni gente
Papa Martino
Non val un quattrino"

they sang in high, shrill voices below the windows of His Holiness. The insult stung and rankled.
"Papa Martino non val un quattrino," muttered the Pope in a miserable voice as he paced up and down, complaining to his secretary.

In 1423 Braccio had reached the height of his power, but his ambition soared still higher, and at this turn in his life his character seems to have undergone a change. His vast plans for conquering Italy had unhinged him, and he became cruel where formerly he had been kind, and deaf to the counsels of his friends. The simplest and the quietest of his days had been spent at Perugia, where his memory still lingers like the aureole around some conquering saint. But looking out across the plains and mountains of Umbria and towards the Marches which were already his, Braccio dreamed his mighty dream: that of becoming king of a united Italy. Aquila alone resisted his power, and in the year 1423, he set out for his last venture. It is said that before he started he left to the care of his wife, Nicolina da Varano, a little casket, with the injunction that she should not open it until after his death, or his return home. When Braccio died Nicolina opened the casket and she found inside a black veil and a sceptre. It was thus the dead man told his wife that the battle of Aquila decided whether she should be a powerful queen or an unhappy widow.

The siege of Aquila lasted for a whole year, and finally, in May 1424, a decisive battle took place in the plain below the town, between Braccio and Caldora, who came to fight him in the name of Martin V. It was a great fight, and it ended in a tragic manner: Braccio, the beloved of the Perugians, got his death-wound at the hands of a Perugian citizen, a *Raspante*, who had never forgiven the return of the nobles to Perugia.

Caldora tended Braccio during his last hours with every possible care. The doctors hoped to save him, they said that the wounds in his head and throat were curable, but Braccio wished to die; he was determined not to survive his defeat. He refused all nourishment and during the three days that he lingered, he never spoke a single word. His dream had faded, and his courage gone.[20]

The Story of Perugia

In the papal circle there was great rejoicing at the news of Braccio's death, for Martin V. knew well that Umbria was once again his own. The Pope indeed was small-minded enough to harbour his enmity to the very last. Instead of allowing the fallen captain to be quietly buried, he had him placed in unconsecrated ground outside the walls of Rome. The bones of the great Braccio had but a troubled career. They were brought to Perugia by Niccolò Fortebraccio, and deposited for a while in the Church of S. Costanzo, where they were met by the municipality and the whole city and then carried in triumphal procession to the Church of S. Francesco al Prato. All the shops were closed as the bones passed up the streets, no bells were rung, horses and men were draped in black. In this century, by a piece of rather questionable taste the bones of the hero were once more taken from their Church, and may now be stared at, like the bones of the Etruscan ladies, under a bit of glass in the museum of the University. Under them are written in Latin the following lines: "O you who pass by, stay and weep. I, born in Perugia, was received in Montone as an exile. Mars subjected to me my native land of Umbria, and Capua too. Rome obeyed me, the world was the spectator and Italy the stage. But Aquila mocked my fall, wherefore my weeping country locked me into this small urn. Ah! Mars raised me up, Mors brought me low. Therefore pass on."

The news of Braccio's death caused the utmost consternation in Perugia. If the great captain had saved the town at a critical point, he may also be said to have created a situation which was perhaps a still more critical one for her citizens. Braccio was a noble. With his advent in Perugia the party of the nobles had returned. Terrible things were in store for the city. For a little while, and partly through the efforts of a rather complicated personality, they were postponed, but the time of terror was at hand.

When Braccio died at Aquila, the Perugians prepared to defend themselves they knew not well from what. "Each man," says Graziani, "furnished himself with flour, the ditches and walls were repaired both of the city and the territory around it, and every one left the open country and took refuge in fortresses and city palaces." Two courses lay open to them, and of the two they selected that which seemed least evil. They submitted themselves once more to the power of the Pope; and on July 29th, 1424, the delighted Martin entered Perugia as its acknowledged lord and ruler.

Like many famous people of that day Martin had studied at the Perugian University, and perhaps he had preserved an affection for the city which he had known in his youth. Anyhow, the terms of peace which he concluded with the citizens were very mild, and as usual, all the privileges obtained from Innocent III. were preserved. But this time it was through the *nobles* that the Pope had been called into the city. The thin end of the wedge was surely and irretrievably driven in, and the power of the nobles was as a matter of fact secure. The Pope himself fostered the growing power, and amongst others, who on the occasion of his advent received rich possessions from him, was Malatesta Baglioni. Martin handed Spello over to his rule, and thus helped to enrich a family whose members were for a period to wrest the power from the Church itself, and to set the town ablaze with crime and bloodshed.

The nobles remained at the head of affairs, but, as we have said, there was one strong personality—a Perugian citizen, Niccolò Piccinino—who made a last effort, as Braccio Fortebraccio and Michelotti had done before him, to become that strange creation of the day: a *condottiere* despot.

Niccolò Piccinino was a follower of Braccio di Montone, and his name remains stamped on the pages of history for successfully leading the Braccian troops to battle, and following out the famous tactics of his master. For twenty years Piccinino maintained a constant rivalry with Francesco Sforza, as Braccio Fortebraccio had done before him with Attendolo Sforza, the ancestor of a line of dukes. The ancestry of Niccolò is both humble and obscure.[21] Some tell us he was the son of a Perugian butcher, others say, of a peasant from Calisciana near the city, but it is difficult to get any satisfactory information about him; he was practically little beyond an adventurer. As quite a boy he left his home in the Umbrian hills, and started out to seek his fortune amongst the captains of adventure in the north. Later in life his career became closely linked with that of Fortebraccio, who loved him because of his bravery and enthusiasm for the soldier's career. Nature had not fitted Niccolò for the camp. His health was bad, he was paralysed in one leg and had to be lifted on to his horse, and because of his miniature figure he got the nickname of "Piccinino" (the Tiny One); but the small body contained an undaunted spirit, and his tactics in the field were quick and decisive. He never knew when he was beaten, but would turn to strike again while the enemy were boasting of their victory. On one occasion Piccinino crept into a sack and had himself carried across the battlefield on a man's shoulder. The enemy (probably Francesco Sforza) imagined him to be at that moment in an opposite direction, and the sudden appearance of Piccinino's head from out of the sack, his piercing eyes gazing at them over his carrier's back, caused general consternation among the soldiers. Whether this strange manœuvre won the day history does not record.

In 1440 Piccinino made a desperate effort to win for himself the government of Perugia, but Papal power was too deeply rooted in the city, and he had to rest content with the title of *Gonfaloniere of the Holy Church*—Supreme Magistrate of the City but acting in the Pope's name.

Perugia had a terrible time under this ecclesiastical and military yoke. Three masters pulled her different ways: Piccinino, the Pope, and the nobles, and each of these three imposed taxes for their different uses. Piccinino's is an unsatisfactory career. It is that of a man pouring old wine into new bottles; the trade of the *condottiere* ruler was practically dead. The Pope's tactics were unsatisfactory also. He tried to conciliate two parties. He encouraged and patronised the nobles and pandered to the populace by encouraging all kinds of extravagant superstition. There is a horrid tale about the burning of a witch at this time; and religious processions assumed such monstrous length that the streets could hardly hold them, and we read that the leading men got entangled in the tail of the procession which had not been able to leave the piazza before those who had left it long ago returned to the starting-point. Passion-preaching, too, became the fashion, accompanied by grotesque miracle-plays in which a barber from S. Angelo represented our Saviour; and all those things only served to increase the morbid passions of the people. In this complicated situation the nobles came off best, and their power grew and strengthened rapidly; but the power was evil. As for the attitude assumed by the former rulers of the city, it is difficult to judge. A sort of stupor seems to have fallen on the hitherto vigilant *Priori*. A feeble effort was made in 1444 to drive out the tormentors by payment of a large sum of money to mercenary soldiers, but these only took the pay and continued to enjoy themselves at the expense of the town.

NICCOLÒ PICCININO

Hitherto, at least, the nobles had been one party, fighting for one cause. But now that the cause was won, now that their own supremacy had been attained, they began to fight amongst themselves. They hated each other with a mortal hatred. We no longer hear of fights between nobles and burghers, but of passionate blood-feuds between the nobles themselves: between the Oddi, Corgna, Staffa, Arciprete, Baglioni, and others, and next we read of cousins murdering each other for the sake of mere ambition. The slightest pretext is seized upon for a skirmish between the men who, through centuries, had stood together in opposition to the outside world. A hundred instances are given of their quarrels at this period. The Della Corgna by way of an example, are one day preparing to enhance the solemnity of a feast-day by decorating the Arco dei Priori with box and laurel boughs, and are interrupted in their pious labours by the Degli Oddi, who begin to pull down the decorations. There is some dispute about precedence, in their quarter of the city—some trifling question as to which family has most right to manage the local festival, a bitter fight ensues, and the whole town is in a tumult.

Again on another occasion, one of Ridolfo Baglioni's bastard sons wounds a certain Naldino da Corciano, a friend of the Degli Oddi, and Naldino hurries off to show his bleeding face to his allies. The Oddi, mad with fury, rush all armed to the piazza, striking at every Baglioni adherent whom they meet upon their way. The Baglioni are not slow to appear, as ready for the fight as anybody. The shops are closed, the citizens arm themselves, a procession wending its way to the Duomo is thrown into utter disorder, and even the women thrust their heads out of the windows and throw down jugs and tiles and pitchers into the street below. The

Bishop, the *Priori*, and the learned doctors of the law leave their houses and exhort the nobles to lay down their arms; and after a while a truce is obtained, and the hubbub for the time subsides.

Such scenes as these were of almost daily occurrence in the city, and it was in vain that the Pope, both by foul means and by fair, attempted to calm the frantic passions of the rivals. [22] It was in vain that S. Bernardino, carrying his crucifix before him, came to preach of brotherly love and unity, in vain the Blessed Colomba uttered mysterious warnings. It was too late either for Pope or Saint to check so strong a flood as the ambition of men like the Oddi and the Baglioni. All over Italy at this period the character of individual families had grown too strong for outer influences to crush it, and the heads of the Guelph families were everywhere attempting to form themselves into ruling princes. In the case of this struggle at Perugia the most successful of the combatants were the Oddi and the Baglioni. The struggle between them was a struggle unto death. Now one was driven from the city gates, and now another; but finally, in 1488, the Oddi were ousted altogether, and from that minute until the time when the great Farnese Pope came down with guns and stones and every implement of war as well as curses, to quell them, the members of the Baglioni family became the dominant faction of the city. They left their country houses for ever. They fixed their mighty eyries on the south side of the city, about where the modern Prefettura stands today; from thence they dominated all the town, and there they lived their wild ill-regulated lives, mingling the most exquisite luxury with cruel vice. They were a splendid and a beautiful race of men, and Italy rang with their great names, but their rule was horrible.

"As I do not wish to swerve from the pure truth," says Matarazzo, who himself adored them, "I say that from the day the Oddi were expelled our city went from bad to worse. All the young men followed the trade of arms. Their lives were disorderly; and every day divers excesses were divulged, and the city had lost all reason and justice. Every man administered right unto himself, *propriâ autoritate et manu regiâ*. Meanwhile the Pope sent many legates, in order that the city might be brought to order; but all who came returned in dread of being hewn in pieces; for they threatened to throw some from the windows of the palace, so that no cardinal or other legate durst approach Perugia, unless he were a friend of the Baglioni. And the city was brought to such misery that the most wrongous men were most prized; and those who had slain two or three men walked as they listed through the palace, and went with sword or poniard to speak to the podestà and other magistrates. Moreover, every man of worth was downtrodden by *bravi* whom the nobles favoured; nor could a citizen call his property his own. The nobles robbed first one and then another of their goods and land. All offices were sold or else suppressed; and taxes and extortions were so grievous that every one cried out. And if a man were in prison for his head, he had no reason to fear death, provided he had some interest with a noble."

PALAZZO PUBBLICO

CHAPTER III

The Baglioni. Paul III. and last years of the City

SO after centuries of steady struggle fate had at last decreed that the nobles should have their way. Because the way of the Baglioni is the most picturesque point in all the annals of Perugia, because it was crowned by one of the most horrible domestic tragedies of Italian history, and because, moreover, it happens to have been so admirably and so vividly recorded, we are sometimes inclined to regard it as the most important fact about the town. We must, however, remember that it was only one of the infinite points which make the city's history, and that the rule of the Baglioni covers a period of not more than fifty years.

By a rare coincidence it happened that exactly at this period, *i.e.*, during the ascendency of the Baglioni, there was living in the city of Perugia a scholar by name Matarazzo or Maturanzio.[23] This scholar took upon himself to record day by day the extraordinary exploits of a family in whose good looks and deeds of violence, their jousts and subterfuges, he may be truly said not only to have delighted but to have revelled. To understand the Baglioni and the fashion in which they were regarded by the men of their day:

terror, hatred, fear, and a cringing admiration being pretty well mixed, one must study the chronicles of Matarazzo in the original.[24] But as it would be impossible, and even impertinent for us to try and retell the tale of this tragic history in new English words, we have quoted at length the words of one who studied it faithfully and recorded it with a strange vibrating echo of the original language.[25] We have merely inserted here and there a few notes and details which seemed to add to the narrative.

"It is not until 1495 that the history of the Baglioni becomes dramatic, possibly because till then they lacked the pen of Matarazzo. But from this year forward to their final extinction, every detail of their doings has a picturesque and awful interest. Domestic furies, like the revel descried by Cassandra above the palace of Mycenæ, seem to take possession of the fated house; and the doom which has fallen on them is worked out with pitiless exactitude to the last generation. In 1495 the heads of the Casa Baglioni were two brothers, Guido and Ridolfo, who had a numerous progeny of heroic sons. From Guido sprang Astorre, Adriano—called for his great strength Morgante—Gismondo, Marcantonio, and Gentile. Ridolfo owned Troilo, Gianpaolo, and Simonetto. The first glimpse we get of these young athletes in Matarazzo's chronicle is on the occasion of a sudden assault upon Perugia made by the Oddi and the exiles of their faction in September 1495. The foes of the Baglioni entered the gates and began breaking the iron chains, *serragli*, which barred the streets against advancing cavalry. None of the noble house were on the alert except young Simonetto, a lad of eighteen, fierce and cruel, who had not yet begun to shave his chin. In spite of all dissuasion, he rushed forth alone, bareheaded, in his shirt, with a sword in his right hand and a buckler on his arm, and fought against a squadron. There at the barrier of the piazza he kept his foes at bay, smiting men-at-arms to the ground with the sweep of his tremendous sword, and receiving on his gentle body twenty-two cruel wounds. While thus at fearful odds, the noble Astorre mounted his charger and joined him. Upon his helmet flashed the falcon of the Baglioni with the dragon's tail that swept behind. Bidding Simonetto tend his wounds, he in his turn held the square. Listen to Matarazzo's description of the scene; it is as good as any piece of the *Mort Arthur*: "According to the report of one who told me what he had seen with his own eyes, never did anvil take so many blows as he upon his person and his steed; and they all kept striking at his lordship in such crowds that the one prevented the other. And so many lances, partisans, and cross bow quarries, and other weapons made upon his body a most mighty din, that above every other noise and shout was heard the thud of those great strokes. But he, like one who had the mastery of war, set his charger where the press was thickest, jostling now one and now another; so that he ever kept at least ten men of his foes stretched on the ground beneath his horse's hoofs; which horse was a most fierce beast, and gave his enemies what trouble he best could. And now that gentle lord was all fordone with sweat and toil, he and his charger; and so weary were they that scarcely could they any longer breathe. Soon after the Baglioni mustered in force. One by one their heroes rushed from the palaces. The enemy were driven back with slaughter; and a war ensued which made the fair land between Assisi and Perugia a wilderness for many months." It must not be forgotten that at the time of these great feats of Simonetto and Astorre young Raphael was painting in the studio of Perugino. What the whole city witnessed with astonishment and admiration, he, the keenly sensitive artist-boy, treasured in his memory. Therefore in the St George of the Louvre, and in the mounted horseman trampling upon Heliodorus in the Stanze of the Vatican, victorious Astorre lives for ever, immortalised in all his splendour by the painter's art. The grinning griffin on the helmet, the resistless frown upon the forehead of the beardless knight, the terrible right arm, and the ferocious steed—all are there as Raphael saw and wrote them on his brain. One characteristic of the Baglioni, as might be plentifully illustrated from their annalist, was their eminent beauty which inspired beholders with an enthusiasm and a love they were far from deserving by their virtues. It is this, in combination with their personal heroism, which gives a peculiar dramatic interest to their doings, and makes the chronicle of Matarazzo more fascinating than a novel."

Matarazzo was not alone in his admiration for the Baglioni. He tells us that whenever the "magnificent Guido," his son Astorre, or his nephew Gianpaolo walked in the piazza every citizen paused at his work to admire them, and if perchance a stranger passed through Perugia he was certain to make every effort to see them. The soldiers would hurry from their tents to see Gianpaolo go by, and anyone walking by this noble's side seemed dwarfed and insignificant by reason of his great stature and his noble form. Gismondo, another of Guide's sons, was universally admired for his splendid horsemanship. He would make his horse leap into the air, while he sat straight and square in the saddle, not stirring hand or foot. The citizens looked on marvelling at these feats of skill and daring. Gismondo was slim, and walked with the lightness of a cat, so that no man in Perugia, however quick of hearing, knew when he was coming. The richest and perhaps the handsomest of the Baglioni family was young Grifonetto Baglioni, whose beauty Matarazzo compares to Ganymede. He was the son of Grifone and Atalanta Baglioni, and nephew to Guido and Ridolfo. His father had been stabbed at Ponte Ricciolo in 1477, and he lived with his young mother in one of the most beautiful houses in Perugia. This palace had been commenced by Malatesta Baglioni and finished by Braccio Baglioni, who, because of the court of learned men he gathered round him, and the splendid festivals with which he honoured the lovely ladies of the city, was called "Lorenzo il Magnifico di Perugia." The palace was entered by a large and richly-ornamented hall, hung with beautiful pictures. At the opposite end of the room was a painting of a woman of most venerable and majestic bearing, and over her head the word *Perusia*. This grave and queenly lady commanded a view of all the celebrated men of the Umbrian city, for on one side of the wall were portraits of the famous captains of adventure, and on the other those of the most learned of the doctors and scholars, with their names and a description of their mighty deeds written in full below them. Grifonetto lived in great magnificence. "He kept numbers of horses, Barbary steeds, to run in the races, jesters and other properties pertaining to a gentleman. He even kept a lion; and all who went to the house compared it to a king's court."

"In 1500, when the events about to be related took place, Grifonetto was quite a youth. Brave, rich, handsome, and married to a young wife, Zenobia Sforza, he was the admiration of Perugia. He and his wife loved each other dearly, and how, indeed, could it be otherwise, since 'l'uno e l'altro sembravano doi angioli di Paradiso?'[26] At the same time he had fallen into the hands of bad and desperate counsellors. A bastard of the house, Filippo da Braccio, his half-uncle, was always at his side, instructing him not only in the accomplishments of chivalry, but also in wild ways that brought his name into disrepute. Another of his familiars was Carlo Barciglia Baglioni, an unquiet spirit, who longed for more power than his poverty and comparative obscurity allowed. With them associated Girolamo della Penna, a veritable ruffian, contaminated from his earliest youth with every form of lust and violence, and capable of any crime. These three companions, instigated partly by the lord of Camerino and partly by their own cupidity, conceived a scheme for massacring the families of Guido and Ridolfo at one blow. As a consequence of this wholesale murder, Perugia would be at their discretion. Seeing of what use Grifonetto by his wealth and name might be to them, they did all they could to persuade him to join their conjuration. It would appear that the bait first offered him was the sovereignty of the city, but that he was at last gained over by being made to believe that his wife, Zenobia, had carried on an intrigue with Gianpaolo Baglioni. The dissolute morals of the family gave plausibility to an infernal trick which worked upon the jealousy of Grifonetto. Thirsting for revenge, he consented to the scheme. The conspirators were further fortified by the accession of Jeronimo della Staffa, and three members of the house of Corgna. It is noticeable that out of the whole number only two—Bernardo da Corgna and Filippo da Braccio—were above the age of thirty. Of the rest, few had reached twenty-five. At so early an age were the men of those times adepts in violence and treason. The execution of the plot was fixed for the wedding festivities of Astorre Baglioni with Lavinia, the daughter of Giovanni Colonna and Giustina Orsini. At that time the whole Baglioni family were to be assembled in Perugia, with the single exception of Marcantonio, who was taking baths at Naples for his health. It was known that the members of the noble house, nearly all of them condottieri by trade, and eminent for their great strength and skill in arms, took few precautions for their safety. They occupied several houses close together between the Porta San Carlo and the Porta Eburnea, set no regular guard over their sleeping-chambers, and trusted to their personal bravery and to the fidelity of their attendants. It was thought that they might be assassinated in their beds. The wedding festivities began upon the 28th of July, and great is the particularity with which Matarazzo describes the doings of each successive day—processions, jousts, triumphal arches, banquets, balls, and pageants."

Perugia, it seems, was turned into a veritable garden of loveliness on this occasion. Rich velvets, brocades, and tapestries hung from the palace windows, their gorgeous colours mingled with long trails of ivy, with many shrubs and the branches of blossoming trees, which also filled the streets. Colossal arches spanned the roads at the different gates into the city. All vied together to erect the finest arch;

and one was hung all over with tapestries showing the military exploits of the young Astorre. As the Roman bride passed in, the ladies of Perugia went to meet her, offering her rich presents. Some were dressed in cloth of gold and silver, others in silk and velvet, and many of them were lovely to behold. But Lavinia Colonna excelled them all by the glory of her broidered gown, and by the pearls and jewels twisted in her hair. Simonetto Baglioni drove round the city in a triumphal car, and as he went he cast great quantities of sugared dainties to the crowd, thus trying, by every means in his power, to add to the merriment of the marriage-day, and to show that love and comradeship united the Baglioni family.

But down in the Borgo S. Angelo men were silent and morose, for they hated these tyrants of Perugia, and held aloof from all rejoicings. They had noted strange auguries of late, and a whisper went round that evil was impending. On the first night of the festivities a terrible storm arose, scattering the decorations in the whirlwind. It was an awful night, and the young Roman bride shuddered, as above the din of the storm, she heard the sinister roars of the Baglioni lions.[27] Lavinia and Astorre were lodged in the palace of their traitorous cousin Grifonetto, and neither dreamt of the treachery that was so near at hand.

"The night of the 14th of August was finally set apart for the consummation of *el gran tradimento*: it is thus that

Matarazzo always alludes to the crime of Grifonetto, with a solemnity of reiteration that is most impressive. A heavy stone let fall into the courtyard of Guido Baglioni's palace was to be the signal: each conspirator was then to run to the sleeping-chamber of his appointed prey. Two of the principals and fifteen *bravi* were told off to each victim: rams and crowbars were prepared to force the doors if needful. All happened as had been anticipated. The crash of the falling stone was heard. The conspirators rushed to the scene of operations. Astorre, who was sleeping in the house of his traitorous cousin Grifonetto, was slain in the arms of his young bride, crying, as he vainly struggled, 'Misero Astorre che more come poltrone!'[28] Simonetto flew to arms, exclaiming to his brother, 'Non dubitare Gismondo, mio fratello!'[29] He, too, was soon despatched.[30] Filippo da Braccio, after killing him, tore from a great wound in his side the still quivering heart, into which he drove his teeth with savage fury. Old Guido died groaning, 'Ora è gionto il ponto mio,'[31] and Gismondo's throat was cut while he lay holding back his face that he might be spared the sight of his own massacre. The corpses of Astorre and Simonetto were stripped and thrown out naked into the streets. Men gathered round and marvelled to see such heroic forms, with faces so proud and fierce even in death. In especial the foreign students likened them to ancient Romans. But on their fingers were rings, and these the ruffians of the place would fain have hacked off with their knives. From this indignity the noble limbs were spared; then the dead Baglioni were hurriedly consigned to an unhonoured tomb. Meanwhile the rest of the intended victims managed to escape. Gianpaolo, assailed by Grifonetto and Gianfrancesco della Corgna, took refuge with his squire, Maraglia, upon a staircase leading from his room. While the squire held the passage with his pike against the foe, Gianpaolo effected his flight over neighbouring house-roofs. He crept into the attic of some foreign students, who, trembling with terror, gave him food and shelter, clad him in a scholar's gown, and helped him to fly in this disguise from the gates at dawn. He then joined his brother Troilo at Marsciano, whence he returned without delay to punish the traitors. At the same time Grifonetto's mother Atalanta, taking with her his wife, Zenobia, and the two young sons of Gianpaolo, Malatesta and Orazio, afterwards so celebrated in Italian history for their great feats of arms and their crimes, fled to her country-house at Landona. Grifonetto in vain sought to see her there. She drove him from her presence with curses for the treason and the fratricide that he had planned. It is very characteristic of these wild natures, framed of fierce instincts and discordant passions, that his mother's curse weighed like lead upon the unfortunate young man. Next day, when Gianpaolo returned to try the luck of arms, Grifonetto, deserted by the companions of his crime and paralysed by the sense of his guilt, went out alone to meet him on the public place. The semi-failure of their scheme had terrified the conspirators: the horrors of that night of blood unnerved them. All had fled except the next victim of the feud. Putting his sword to the youth's throat, Gianpaolo looked into his eyes and said, 'Art thou here, Grifonetto? Go with God's peace: I will not slay thee, nor plunge my hand in my own blood, as thou hast done in thine.' Then he turned and left the lad to be hacked in pieces by his guard. The untranslatable words which Matarazzo uses to describe his death are touching from the strong impression they convey of Grifonetto's goodliness: 'Qui ebbe sua signoria sopra sua nobile persona tante ferite che suoi membra leggiadre stese in terra.'[32] None but Greeks felt the charm of personal beauty thus.[33] But while Grifonetto was breathing out his life upon the pavement of the piazza, his mother, Atalanta, and his wife Zenobia, came to greet him through the awe-struck city. As they approached, all men fell aside and slunk away before their grief. None would seem to have had a share in Grifonetto's murder. Then Atalanta knelt by her dying son, and ceased from wailing, and prayed and exhorted him to pardon those who had caused his death. It appears that Grifonetto was too weak to speak, but that he made a signal of assent, and received his mother's blessing at the last: "And then the noble stripling stretched his right hand to his youthful mother, pressing the white hand of his mother;

and afterwards forthwith he breathed his soul forth from his beauteous body, and died with numberless blessings of his mother instead of the curses she had given him before."

"After the death of Grifonetto and the flight of the conspirators, Gianpaolo took possession of Perugia. All who were suspected of complicity in the treason were massacred upon the piazza and in the cathedral. At the expense of more than a hundred murders, the chief of the Baglioni found himself master of the city on the 17th of July. First he caused the cathedral to be washed with wine and reconsecrated. Then he decorated the Palazzo with the heads of the traitors and with their portraits in fresco, painted hanging head downwards, as was the fashion in Italy. Next he established himself in what remained of the palaces of his kindred, hanging the saloons with black, and arraying his retainers in the deepest mourning. Sad, indeed, was now the aspect of Perugia. Helpless and comparatively uninterested, the citizens had been spectators of these bloody broils. They were now bound to share the desolation of their masters. Matarazzo's description of the mournful palace and the silent town, and of the return of Marcantonio from Naples, presents a picture striking for its vividness.[34] In the true style of the Baglioni, Marcantonio sought to vent his sorrow not so much in tears as by new violence. He prepared and lighted torches, meaning to burn the whole quarter of S. Angelo; and from this design he was with difficulty dissuaded by his brother. To such mad freaks of rage and passion were the inhabitants of a mediæval town in Italy exposed! They make us understand the *ordinanze di giustizia*, by which to be a noble was a crime in Florence.

"From this time forward the whole history of the Baglioni family is one of crime and bloodshed. A curse had fallen on the house, and to the last of its members the penalty was paid. Gianpaolo himself acquired the highest reputation throughout Italy for his courage and sagacity both as a general and a governor."

Gianpaolo is the last member of the Baglioni brood who succeeded in ruling over his native city, maintaining the despotic traditions of his predecessors by a system of unconscionable brutality. The personality of this tyrant is strongly brought forward in Italian histories. Frolliere gives the following account of the fascination of the outward man:

"Gianpaolo during his life-time was the favoured one of Heaven and of fortune. He was handsome and of a gracious aspect, pleasant and benign; eloquent in his conversation, and of great prudence; and every gesture harmonised with his words and manner. In his desire to please all, even strangers, if perchance he was unable or unwilling to serve them, he showed himself so gracious and so willing, that they left him satisfied and pleased. He was much given to the love of women and he was greatly loved by them by reason of his delicate and lordly bearing. He was, indeed, a valiant and a gallant knight, of admirable and almost divine talent and resource, as was shown in many of his enterprises and his actions."[35]

But there was a very different side to this in the character of Gianpaolo, and we hear that on one occasion

... "he had it in his mind to murder four citizens of Perugia, his enemies. He looked calmly on while his kinsmen Eusebio and Taddeo Baglioni, who had been accused of treason, were hewn to pieces by his guard. His wife, Ippolita de' Conti, was poniarded on her Roman farm; on hearing the news, he ordered a festival in which he was engaged to proceed with redoubled merriment."[36]

Gianpaolo was also a good diplomatist, as cautious as he was cruel, and one of the most striking pictures in Perugian history is that of his reception of Julius II. in 1506, on which occasion the Pope came to visit the tyrant in person. The Baglioni was perfectly well aware that Julius had come for the purpose of re-establishing papal dominion in the city; but he was too cautious to shove His Holiness over a wall which he was building at the time, and thus to counterfeit the papal plans and set all Italy ablaze with admiration at the audacity of his action:

"While Michelangelo was planning frescoes and venting his bile in sonnets, the fiery Pope had started on his perilous career of conquest. He called the cardinals together, and informed them that he meant to free the cities of Perugia and Bologna from their tyrants. God, he said, would protect His Church; he could rely on the support of France and Florence. Other popes had stirred up wars and used the services of Generals; he meant to take the field in person. Louis XII. is reported to have jeered among his courtiers at the notion of a high-priest riding to the wars. A few days afterwards, on the 27th of August, the Pope left Rome attended by twenty-four cardinals and 500 men-at-arms. He had previously secured the neutrality of Venice and a promise of troops from the French court. When Julius reached Orvieto, he was met by Gianpaolo, the bloody and licentious despot of Perugia. Notwithstanding Baglioni knew that Julius was coming to assert his supremacy, and notwithstanding the Pope knew that this might drive to desperation a man so violent and stained with crime as Baglioni, they rode together to Perugia, where Gianpaolo paid homage and supplied his haughty guest with soldiers. The rashness of this act of Julius sent a thrill of admiration throughout Italy, stirring that sense of *terribilità* which fascinated the imagination of the men of the Renaissance. Machiavelli, commenting upon the action of the Baglioni, remarks that the event proved how difficult it is for a man to be perfectly and scientifically wicked."[37]

The Story of Perugia

* * * * * * *

"At last the time came for Gianpaolo to die by fraud and violence. Leo X., anxious to remove so powerful a rival from Perugia, lured him in 1520 to Rome under the false protection of a papal safe-conduct. After a short imprisonment he had him beheaded in the Castle of S. Angelo. It was thought that Gentile, his first cousin, sometime Bishop of Orvieto, but afterwards the father of two sons in wedlock with Giulia Vitelli—such was the discipline of the Church at this epoch—had contributed to the capture of Gianpaolo, and had exulted in his execution. If so, he paid dear for his treachery; for Orazio Baglioni, the second son of Gianpaolo and captain of the Church under Clement VII., had him murdered in 1527, together with his two nephews Fileno and Annibale. This Orazio was one of the most bloodthirsty of the whole brood. Not satisfied with the assassination of Gentile, he stabbed Galeotto, the son of Grifonetto, with his own hand in the same year. Afterwards he died in the kingdom of Naples while leading the Black Bands in the disastrous war which followed the sack of Rome. He left no son. Malatesta, his elder brother, became one of the most celebrated generals of the age, holding the batons of the Venetian and Florentine republics, and managing to maintain his ascendency in Perugia in spite of the persistent opposition of successive popes. But his name is best known in history for one of the greatest public crimes. Intrusted with the defence of Florence during the siege of 1530, he sold the city to his enemy, Pope Clement, receiving for the price of this infamy certain privileges and immunities which fortified his hold upon Perugia for a season. All Italy was ringing with the great deeds of the Florentines, who for the sake of their liberty transformed themselves from merchants into soldiers, and withstood the united powers of pope and emperor alone. Meanwhile Malatesta, whose trade was war, and who was being largely paid for his services by the beleaguered city, contrived by means of diplomatic procrastination, secret communication with the enemy, and all the arts that could intimidate an army of recruits, to push affairs to a point at which Florence was forced to capitulate without inflicting the last desperate glorious blow she longed to deal her enemies. The universal voice of Italy condemned him. When Matteo Dandolo, the Doge of Venice, heard what he had done, he cried before the Pregadi in conclave, 'He has sold that people and that city, and the blood of those poor citizens ounce by ounce, and has donned the cap of the biggest traitor in the world.' Consumed with shame, corroded by an infamous disease, and mistrustful of Clement, to whom he had sold his honor, Malatesta retired to Perugia, and died in 1531. He left one son, Ridolfo, who was unable to maintain himself in the lordship of his native city. After killing the papal legate, Cinzio Filonardi, in 1534, he was dislodged four years afterwards, when Paul III. took final possession of the place as an appanage of the Church, razed the houses of the Baglioni to the ground, and built upon their site the Rocca Paolina....

... "Ridolfo Baglioni and his cousin Braccio, the eldest son of Grifonetto, were both captains of Florence. The one died in battle in 1554, the other in 1559. Thus ended the illustrious family. They are now represented by descendants from females, and by contadini, who preserve their name and boast a pedigree, of which they have no written records."[38]

* * * * * * *

Thus the Baglioni practically killed themselves—stamped out their own power through their own passions. It remained for the Church to crush if possible the spirit of liberty and of self-government in the people of Perugia. It is as though a mighty wheel spun round and we next find the city wholly and entirely in the clutches of Rome.

When the last strong member of the terrible brood, Ridolfo Baglioni, forced his way back into Perugia with the evident intention of ruling there, he seems to have ignored the fact that he had something more powerful to face than the opposition of the people. Ridolfo set fire to the people's palace, but he went much further, he assassinated the Pope's Legate. This outrage gave the final push to Rome, who had so often and so impotently interfered before, and Paul Farnese, the reigning Pope, listened, we hear, with the profoundest displeasure to the account of this barefaced murder. He at once took the high hand. He sent troops from Rome to drive out Ridolfo, who retired before them to seek a better fortune elsewhere. He then had the walls of Spello, Bettona, Bastia, and other strongholds of Ridolfo Baglioni demolished, and finally, in order to make his policy more permanent and decisive, the great Farnese Pope arrived in person at Perugia.

Paul's arrival is one of the most impressive points in the annals of the town. The rule of the Baglioni had been so powerful and so picturesque that in tracing it one is inclined to ignore the undercurrent of affairs in the city. As a matter of fact the old order of rule had not really died out under that of the nobles, and in the description of Paul's reception we find the familiar names of companies and *Priori* occurring again and again with all their followers and titles.

The Perugians, wearied to death by the despotic rule of the nobles, hailed the advent of a much more despotic Pope with blind and excessive joy. Paul came in triumph, and in triumph he was received. Great arches were built for him and for his cardinals to pass beneath, and since the town had not sufficient money to spend on his reception they even melted down a beautiful silver ship belonging to the city plate chest. It was on the last day of August 1535, and at about midnight, that "His Blessed Holiness" arrived at the gates with fourteen cardinals and some companies of 600 or 700 horse and 700 infantry. The Pope rode up on horseback, dressed in scarlet. Drums and tambours heralded his approach. The cardinals rode by two and two. On either side of His Holiness rode his two nephews: the Cardinals Alexander Farnese and Guido Ascanio Sforza. The *Priori*, all in new and gorgeous robes, preceded by the Holy Eucharist, came out to meet him, and through their ambassador or *nunzio* they presented to His Holiness a silver basin containing the keys of the city. Then a learned doctor of the University delivered "a short but elegant address," to which the Pope listened attentively, and for that night the Pope turned in to sleep in the monastery of S. Pietro. The following day he entered the city with extraordinary pomp and took up his abode in the Palazzo Pubblico, where the *Priori* had vacated their own rooms in order to give him proper space; and thither all the professors and all the members of the city guilds and confraternities arrived that afternoon to kiss his foot.

Paul's first visit to Perugia may be called a triumphal progress rather than anything else. He gave great gifts of grain to the city, and he conferred countless benefits upon its churches and its clergy. But he came to rule, and not to pamper or caress. For a time all went well. The convents and the monasteries grew fat and prosperous, the Baglioni were away, and the people apparently at peace; but storms were brewing. After three years of passive submission Perugia found cause to revolt against her new ruler as she had done against her old. In 1538 Paul III. sent out his decree for raising the price of salt by one half in all the pontifical states, and the Perugians revolted at once against an imposition which they had good reason to feel unjust.[39]

Revolution was declared. Alfano Alfani, the chief of the magistrates, tried to calm the fury of his countrymen, and at first only humble entreaties were sent down to Rome imploring Paul III. to remove a tax so odious to the people. But the Pope was too much in need of money to listen to these prayers. His only answer was an excommunication, which punishment was not unfamiliar to the people of Perugia. During the month of March 1539 the city lay under an interdict, no masses were said, no sacraments given, and the churches seemed as the monuments of a people long since dead. Every day the murmurings of the Perugians grew and strengthened, and finally they took the high-handed measure of arranging matters for themselves. They elected twenty-five citizens who were called "the twenty-five defenders of justice in the city of Perugia," and before many days were out the "twenty-five" had obtained unlimited power. They exercised an independent and undisputed authority and pushed the *priori* entirely to one side. Their endeavours to protect their liberty and resist the Pope's authority soon roused his anger. The Farnese was not a person to be trifled with, and this barefaced rebellion of the little Umbrian city had to be crushed by prompt and powerful means; so the Pope sent his son, Pier Luigi Farnese, at the head of 10,000 Italians and 3000 Spaniards to meet the rulers in the field.

A strange piece of history follows. The Perugians veer round utterly and call in as their leader Ridolfo Baglioni to help them against a Pope, whom but three short years ago they had welcomed as their best benefactor.

Ridolfo went forth to fight against the Papal troops with a mighty flourish of trumpets, but we only hear faint rumours of a skirmish near Ponte S. Giovanni where one or two men were killed, and a few more tumbled off their chargers. The whole account reads like a farce, and yet we know that men and women regarded it with deadly earnest at the time. The city was all unhinged. An extraordinary religious phase which had nothing to do with the Church came over her. The large crucifix which is still to be seen in S. Lorenzo, was placed above the main entrance to the Duomo, and here the people came to pray and tell their beads with an unwonted fervour. Continual processions wound their slow way up from S. Domenico to the Cathedral square, and we hear that the cries for mercy were deafening throughout the city.

The Story of Perugia

On a dark night, by the flickering light of many torches, Maria Podiano, the Chancellor of the Commune, delivered a touching oration, and in the sight of all the citizens he placed the city keys at the foot of the great crucifix on the outside of the Cathedral—Christ was to be their defender, Christ their leader, to fight against a Pope![40]

But it was impossible that Perugia should be able to stand against such an army as that of Paul III., and Ridolfo Baglioni was the first to see that his side must lose. With less loyalty than might have been expected from this would-be despot of Perugia, he edged towards peace, and finally, on the 3rd June 1540, peace was concluded between Pier Luigi Farnese and Ridolfo Baglioni. Thus it happened that once again Perugia was cast under the shadow of Pontifical Rome. Neighbouring towns had abandoned her at the moment when she wrestled for her liberty; Ridolfo Baglioni had given her but a half-hearted help, and the Perugians were driven to confess that the only course which now lay open to them was an apology to the Pope. Twenty-five ambassadors were therefore sent to Rome. Dressed in long black robes with halters round their necks, the unhappy Perugian envoys crouched in the portico of S. Peter's awaiting their absolution.

Pardon was obtained, but at a heavy price. The ambassadors returned home bearing the news that Paul had forgiven the city; but the titles of Preservers of Ecclesiastical Obedience, borne by the Pope's magistrates, warned Perugia quite sufficiently that her old forms of government were wiped away for ever. A few days later and the foundations of Paul III.'s fortress were laid on the site of the razed palaces of the Baglioni, and the citizens were compelled to lend their help in the erection of this colossal stronghold which was to prove their bane for centuries to follow. On its inner walls it bore the following inscription, which fully indicated the feelings and intentions of the indomitable Farnese: *Ad coercendam Perusinorum Audaciam.*[41]

Writhing beneath the yoke of priests, the Perugians soon regretted even the rule of the Baglioni: "Help me if you can," Malatesta Baglioni had cried as he lay dying at Bettona in 1531, "for after my death you will be made to draw the cart like oxen"; and Frolliere, chronicling these words, remarks: "This has been fulfilled to the last letter, for all have borne not only the yoke but the goad."[42]

In the same year (1540) as that in which Paul III. laid the foundations of his famous fortress, a society, which proved of invaluable service in furthering the work and wishes of the Papacy, sprang forth into vigorous life, and gradually the chief power in Perugia fell into the hands of the Jesuits. These agents of the Pope proceeded to convert the city wholesale by means of religious ceremonies, general confessions, preachings in every square, and in all the corners of the streets, and colossal processions, headed by missionaries wearing crowns of thorns and bearing enormous crosses. Industries died out, poverty, famine, and pestilence decimated the city, and in 1728, from a petition presented to Clement X., it appears that Perugia was reduced to such a state of wretchedness as to bring tears to the eyes of those who remembered her former prosperity.

* * * * * * *

The final history of Perugia, down to the present day, may be compressed into a very few lines. Up to the end of the last century, she was practically ruled by the Popes, and was a city of the Papal States. Her immense convents and churches were filled with monks and nuns. In 1549, Julius III. restored to her some of her ancient privileges of which Paul had deprived her, and in some sort she regained her old forms of government, but she could never again be called by her historians an independent State. In 1797, during the general upheaval of Europe which followed the revolution in France, she underwent a quite new phase, and became a French Prefecture under the title of *Departimento del Trasimeno*. General la Valette levied tribute from the citizens, who were further harassed by the sudden break up of the Roman Republic and an Austrian occupation.

After the Battle of Marengo, in 1800, Perugia ceased to be Pontifical, and in 1809 she was formally annexed to the French Empire, and made a canton of Spoleto under a sub-prefect. By Napoleon's orders the convents of both sexes and of all orders were suppressed, the bishops and prelates were sent to Rome in carriage loads, and the poor monks and nuns were unfrocked and literally carted through the streets to their homes. When a turn came in the fortunes of the empire, Perugia became the victim of another change, and with the partial introduction of the papal sway, the monks and nuns returned to their convents.

FORTRESS OF PAUL III. SHOWING THE UPPER PART NOW OCCUPIED BY THE PREFETTURA, ETC., AND THE LOWER WING WHICH COVERED THE SITE OF THE PRESENT PIAZZA D'ARMI
(From a water-colour sketch now in the possession of Madame Brufani at Perugia.)

The Story of Perugia

In spite of its tyrannies, the Napoleonic occupation had given the Perugians a taste for better things than a papal despotism, and they never again found rest in the care of the Pope. They fretted and chafed under the Pope's people; the Pope's fortress became a veritable eye-sore to them, the daily sight of its walls burned into their hearts like red-hot nails, and whenever they could they pulled a part of it down.

At last, in 1859, they rose in open rebellion, and Papal troops were sent by Pius IX. to besiege the town. Some 2000 of the Swiss Guard, led by Colonel Schmid, arrived from Rome to quell the insurrection. Bonazzi gives a vivid account of the atrocities these men committed in the city. They killed all whom they laid hands on in their raids as they passed through the streets, crying aloud as they went that "their master the Pope had given them orders that none should be spared." S. Pietro was forced, and, notwithstanding the protests of the Abbot and his monks, its vestments were torn to threads, gold and silver ornaments carried away, and not even the archives with their wealth of long accumulated missals escaped the vandalism of the papal troops. (See p. 162.)

In 1860 the Swiss were finally dislodged by Victor Emanuel's envoy, General Manfredo Fanti; and, unarmed and closely guarded by a double file of the King's soldiers, the last representatives of papal power were driven from the fortress of Paul III., and having passed a night in the cathedral, they were ousted for ever from the precincts of Perugia. Paul III.'s fortress had now been entirely pulled down by an infinite number of willing hands, and the present great buildings of the Prefettura, which represents the modern government of a prosperous town, took their place on the former site of the Baglioni palaces.

* * * * * * *

With the loss of Perugia's independent existence in 1540 the light of romance was lost to her history. But from that minute, and in spite of all her anguish and humiliation, she learned the final lesson of how to live at peace within herself, and be at peace with all her neighbours. This lesson she had never learned through all her battlings in the past. She had risen fighting, and fighting she had flourished. It would be inaccurate to say that fighting she fell.

Perugia never fell. She was merely caught and tamed. Anyone familiar with the cities of Umbria will at once recognise in this, their head, something forcible, strong, grand, and enduring, which neither nobles, emperors, nor popes were able to beat out of her; something which has kept her what she was at the beginning: Perugia, the city of plenty, and fitted her to be what she is now: Perugia the capital of Umbria; as grand in her unity with her great mother, as she was powerful in her strife.

CHAPTER IV

The City of Perugia

"C'est une vieille ville du moyen âge, ville de défense et de refuge, posée sur un plateau escarpé, d'où toute la vallée se découvre."—H. Taine, *Voyage en Italie*.

HAVING glanced thus rapidly over the history of Perugia we turn with fresh interest to examine the city itself, and to trace through what remains of its earliest walls and houses, the character of those same fascinating, if pugnacious persons, who built those walls, fought over them, lived and died within them.

Perugia is an excellent mirror of history, combining on its surface not only a reflection of the immortal past but of a prosperous present, and with the exception of ancient Roman influences, which, for some obscure reason, have almost entirely vanished, it would be difficult to find a nest of man more perfect or unchanged in all its parts. Battered and abused by warfare and by weather the stones of the middle ages may be and are, but they have not been destroyed, and there is something grand and clean in the modern buildings which confirms, rather than destroys, the æsthetic charm and splendour of the old.

The Story of Perugia

Perugia is very distinctly the living capital of the province. After travelling through Umbria and studying one by one the little dreamy old-world cities—each perched upon its separate hillside, which seem to have fallen asleep long centuries ago, letting the silence of the grass close in on their paved streets, as the need of self-protection vanished—one returns to Perugia and recognises that she, at least, has never died. She is often very silent, very brown and grim; she has her dreams, but the hope in her: the desire for rule and power, has never really vanished. The most remarkable change about the town, if we are to take what we read of her history for certain fact, is the change in her people. The inhabitants of Perugia, in every class, are unmistakably gentle and amiable, both in mind and manner. They are courteous to strangers, kind, helpful and calm. Even the street boys ask one for stamps instead of pennies. In their leisure they are gay, and in their work persistent. They are never frantic or demonstrative. As one sits at one's window on warm spring nights, one almost wishes the people in the street would either fight or sing, but they do neither. They take their pleasures calmly, and hang upon their town walls by the hour, gazing out upon a view they love. Perhaps in their inmost hearts they are counting the numberless little cities, all of which their fathers won for them in battles of the past. The fact of their supremacy may make them thrill, but there is nothing to mark their triumph in their faces.

The Story of Perugia

PERUGIA FROM THE ROAD TO THE CAMPO SANTO

This is no place in which to discuss the rapid change of personality in the Perugians. We note it as a fact, and pass to a description of the town itself, which certainly contains abundant marks of that same "warlike" character which time has washed away from the minds of its inhabitants.

The city is built, as we have shown in our first chapter, on one of the low hills formed after thousands of years by the silting up of the refuse brought down by the Tiber, and not, as one naturally at first imagines, on a spur of the actual Apennines which are divided from her by the river. Much of the power of the town in the past may be traced to her extraordinary topographical position. Perugia stands 1705 feet above the level of the sea, and 1200 above that of the Tiber. She stands perfectly alone at the extreme edge of a long spine of hill, and she commands the Tiber and the two great roads to Rome.[43] But looked at from a merely picturesque point of view, few towns can boast of a more powerful charm. Perugia, if one ignores her history, is not so much a town as an eccentric freak of nature. All the winds and airs of heaven play and rush around her walls in summer and in winter. The sun beats down upon her roofs; one seems to see more stars at night, above her ramparts, than one sees in any other town one knows of. All Umbria is spread like a great pageant at her feet, and the pageant is never one day or one hour like the other. Even in a downpour, even in a tempest the great view fascinates. In spring the land is green with corn and oak trees, and pink with the pink of sainfoin flowers. In winter it seems smaller, nearer; brown and gold, and very grand at sundown. On clear days one can easily trace a whole circle of Umbrian cities from the Umbrian capital. To the east Assisi, Spello, Foligno, Montefalco, and Trevi. The hill above Bettona hides the town of Spoleto, but its ilex woods and its convent of Monte Luco are distinct enough. To the south Todi and Deruta stand out clear upon their hillsides; and to the east the home of Perugino, Città della Pieve, rises half hidden in its oakwoods. Early in the mornings you will see the mists lift slowly from the Tiber; at night the moon will glisten on its waters, drawing your fancy down to Rome. Strange lights shine upon the clouds behind the ridge which covers Trasimene, and to the north the brown hills rise and swell, fold upon fold, to meet the Apennines. In autumn and in winter the basin of the old Umbrian lake will often fill for days with mists, but the Umbrian towns and hamlets rise like the birds above them, and one may live in one of these in splendid sunshine, whilst looking down upon a sea of fog which darkens all the people of the plain.

The inhabitants of Perugia swear by the healthy nature of their air, and indeed, were it not for the winds, the most fragile constitution would probably flourish in the high hill city. But it must be confessed that there come days when man and horse quiver like dead leaves before the tempest, and when the very houses seem to rock. Indeed, it would be almost impossible to exaggerate the arctic power of a Perugian whirlwind. Yet the average temperature is mild, and myrtles grow to the size of considerable trees in the villa gardens round the town.

To fully understand the city of Perugia, the marvellous fashion of its building, and the way in which its houses have become a part of the landscape and seem to creep about and cling to the unsteady crumbling soil, one should pass out into the country through one of its gates, and, rambling round the roads and lanes which wind beneath its walls, look ever up and back again towards the town. In this way only is it possible to understand what man can do with Nature, and how, with the centuries, Nature can gather to herself man's handiwork and make of it a portion for herself. Birds and beasts have built in this same fashion, but rarely except in Umbria have men.

"The unstable quality of the soil on which Perugia is built," writes Mariotti, "has made strong walls and very costly buildings a necessity," and he goes on to point out the different and expensive ways in which the town has been bolstered up with solid masonry. The Etruscans were the first to recognise this necessity. They may have been a peaceful and a rather bourgeois set of human beings, differing in all ways from their combative successors, but they understood the science of building, and their walls, which encompassed only about one-third of the space covered by the mediæval town, remain a monument of splendid solid masonry wherever they can be traced.

ETRUSCAN ARCH. PORTA EBURNEA

The Etruscan walls are a marked feature of some Umbrian cities, and although it is rather the fashion to dispute their authenticity in Perugia, the bits which remain of them there are probably quite genuine. They have, however, become such a part of the mediæval and the modern town, and are often so embedded in later buildings, that without close study it is difficult to trace them; we have therefore marked their course in red on the map of the town.

Five of the present gates of the town, namely, *Porta Eburnea, Porta Susanna, Porta Augusta, Porta Mandola,* and *Porta Marzia* are the genuine old gates of the Etruscan town, and although the Romans altered them a little, enlarging them from below, a great part of their masonry is the work of the Etruscans, and from three to four thousand years old. Of these gates, the *Porta Augusta* is familiar to every one, as it is one of the most remarkable and impressive features of the town. Rome and the Renaissance have combined to give it a fantastic and a fascinating appearance, even as these same influences have made a miniature museum of the now disused *Porta Marzia*. Strangely enough the work of the Etruscan masons is far better preserved than any which followed them, and the great blocks of travertine neatly placed (as some suppose without mortar) on one another, are easily distinguishable from those built above and below them. Perugia always felt a certain respect for her oldest walls, and even in the fifteenth century, when she was in her prime, and bristling with new towers and churches, the work of the dead people was respected. In 1475 we read that a law was passed for the preservation of the Etruscan walls, as "they were very marvellous, and worthy to be preserved into all eternity."

MEDIÆVAL STAIRCASE IN THE VIA BARTOLO

Beyond the city walls nothing remains of the Etruscans at Perugia, except what is found in their tombs. That the town was rich in temples and other beauties we may gather, but these, together with the houses, were destroyed when Augustus took the town in 40 B.C., and when her devoted citizen, Caius Cestius, set fire to his native city, to cover her disgrace. Of the Roman occupation, which covered a period of many centuries, no trace remains in Perugia. The present town is therefore a monument of the purest mediæval building crowned by some rare and beautiful bits of Renaissance architecture.

But before entering into a description of the city, it may be well to insist once more on the fact already made plain in our history, that if men made Perugia, men also marred her. [44] The impatience of man is everywhere discernible in her streets her palaces and churches, and only the latest buildings have their towers and stones intact. The towers of S. Pietro, S. Domenico, and others have had their tops all truncated by popes, by nobles, and by people in moments of their fury or their vengeance. The city was built for warfare and defence, and not for beauty, luxury and peace. In these comparatively quiet times of ours we go about in foreign towns and look for art, and art alone. We seem to forget that art is but a small affair—a little landmark in the history of nations. There is an art in Umbria, an art so pure, so sweet, so tender that thinking of it we may easily forget the history of her men, or, if remembering, we seem to dream a dual dream. The art of Perugia was, maybe, the outcome of her almost fanatical religion, but the wars of her inhabitants have always been her life-blood. The very first walls were built for defence, or, as some say, to store the crops, the corn and hay, in; and the houses of the earliest mediæval town were also built purely with a view to personal safety and protection. Bonazzi gives a curious account of the growth of the city, and the almost fantastic fashion in which its inhabitants hammered its houses together, and then proceeded to live in them. "There were," he says, describing the town in about 1100 and 1200, "few monuments or buildings of importance up to the sixteenth century. The houses were all on one floor, the sun barely reached them; some of them were of stone and bricks, but the greater part of mud, clay and straw. Hence incessant and considerable fires, increased by the lack of chimneys. And they were so inconveniently arranged that often eight or ten persons slept in a single room. A motto, a saint, some small sign took the place of our modern numbers, and the lamp which burned in front of the many shrines served to light the streets at nightfall. There were no flags or pavements then upon the streets, which took their names from the churches or houses of the nobles which happened to look down upon them; these were narrow and tortuous, simply because they grew without any method or premeditation, they were horrible to behold as all the dirt was thrown into them, and because of the herds of swine which passed along them, grunting and squeaking as they went."[45] Bonazzi next goes on to trace the topography of the mediæval town, which was much smaller than the present one, and lacking in large monuments. There was no Corso in those days, no Piazza Sopramuro, no Palazzo Pubblico. Where the present cathedral now stands there was only the little old church of S. Lorenzo and a big and beautiful tower with a cock on the top of it. The towers of Perugia were a most marked feature of her architecture and, indeed, in old writings she is always mentioned as *Turrena* because of them.[46] "About this time," says Bonazzi, "another great work began in our city, which was continued into the following centuries. The feudal lords who came in from their own places in the country to inhabit the town, brought with them each the tradition of his own strong tower in the abandoned castle. Great therefore was the competition between them of who should build the highest, and this each noble did, not so much for decoration as for a means of defence and of offence, and according to the amount of power possessed by himself or by his neighbour.... In the shadow of the massive feudal towers," Bonazzi writes in another place, "like grass which is shaded by giant plants, rose the little houses of the poor. The more elegant houses were of terra-cotta (bricks) without plaster or mortar, and their windows were arched in the Roman fashion.[47] After 600 they were roofed with flat tiles in imitation of the Lombards."

The city gates were always closed at nightfall, and some of the streets were blocked by means of huge iron chains which stretched across the road, preventing the passage of horse or carts, from one house to another. One can still see the hooks and holes belonging to these somewhat barbaric defences in some of the more solid houses of Perugia; and in the neighbouring town of Spello the chains themselves have been left hanging to one of the houses. In 1276 we read that the law of closing the city gates was abolished, but a little later on it was again found necessary to barricade the town at nightfall, and during some of the fights between the nobles in 1400 and in 1500 we hear of the difficulties which one or the other party had to combat in the "chains across their path."

Strange scattered relics of this nest of mediæval man linger and come down to us even in the nineteenth century. Amongst these are the *porte del mortuccio*, or doors of the dead. All the best houses had these doors alongside of their house-doors, but they are bricked up now and quite disused, and might easily be ignored in passing through the streets. The *porta del mortuccio* is tall, narrow, and pointed at the top; it is, indeed, just wide enough to pass a coffin through. It seems that in very early days, even so far back as the Etruscans, there was a superstition that through the door where Death had passed, Death must enter in again. By building a separate door, which was only used by the dead, the spirit of Death passed out with the corpse, the narrow door was closely locked behind it, and the safety of the living was secured, as far as the living can secure, from Death. Other charming details of the mediæval city are the house doors. They are built of travertine or *pietra serena*, and have little garlands of flowers and fruit bound with ribbons, and delicate friezes above them. Some of them have very beautiful Latin inscriptions, which show a strong religious sentiment. We quote a few of them here: *Janua coeli* (door of heaven, over a church); *Pulchra janua ubi honesta domus* (beautiful the door of the house which is honest); *A Deo cuncta—a domino omnia* (all things from God); *Ora ut vivas et Deo vives* (pray to live and thou shalt live to God); *Prius mori quam fædari* (die rather than be disgraced); *In parvis quies* (in small things peace); *Solicitudo mater divitiarum* (carefulness is the mother of riches); *Ecce spes I.H.S. mea semper* (Christ always my hope).

Over one or two of the doorways in Perugia you will find almost byzantine bits of tracery with figures of unknown animals—beasts of the Apocalypse—carved in grey travertine all round them. One of the very earliest bits of mediæval building is the fragment of a door of this sort, belonging to the first palace of the *Priori*, which is now almost buried in the more modern buildings of the sixteenth century. There is another amusing procession of beasts over a gateway below S. Ercolano. These odd animal friezes were probably first designed for some sort of closed market where beasts were sold, and the old Pescheria has medallions of *lasche* on its walls.

As for the ways and manners of the people who inhabited this mediæval city, Ciatti and other writers supply us with plenty of fantastic information:

"Perugia lies beneath the sign of the Lion and of the Virgin," Ciatti says in his account, which is as usual, unlike the account of anybody else, and highly entertaining, "and from this cause it comes that the city is called *Leonina*[48] and *Sanguinia*, and the habits of the Perugians are neither luxurious nor effeminate. Like those of whom Siderius writes, they came forth strong in war, they delighted in fish, were humorous in speech, swift in counsel, and loved the law of the Pope.... The women," he continues with a certain monastic indifference to female charm, "were not beautiful, although Siderius calls them elegant;[49] the genius of Perugia was ever more inclined to the exercise of arms than the cultivation of beauty, and many famous captains have brought fame to this their native city through their brave deeds. In Tuscany the Sienese have the reputation of being frivolous, the Pisans astute and malicious, the Florentines slow and serious, and the Perugians ferocious and of a warlike spirit."

Concerning the clothes and the feasts of this combative race of people who lived for warfare rather than for delight, we hear that they were accustomed to wear a great deal of fur, the nobles using pelisses of martin and of sable, the poor, sheep or foxes' skins. The fur tippets still worn by the canons of cathedrals in Italian towns in winter are probably a remnant of these days. For the rest an adaptation of the Roman tunic was perhaps worn by the men, whilst the women kept to the tradition of the Etruscan headgear. "Victuals," Bonazzi tells us, "were of a coarse description, more lard and pepper was eaten in those days, than meat and coffee in ours. But at the feasts of the priests and nobles an incredible quantity of exquisite viands was consumed; great animals stuffed with dainties were cooked entire, and monstrous pasties served at table, from which, when the knife touched them, a living and jovial dwarf jumped out upon the table, unexpected and to the great delight of all the company."

* * * * * * *

But from the Age of Darkness men awoke both in their manners and in their buildings. Perugia of the Middle Ages shook the sleep from off her heavy eyelids, and with that passionate impulse towards Light which was perhaps the secret of the Renaissance, she too strove toward the Beautiful, and in a hurried, fevered fashion, she too decked herself with fairer things than castle towers and hovels. The fourteenth and the fifteenth centuries were, as we know, the Age of Gold in later art, and Perugia, in spite of all her tumults, in spite of her feuds, and even her passionate religious abstinences, woke with the waking world. Most of her churches, and most of those monuments which mark her as a point for travellers, date from that period. "And at that time," says the chronicler Fabretti, "there was so great a building going on in different parts of the city that neither mortar nor stones nor masons could have been procured even for money, unless a number of Lombards had come in to build. And they were building the palace of the *Priori* (Palazzo Pubblico), they were building S. Lorenzo, Santa Maria dei Servi, S. Domenico, S. Francesco, the houses of Messer Raniero ... the tower of the Palazzo, and numerous other houses of private citizens all at that same time."

But it was not merely a love of beauty which prompted the Perugians to this sudden departure in the way of architecture; the spirit of the great saint of Umbria had much to do with it. In Perugian chronicles and histories we find a strange silence about the influence of S. Francis on a city which was only separated by some fourteen miles from Assisi. Yet it is not possible that so strong a force as that of this man's preaching could have been kept outside the walls of the neighbour town, and Ciatti declares that at one time nearly a third part of the inhabitants of Perugia took the Franciscan habit. In 1500 and 1600 there were more than fifty convents in Perugia, many of which had sixty to eighty inhabitants, but that was during the rule of the popes. Of the great period of building in the fourteenth century, which included many fine churches and convents, the buildings of the people and not of the priests remain intact. The splendid Palazzo Pubblico and Pisano's fountain in the square belong to this period. But because the work of the Renaissance is so conspicuous and charming we have described it in another place, and in our description of the town have lingered rather over the fragments of the Etruscan and the mediæval city.

As it would be impossible in this small book to give anything beyond a cursory sketch of all the different buildings of the town, we have decided to deal with the details of some of the principal ones, leaving the rest for the discovery of those whose leisure and intelligence will always make such exploration a delight. There is no lack of excellent guide-books to Perugia. Of the fuller and rarer ones we would mention those of Siepi and Orsini and the more modern one of Count Rossi Scotti. These are in Italian. Murray's last edition of "Central Italy" contains clear and excellent general information, and there are several small local guides—the best of these by Lupatelli—which can be had in the hotel. No one who really desires to study the town should fail to read the fascinating books of its best lover, Annibale Mariotti; and the works of Conestabile and Vermiglioli are invaluable for students. All these can be had in the public library of the town where there is a pleasant quiet room in which to study them, and the excessive courtesy of whose head—Count Vincenzo Ansidei—makes research an easy pleasure there.

The topography of Perugia is simple: "The entire city," says Mariotti, "since the very earliest days, was divided into five quarters or *rioni*, which from the centre, that is to say, the highest point of the town, and with as gentle an incline as the condition of the ground allows, stretch out in five different directions like so many sunbeams across the mountain side. These gates are: *Porta Sole* to the east, *Porta Susanna* to the west (formerly called Trasimene), *Porta S. Angelo* (formerly Porta Augusta) to the north, *Porta S. Pietro* to the south, and *Porta Eburnea* to the southwest. Each of these separate gates bears its own armorial design and colour. Porta Sole is white and bears a sun with rays; Porta Susanna blue, with a chain; Porta S. Angelo red, with a branch of arbutus; Porta S. Pietro yellow, with a balance, and Porta Eburnea green, with a pilgrim's staff."

Owing to the extraordinary situation of the town there are hardly any level squares or streets. The two considerable flat open spaces on either side of the Prefettura, the site of the Prefettura itself and of the hotel Brufani are artificial spaces, the result of the demolition of Paul III.'s fortress (see chap. vi.). We imagine that many intelligent persons have passed through the comfortable hotel of Perugia not realising at all the artificial nature of the ground on which it stands. The Corso and the Piazza di S. Lorenzo may be said to be the heart of the town; its pulse beats a little lower down in the Piazza Sopramuro where fruit and vegetables are sold and where there is a perpetual market-day.[50] The other big open square is the Piazza d'Armi, on a lower level of the hill and to the south of the town. There the cattle fair is held on Tuesdays, and there the beautiful white Umbrian oxen, with skins that are finer than the cattle of the plain, and the grey Umbrian pigs, and tall Umbrian men and girls can be seen in all their glory. Here too is the convent of S. Giuliana with its splendid cloisters and little Gothic campanile, and here above all do the soldiers of Perugia practice their bands, their horses, and their bugles every morning.

There are three things lacking in Perugia, as there are naturally in all hill-cities, and these are gardens, carriages, and running water. But all these wants have been delightfully overcome by the inhabitants. As a matter of fact, there are plenty of hidden gardens, behind the houses in the town, but in almost every house you will see that iron sockets or rings have been fastened to the walls below the windows, and in these, pots of geraniums, daisies, and carnations are hung and tended with excessive care. Some of the better palaces or convents have stone brackets in the shape of shells for window gardens, and even in the dusk of grim December days the old stone walls seem green and living. The lack of carriages is really only felt in winter when the inhabitants seem to fall for the while asleep, leaving the streets to assume their mediæval character, and to be swept by winter hurricanes; in spring and summer the place is gay enough; indeed the Corso is a very good specimen of Umbrian Piccadilly on a fine May evening, and there are plenty of carriages in the tourist season. But go into any palace of Perugia and you will find the sedan chairs of our grandfathers ready for instant use, proving that carriages are quite a modern innovation in the town.

PIAZZA SOPRAMURO, SHOWING THE PALACE OF THE CAPITANO DEL POPOLO AND THE BUILDINGS OF THE FIRST UNIVERSITY OF PERUGIA

The need of running water is, of course, the most serious point about so big and prosperous a city, and a running stream to turn a paper mill would heal more ills than all her pictures and her wide calm view. The great rushing stream of the Tiber down at the foot of the hill seems like a sort of solemn mockery to people who have only wells and a little river from the hill to drink from and to wash their linen in. We have realized this on winter nights when the Tiber was out in flood in the moonlight down below our windows, and small drops freezing, one by one, on Pisano's fountain behind us in the square.

Yet the town is prosperous. Its inhabitants and those of the commune have increased by some six thousand since the days of its first prosperity. Commerce, it is true, seems somewhat at a standstill. There is the commerce of travellers, which is by no means inconsiderable; and there is the commerce of Mind. This last Perugia has always had since the days when she grew powerful, and the University of Perugia has played a constant and important part throughout her annals. It was founded in the beginning of the fourteenth century, and its management, like other things in the city, was chiefly in the hands of the people and their representatives, the *Priori*. Five *Savi*, one from each *rione*, were told off to regulate its affairs and to elect its professors. Urban VIII. brought it under the management of the Church, but this did not in any way alter its first rules and laws. We hear that "the Emperor Charles IV. bestowed upon the University all those distinctions which were enjoyed by the most celebrated universities of the Empire," and Napoleon confirmed these and added much to the magnificence of Perugia's university. It was during the Napoleonic rule that the college was transferred from its old quarters in the Piazza Sopramuro to the vast new buildings at Montemorcino. Her three main branches of study are jurisprudence, science, and theology. Several of the popes studied in Perugia. S. Thomas Aquinas lectured here, and many distinguished men of science and of law passed through their first schools in the Umbrian hill town. The two great lawyers Baldo Baldeschi and Bartolo Alfani were students in the University of Perugia, and Alberico Gentile, who afterwards lectured in Oxford, studied here at the University. The affairs of war were never allowed to interfere with those of the mind, and we hear that a guarantee of safe conduct was given to any scholar who came here from a distance.

The arts of peace, such as the manufacture of wool and silken stuffs, were known in the middle ages in spite of the want of water (the hand and foot looms of Perugia are almost prehistoric in their simplicity), and in 1297 we hear of the magistrates of Perugia sending an embassy into Lombardy to fetch two friars thence who should teach their townsfolk the secrets of weaving. This art was zealously kept up for many years, but finally it fell into decay. A branch of it has lately been revived by a Milanese lady, and thanks to her efforts we are again able to buy the strange flame-patterned carpets which we find on the altars of so many of the older Umbrian churches.

Except in the Corso, life seems very quiet in Perugia. Yet though there is poverty, there is none of that feeling of decayed splendour, of arrested magnificence and luxury which we feel in so many cities of Italy. The Perugians were probably never very luxurious. There are one or two beautiful old palaces, but they are plain to look at, and the palaces of the nobles had a bad time of it and were constantly pulled to bits as their different owners were driven into the country. The town is a town of a strong people; it is dignified and peaceful. When the wind is not battering about its roofs and howling through its narrow streets one becomes aware of an extraordinary silence.

And in that silence the questions rise—one cannot stifle them: Where are the *Beccherini* and where are the *Raspanti*? Are the Baglioni really dead, and the Oddi, where are they? And the Flagellants and the *Penitenti*—have even their ghosts departed? Will not a pope ride in at the gates with his nephews and his cardinals and take up peaceful quarters in the grim Canonica? Will not some warlike Abbot come and batter down the church towers to build himself a palace?

Will no procession pass us with a banner of Bonfigli, and women wailing that the plague should be removed?...

The snow falls silently upon the roads in winter. No blood of nobles stains it. In May all Umbria is green with crops. No *condottiere* comes to trample down the corn. But high upon her hill-top Perugia stands as she stood then, and in her silence seems to wait for something yet to come.

* * * * * * *

Before closing this chapter we would once again repeat that no one with a few hours' leisure should forbear to wander round the outer walls of the town before leaving Perugia. With only one break: that which is formed by the deep ravine (or *bulagnjo* in the local dialect) between Porta Sant Antonio and Porta S. Angelo, one can walk on quite good paths and roads under the outer walls of the entire city. The Via della Cuparella is a pleasant lane reached by passing out through Porta Eburnea. It skirts under the mediæval and Etruscan walls to the west of the town and re-enters the city again a little below Porta Susanna. This lane is one of the most sheltered corners in Perugia, and we have wandered up and down it in the early days of January, and found the sleepy lizards basking on its banks and yellow aconites in all the furrows. The trees bud early there; their young green shimmers like a vision of immortal youth against the grim walls of the mediæval and Etruscan city up beyond.

Another charming walk is that along the eastern side of the town, passing out through Porta S. Ercolano and through the Corso away along the broad high-road to the convent of Monte Luce, which is quite one of the most fascinating buildings of Perugia, with its front of white and rosy marble, its court-yard and rose window, and the splendid block of its nunnery walls covering the crest of the hill behind the church. The convent was built early in the thirteenth century on the site, some say, of an Etruscan temple dedicated to the Goddess Feronia, but more probably in the sacred wood or *lucus* from which it derived its name. It was one of the most prosperous convents of the country, and Mariotti gives a delightful account of a visit paid by the great Farnese Pope, Paul III., to its Abbess. The Pope, it seems, gave himself the permission to visit the nuns, who received him, "marvelling," as the most learned nun of her day relates, "that the Vicar of God on earth should so far humiliate himself as to visit such vile servants, as we were." The Pope came into the church and took the seat prepared for him in the choir, "all of his own accord, without being helped by anybody, and like a meek and gentle lamb ... and being seated, he said to the sisters, 'Come everyone of you and kiss my foot.' " Then the Abbess and the sisters kissed the feet of the Pope. A long conversation and exchange of compliments followed, and finally at sundown the Pope departed, "very greatly edified."

CONVENT OF MONTE LUCE

From Monte Luce one road winds down to the Tiber, passing under the charming villa of Count Rossi Scotti, and another back into the city, first through a strange row of wooden booths which are opened on the feast day of Monte Luce (August 15th), and then on through the walls of Mommaggiore's fortress and back into the town through Porta S. Antonio.

But it is not possible to describe all the details of a place which, like all fair things, should be explored to be enjoyed. The discovery of its hidden lanes, its little wayside villas, and its churches must be left as it was left to the present writers, who never will forget the tramps they took in the brown winter twilight, the drives on warm spring afternoons when honeysuckle scented all the hedges, and the strange excited feelings which possessed them when they found the hidden wayside house or chapel, which had no written record to tell them who had built it, and nothing but its own Perugian charm to endear it to them, and to give it history.

CHAPTER V

Palazzo Pubblico, The Fountain, and the Duomo

IN Professor Freeman's small sketch of Perugia he says very truly that the most striking points of the city—that is to say, of the Mediæval and Renaissance period—are those which are gathered together in the *Piazza di San Lorenzo*.

The whole atmosphere of the square is unique and impressive: individual as are the piazzas of the largest and the smallest towns in Italy which have battled for their independence throughout the course of centuries. The buildings have been changed about, burnt, battered and rebuilt, but the spirit of the middle ages has never really left them. Sitting on the steps of the Duomo we seem to feel it creep up round our feet telling us stories of a past which is immortal. It was here that the people of Perugia fought and judged, preached and repented, loved maybe, and most certainly hated. It was in this little pulpit above our heads that S. Bernardino preached, and saw the books of necromancy and the false hair of the ladies burned; here that the *Podestà* and the people received ambassadors with deeds of submission from terrified neighbour towns. On the spikes of the railing round the fountain one set of nobles stuck the heads of others whom they hated, whom they slaughtered; and down those steps of the palazzo opposite, the great procession of the *Priori* came on days of solemn ceremony, and up through the dark gateway of the Canonica the Pope and all his cardinals passed in when they arrived from Rome. Truly the spirit of the past history is not dead. It is painfully and supremely living. The Piazza di S. Lorenzo on a December night with windstorms hurrying the sleet across its great grim walls is more absolutely filled with the *terribilità* of humanity than anything we ever realised.

One strange fact to trace in the square is the splendid preservation of the municipal buildings as compared to the almost ruinous condition of those of the church. The strife between the people and the papacy is carved as it were upon the very hearts of the monuments, and whereas the palace of the people has remained comparatively perfect—a beautiful finished building which delights the eye—the palace of the popes has been battered and abused almost to destruction at the hand of man, of fires and of time. Almost the only lovely detail which still clings to the face of the cathedral is the small pulpit whence the saint of Siena preached to the people; and this in itself is a symbolical fact, for it was the power of a single human *soul* which, for an instant tamed, if it could not quell, the passion of the Perugians. The power of the church, as church, never really mastered them. Paul III. mastered them, but he did so in the character of a warrior and tyrant.

As far as position goes the cathedral entirely dominates the municipal palace. It stands so high that in any distant view of the city it seems to soar above the other buildings. As we have seen before, the Perugians had but little patience with architectural or æsthetic matters. "They always preferred Mars to the Muse," says Bonazzi. Some grim and enduring respect kept their hands off their municipal palace when once it had been completed to their satisfaction, they took the precaution of putting a large iron fence round their fountain, but their cathedral suffered. They were zealous during the time of their prosperity to have a large and splendid church, but they never found time to finish or adorn it. They left the brickwork naked, hoping for some chance fight to furnish them with marbles for it, and in 1385 they were able to secure those which had been prepared for the cathedral of Arezzo. But they did not keep them. Pellini gives a weird account of the bringing of these marbles. "These things being accomplished," he says, referring to a very inhuman siege and conquest over the unfortunate Arezzo, "some outward sign of the acknowledged victory was necessary; so many marble stones were brought back to Perugia with some paintings upon them which had been formerly in the cathedral of the city; and the oxen and carts which brought them hither, with all the men who worked to bring them, were dressed out by our city with red cloth; but of those said stones, although they were certainly put up outside the walls of our cathedral, no sign at all remains." A little later Pellini explains their loss, for the people of Arezzo got back their marbles. "They started on their journey back to Arezzo," says the faithful historian, who will acknowledge no possible conquest of his own city, "and were put up on a part of their church where they may now be seen, white and red in colour, and very lovely to behold."

PIAZZA DI S. LORENZO, SEEN FROM UNDER THE ARCHES OF THE PALAZZO PUBBLICO

Throughout the history of Perugia, in the fifteenth and sixteenth centuries, we hear of fights and skirmishes in the square, but it was always the cathedral and not the palace which was turned into a fortress. In 1489 one of the endless fights between the Baglioni and the Oddi occurred, and the cathedral became a castle. Guido Baglioni arrived in hot haste from Spello, and proceeded to turn the Oddi out of Perugia. "Girolamo della Penna," says Villani, "deserted his brother Agamemnon and joined the Signori Baglioni, taking with him Silvio del Abate and others, and, together with the Baglioni, they took possession of S. Lorenzo, placed artillery there, and fortified the church, its loggia, and its roof in every way they knew of." The Duomo, on this occasion, proved such an excellent stronghold, that the Oddi outside were entirely discomfited, and had to abandon the siege and retire once more to the country. Another remarkable instance of fighting between the two pugnacious families is given by Fabretti, which illustrates, moreover, the slight power possessed by the Pope at that period. "At the end of October 1488 there was a great fight in the Piazza degli Aratri, and then the Baglioni collected in the piazza, and an ever-increasing throng of supporters assembled round them. And on that same day the brother of the Pope (Innocent VIII.) arrived, and as he passed by the piazza the people called out, '*Chiesa, chiesa.*' He was accompanied to the steps of the Palazzo Pubblico by Guido and Grifonetto Baglioni, who hoped that he might manage to arrange matters. But the *Priori* looked out of the windows above them, and seeing the Baglioni in the street below, they began to throw down large and heavy stones in the hopes of wounding Guido Baglioni. The hubbub continued with renewed force, and only at dusk did stillness fall upon the city."

Palazzo Pubblico.

Having glanced thus rapidly over the general historical interest of the piazza, it may be well to describe the buildings separately, taking the *Palazzo Pubblico* first. Anyone who comes to Perugia, even for a single afternoon, will naturally hurry to this point and spend an hour or two in the Cambio and Pinacoteca; but if a little time remains he should wander further through its public corridors and halls and archives, its council chambers, library, and prisons. All these are gathered together with a certain indifference to the first lines of architecture in the shell of the massive old buildings, and by penetrating these mysterious regions one seems better able to understand the spirit of historical Perugia. The iron force of the people's law—that force which alone kept head above the breakers of foreign wars and civil discord in the past—slumbers, but is not dead, in the halls where it once reigned. A hum of modern life, a host of modern busts and portraits now clash with, now mellow, the sombre walls and passages. At the other end of the Corso there is a grand new Prefettura, where the Prefect of all Umbria manages Umbrian matters, but the pulse of the old city beats on in its old veins. The *Priori*, with their golden chains and crimson gowns, have vanished, but the men and women of the land are pretty much the same. They wear big collars of foxes' fur on their long winter cloaks, just as they did in mediæval times, and they bring their claims of business into their first house of business, they swarm and hum within the corridors, and trample up and down the wide stone staircase with dignified determination stamped upon their features. In the rooms to which they go the clerks sit writing steadily amidst their piles of archives and of blue-books. Few probably of all these people know, and fewer care, about the Peruginos and Bonfiglis in the rooms above; for the natural man or woman desires to pray before his saints and not to pay to stare at them.

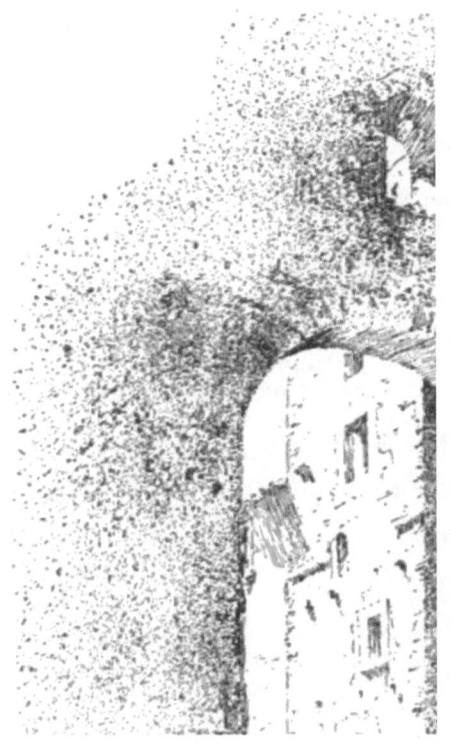

REMAINS OF THE FIRST PALAZZO DEI PRIORI IN THE VIA DEL VERZARO

We hear that the present palace was finished in the middle of the fourteenth century. Long before that date there had been a public hall where the rulers of the city met to discuss and settle its affairs.[51] But this building was comparatively small and cramped, and the new meeting-house was undertaken with superb disregard to expense. A rough calculation from the many bills shows us that upwards of 14,041 *libre* was spent on the building of it, but it took nearly one hundred and thirty years to build, and the fact that it was finished at different periods—a bit being added at intervals down the Corso—may account for the waving and irregular line of the east front, which is one of its most marked features.

The first architects employed were natives of Perugia: Fra Bevignate and Messers Giacomo di Servadio and Giovanello di Benvenuto. The original plan of the building was probably a perfect square, reaching from its present north front down to where the great door now stands. One should examine the building from the back in order to understand it fully. At one time we hear that Lombard workmen were called in to assist in the "very heavy labour," which, perhaps, gives a certain Lombard look to parts of the brickwork round the windows.

The citizens took a vast interest in the erection of their public palace, and allowed many private houses and even churches to be pulled down in order to make room for it. As for the decoration of the cathedral, so also for that of the palace, a neighbouring town was ransacked to furnish ornaments, and the unhappy Bettona was stripped of marbles to supply the magnificent *Priori* with their pillars and their friezes. Different portions of the huge edifice were given to the principal city guilds to decorate, and it was probably a spirit of emulation in these societies which produced the costly beauties of the separate parts. The chapel was decorated by the Merchants' Guild, and also the principal door, which was dedicated to St Louis of Toulouse. It is a beautiful piece of work, rich and lovely in its smallest detail, and carved in the grey stone called *pietra serena*, which always looks a little cold and dusty, like the fur on a grey mole's back, but which lends itself to a certain attractive style of polished carving peculiar to old doorways in Perugia.[52] Through it one passes into an immense hall, from which a staircase leads into the rooms of the palace above. In former times there were no steps, and persons of distinction and of wealth rode up on horseback to the council chambers.

A splendid open-air staircase leads up to the north entrance of the palace, which is, perhaps, the most impressive architectural point in all Perugia. Some years ago this fine outer staircase was pulled down; but it has been rebuilt with extreme care and taste, and probably exactly on the original lines. One can fancy the great procession of the *Podestà* and the *Priori* proceeding up and down these steps on days of solemn ceremony. "Four mace-bearers went before them," we are told, "bearing in their hands a silver staff richly covered with beautifully wrought figures, with the griffin on the top in enamelled relief. Without these mace-bearers it was not lawful for magistrates to go out." Each of the ten *Priori* wore round his neck "a heavy golden chain, the emblem of his office; and on solemn occasions the magistrate was preceded by six trumpeters to herald his approach with silver trumpets, which same were about four metres in length, beautifully enamelled, and with streamers of red satin on which the white griffin of the city was depicted."

The principal door, from which the *Priori* probably emerged, is guarded by great brazen beasts: a griffin and a lion, emblems of the city and the Guelphs. These creatures are very typical creations from the brain of some Perugian artist, and among the most impressive objects of their sort in Italy. They were originally made for a fountain in the square by a certain Maestro Ugolino, who received the modest sum of ten pounds for making them. In 1308 the fountain was destroyed, and a little later they were hoisted up to their present position. Long chains and keys hung from their claws in early days. "At the feet of these beasts," says Rossi, "the bars and keys of the doors of Assisi were hung as glorious trophies in 1321; and in 1358 the keys of the Justice Hall of Siena. The undisciplined militia which entered Perugia on the 3rd August 1799 pulled them down secretly, ('in the silence of the night' Mariotti says,) and thus took from the citizens of the present day the satisfaction of restoring to their rightful owners these disgraceful mementos of patriarchal warfare with cities, who to-day are their best friends. The fragments which remain have not the slightest historical interest; they are merely the bars from which the above-mentioned articles once hung."

The door with the brazen beasts above it leads straight into the *Sala dei Notari*—a splendid vaulted hall, its ceiling covered with frescoes, surrounded by high wooden stalls and steps of walnut. This big hall was given over to the lawyers of Perugia in 1583. They bought it, and their Collegio down below, from the city for the sum of 1000 *scudi*; and they at once decorated their fine new quarters, and settled comfortably into them, doing all their business there till early in the century. By the code of Napoleon they were, however, deprived of their privileges, and during the imperial French rule the hall was used as a criminal court. The lawyers seem to have been utterly unhinged in their arrangements. They never returned to the pleasant haunts from which the Emperor ousted them, and the big hall is now used for public concerts and lectures.

The room which corresponds with this one on the upper storey is now the Public Library, with a magnificent collection of over 50,000 volumes, some valuable manuscripts and beautiful painted missals.

Leaving the *Sala dei Notari* one crosses the main staircase of the palace, and passes into the living heart of the building, into a network of separate rooms and offices which it is not necessary to describe at length. The *Sala del Consiglio Comunitativo*, or *d'Udienza*, is beautifully decorated with crimson damask, and delicate arabesques, and has a fine open fire-place carved in *pietra serena*. Adone Doni's picture of Julius III. is hung in this room, and from it one can gain a pretty accurate knowledge of what the *Priori* and the potentates of Perugia looked like in their gala clothes. In the *Sala degli Archivi* there is a fresco of Parnassus by Baroccio. The colour is very fresh still, and the nymphs seem hopelessly out of place above the piles of dusty archives.

There is a curious history connected with the *Sala del Malconsiglio*—that room with the exquisite fresco by Fiorenzo di Lorenzo over its main entrance door.[53] It was here that the celebrated debate took place concerning the English prisoners (Hawkwood's men) whom the Perugians succeeded in capturing during the great fight down by the Tiber. The prisoners concocted a letter as they lay in their cells, and in the most pathetic terms they appealed to their capturers; "We too are Christians," they urged, "but we die of thirst. Have mercy upon us, have mercy on your poor captives, *your English vassals.*" The Perugians, moved, or more probably flattered by the cringing words, in a moment of ill-timed leniency, let their captives free. They lived to regret the action. A short time later Hawkwood and his men attacked them in another battle on the bridge of S. Giovanni. The English gained an easy victory, 1500 of the Perugians fell, and the *Podestà* and the German captain of their troops were taken prisoners together with a host of other men. Thus it came about that the room in which the council met to decide the release of the English was thenceforth called the

Sala del Malconsiglio in memory of the lamentable decision witnessed by its walls.

Hawkwood's men were not confined, as it happens, in the prisons of the Palazzo Pubblico, but no pity can be too great for those who were, for the Perugians were by no means dainty in their treatment of prisoners in mediæval times. The street which runs from the *Piazza* down into the *Via dei Priori* is still called the *Via della Gabbia* because of the large iron cage which used to hang above it from the upper windows of the palace. In this cage the Perugians were wont to imprison thieves and other malefactors, and not even the clergy escaped the horrid degradation. In 1442 we read of a priest, Angelo di Marino, who robbed Roberto di Ser Francesco di Ferolo of some of his possessions: "the missing articles," says Fabretti, "were found concealed in the campanile and under the altars, and, together with Angelo, the brothers of the priest were discovered to be accomplices, also a friar of S. Fiorenzo and many other priests and excellent citizens. On the 29th the said Angelo was put into a round cage, and with a cord he was dragged up into the corner wall of the Palace of the Podestà and there he remained for two days, and in the night he was put into prison and in the loggia of that palace twelve sacks of stolen goods were stored and round that cage there was a garland of false keys ... and on the 28th of January the said Angelo was once again put back into the cage at midday, and it was very cold and there was much snow, and he remained there till the first day of February, both night and day, and that same day he was brought out dead and laid upon his bier in the piazza, and he was buried in the passage of S. Lorenzo which leads into the cloister."

OLDEST PART OF THE PALAZZO PUBBLICO

A big "open-air" prison looked into the *Via della Gabbia*: a sort of large cavern in the fathomless walls of the old building, and here no doubt the wretched prisoners sat huddled in chains together, a prey to all the pigs and passers-by. A corkscrew staircase leads up from the lower prisons to the higher storeys of the palace, and into this, merely in the thickness of the wall, separate cells are built, windowless, undrained, airless places, where other unfortunate persons were put by the "men of warlike spirit."

There were even rougher modes than these of dealing with malefactors. On one occasion we hear of the most barbarous butchery of some gentlemen whose offences were purely political. Some were "thrown from the windows of the Palazzo Pubblico, and others were hanged from the *lumiere*, or long spikes which project from its lower walls." The *lumiere* were intended for the heads of Perugia's enemies, and one can fancy the faces of the butchered men looking down on the unforgiving citizens, whilst their blood dripped into the street. All through Perugia's history we find references to the *lumiere*: "On the 3rd of July 1541, the head of Ciancio de Burelio was borne along by one of the twenty-five rebels of the Pope, a student killed him: his head was put on a *lumiere* outside the Palace of the *Podestà*" (Fabretti, iii. 22).

There were strange ways of catching prisoners in Perugia. We find one statute which shows us that every artizan was obliged to hang certain hooks and gaffs to his house walls "ready to help in the capture of a criminal, and all were expected to help in this said capture."[54]

But if there was rude cruelty shown to prisoners it is fair to say there was also an occasional rude mercy. No doubt the latter was excited in the Perugians by their extreme religious superstition. We hear of an old custom of liberating prisoners "*pro amore Dei*." "Every six months, two *buon' uomini* (or good men) were chosen to elect certain officials who were given full power to let out five condemned prisoners on Holy Friday, two at Christmas, two on the feast of S. Ercolano, and two on Corpus Domini. Also two women on every feast of the Virgin Mary. In the choice of women, only those condemned for minor offences must be liberated. The men let out must have suffered six months' imprisonment, and the women one month, and neither must have been liberated in this manner (*pro amore Dei*) on previous occasions." Also there was to be strict silence on the nature of the offence. The *Podestà* published the names of the freed prisoners in three parts of the town so that the citizens might protest if they happened to be so minded. Three days later the prisoners were free and went to render thanks in the Church of S. Ercolano, after which they presented themselves before the civil authorities at the Palazzo Pubblico. These *scarcerati pro amore dei*, as they were called, were excluded from all public offices, "it not being decent," says the statute, "that they should be on the same level as the rest of the Perugians."

The Fountain.

There is one remarkable object in the Piazza of S. Lorenzo which has little or nothing to do with individual factions or with the affairs of Church and State, and this is the famous fountain which we are told was ever "dear as the apple of their eye to the people of Perugia." Indeed the citizens were in the habit of declaring that their fountain was "unique not only in Italy but in the entire world."

This beautiful bit of early Renaissance sculpture needs but a slight description here, for its form is familiar to most people either through engravings or through photographs. It is, however, a rather common error to suppose, as Vasari himself did, that the Pisani were the sole architects of the fountain. The only certain work which they did for it was the ornamentation of the panels and probably the statues. The whole plan of the fountain was supplied by the Perugian architect, Fra Bevignate, and it was he who called in other sculptors to help in the building.[55] In 1277 he applied to Charles of Anjou for permission to employ the Florentine, Arnolfo di Lapo, to help with the sculptures on the second basin, and in the same year a certain Rosso designed and made the third bronze basin with its pillar and its ornaments of Nereids and of griffins on the top.[56]

The fountain rises from the square—a broad pile of marble now almost black with age, upon a circle of stone steps. The second basin is supported on a forest of slender columns which give an airiness and a necessary lightness to the whole. The designs upon its panels, which are infinite in their variety, were made by Niccola Pisano and carried out by his son Giovanni. These two big marble basins are crowned by a third in bronze with the figures of three Nereids rising from it, and bearing on their heads the eternal griffin of Perugia, without which fascinating beast no single house or building in the city would ever seem complete.

Niccola Pisano and his son must have studied the tastes of the Perugians with exquisite care and tact, combining these with the more general artistic taste of the age in which they worked. The panels on the first large basin are a fascinating study: the months of the year, and Æsop's fables, scenes of domestic life and Roman legend, the griffin and tales from the Old Testament, the Umbrian saints, the sciences and arts, all wonderfully intermingled upon the separate panels. Even the old joke about the fishes is gracefully treated by the Florentine sculptor, for Lake Trasimene, as a beautiful woman, clasps three large *lasche* in her rounded arms. S. Ercolano, too, is here in all his glory, together with S. Louis of Toulouse and S. Costanzo.

One cannot help wondering how Perugia got her drinking water in early days. We may imagine that it was entirely through wells, and wells on the top of a hill are apt to run dry. Thirst, therefore, was probably a far stronger factor in times of siege than the cowardice of her inhabitants, and the city must often have been driven to capitulate through the terrible need of water, rather than through the fear of foreign arms. As the city grew, a sense of inadequacy on this particular point grew too, and people began to wonder how water could be procured from some fresh running spring upon the neighbouring hills; yet to bring it up to such a height seemed to the Perugians an almost insuperable difficulty. An early genius nearly solved it for them, but like other early geniuses he failed. In 1254 Frate Plenario, an obscure preaching friar, wandering through the woods and hills around Perugia, conceived, what in those days seemed the most hazardous scheme, of bringing water into the piazza of the city by means of a large aqueduct from the hill of Monte Pacciano, which lies three miles or so to the north of the town. Plenario urged his scheme upon the magistrates, they approved it, and after certain difficulties as to the necessary funds they determined to embark on the adventurous undertaking. Frate Plenario was put at the head of the works, and Messer Bonomi chosen as architect. But the plan was large, the execution very difficult. The arches were built too small and fragile, and carried at too low a level. They fell to ruin in the woods, and the poor little priest and his friend Bonomi vanished with the desolation of their works. Their plans, however, never died, they merely remained to be carried out by stronger if not subtler minds.

THE REAPER. DETAIL IN PANEL ON THE FOUNTAIN

In 1274 the question of a fountain again became paramount in Perugia. More solid channels were built across the hills and the ambitious magistrates called in the most skilled sculptors of the day to decorate a receptacle for the precious water when it should arrive. It came for the first time on the 15th of February 1280, and we can fancy the joyful pride of the citizens as they saw it running over the lovely marble and brass basins which had been so carefully prepared for it.

The most elaborate and stringent laws were made for the guardianship of the fountain and the use of its waters. It was enclosed, as it is to-day, with iron railings, and was, as the ever sarcastic Bonazzi rightly says, "the subject of most grave solicitude." We hear that there were seven troughs which gathered the water outside the railing, but "beasts, barrels, unwashed pots, and unclean hands were forbidden the use of the water, and indeed this was guarded with such jealous care that it seemed as though the people of Perugia had built their fountain for the sake of beauty only.... Yet," adds Bonazzi, "the five hundred florins which were annually given over to its maintenance, without counting extra expenses and the wages of its special porters and superior officers, would have been ill-spent indeed if beauty had been missing in the monument."

But if it was difficult to bring the water it was equally difficult to keep it always running. The elegant pile of marbles, the thing that the *Podestà*, the priests and the people all combined in literally doting on, was for ever running dry, and growing lifeless. In this nineteenth century the Prefect of Perugia is about to send some forty miles instead of three to fetch his people water, but the great fountain will be there to hold it when it comes, and the first aqueduct will remain to break with exquisite lines the little copses and the fields away to the north of the city.

GEOMETRY. DETAIL IN A PANEL OF THE FOUNTAIN

We know of few lovelier points about Perugia than the place where its water is stored on the lower hills of Monte Pacciano—low wooded hills where the white heath grows in spring-time amongst the copses of crimson-stemmed arbutus, and where one can lie for hours on the turf looking away to Trasimene, and all the waving hills and smaller hill-set cities of the Umbrian country. Here the Perugians catch and store their drinking water in three great reservoirs. The first of these was built some time at the end of the thirteenth century. The masonry is rough and massive, and the water seems more green and more mysterious in the mediæval basin than in those of this practical nineteenth century. We went there late one April afternoon, and lingered long in the cool and cavernous places where the water is gathered together. As we came home we traced the course of the old aqueducts which have long since been abandoned. The springs to-day are carried underground in a sort of switchback fashion over the sloping hillsides. But the ruins of the earlier conduit remain in their old places. Seeing them, we thought of the times in which they had supplied the men and horses crawling home from some hot skirmish on the plain, and of how the water had washed the blood of nobles from the steps of the Duomo and quenched the thirst of preaching friars and painters. How dead, how *gone*, that passionate past, how hum-drum, and how dreary seemed the clatter of the table d'hôte when we got back that evening.

But in describing the water supply of the city, we have wandered rather far afield from the subject of the piazza. A great flight of steps leads from the back of the fountain up to the cathedral.

ON THE STEPS OF THE CATHEDRAL

Cathedral of S. Lorenzo.

As we have pointed out at the beginning of this chapter, the Church has suffered terribly, both from neglect and warfare. The outer walls look very brown and bruised and naked too, without their marbles, but as such they form a monument of history which few would wish to alter. The first old church was pulled down in 1200 in order to make room for a superb new cathedral which was to take the place of the old one down outside the city walls at Porta S. Pietro, and the citizens met in solemn conclave to talk their project out, they even appointed their architect, Fra Bevignate, to make their plans for them. But the Perugians were full of wars, and other business and buildings at that period, and they soon found that their funds were far too low to allow of a new cathedral. They therefore let the matter drop, and some years passed before they made another effort. In 1345 the Bishop laid the foundation stone of S. Lorenzo. It was a solemn occasion, and all the clergy were present at the ceremony; but the stone, when laid, remained in solitary state for the rest of the century, and the people of Perugia were forced to pray and sing, to marry and baptise elsewhere, for another hundred years went by before the building was completed. Other catastrophes awaited it when finished, for the inexorable French Abbot Mommaggiore was at that time building his fortress at Porta Sole, and in doing this he found it necessary to knock down a great part of the new cathedral. Finally, in the middle of the fifteenth century, Bishop Baglioni, whose beautiful tomb stands to the right as one enters the cathedral, put the place in comparative order again, and it only remained for his descendants to use it as their fortress in the years to come!

There is a feeling of great warmth about the interior of S. Lorenzo, which is built in the form of a Latin cross with three naves. The ceiling is badly painted, much of the glass is poor, the twelve tall columns covered with a sort of stucco which imitates a stone no one has ever seen and only the artist dreamed of; but with all these faults the church has charm, and none of that desolate chill which the outside walls suggest. The clergy are rich at Perugia; the people have never lost their strong religious sense, which the advance of civilisation has turned from a wild fanaticism to a tone of more sober devotion, and the services are always impressive in S. Lorenzo—the whole body of the choir filled with choristers, the priests forming themselves into splendid coloured groups around the bishop's chair, and up against the woodwork and red damasks on the stalls.

Something of the life of the city, and much of the lives of the popes, has crept into the inner walls of the cathedral. The chapel of S. Bernardino stands to the right as one enters. This belonged to the Merchants' Guild of Perugia, and by them it was magnificently decorated. The merchants purchased their rights to the chapel in 1515, and they at once began to adorn it with splendid woodwork. They were naturally anxious to get a really good picture for their altar, but they took their time to select a suitable artist. Finally, they decided on Federigo Baroccio, of whose skill they had heard great things, and they sent their captain to Urbino where Baroccio lived, begging him to come and paint their altar. The subject chosen was the "Descent from the Cross."

Federigo came and finished his picture between 1567 and 1568. Tradition says that he was suffering from the effects of poison which a jealous person had administered to him in Rome, as he painted. Be this as it may, his picture gave the utmost satisfaction not only to the Merchants' Guild but also to "the whole city of Perugia," and it scarcely looks like the work of a man who was sickening from the effects of fatal drugs, but rather like that of one with all his health and wits about him. The figures are full of action, and although the colour is so warm and glowing, the atmosphere is one of storm and tempest. To the left of the cross the Magdalen strains her white arms to the unconscious Virgin whose figure is supported by a radiant woman in a yellow gown. To the right S. John stretches forward to catch the body of the falling Christ, whilst a young man, leaning backwards in a hurricane of wind, supports Him to the left. The only quiet points in this over-dramatic composition are the fainting figure of our Lady and that of her dead Son. Looking at it one is reminded of Tintoretto's work in its extravagant sense of action, but the touch of sentimentality throughout is foreign to the Venetian painter.[57]

Baroccio was a native of Urbino, born there in 1528. He studied painting with the Zuccheri and also with Michelangelo, Titian, and Raphael, and he had in his day a great reputation for his treatment of sacred subjects. It seems that he fell in love with the city of Perugia, for he stayed on painting there long after his work was finished, and he would often come again like the popes and other tired persons of distinction. He adopted a child of Perugia, Felice Pelegrin, and took him back to Urbino, where he educated him as a painter. Felice became distinguished in his way, and his success encouraged the generous Federigo to adopt another child, Felice's brother. But the second experiment was not so happy. The boy grew into an astonishingly beautiful young man; women idolised him and he was murdered by some jealous rival when still comparatively young.

To the left of Baroccio's picture there is a fine glass window designed by Arrigo Fiammingo in 1565. The window has been restored, but is beautiful in parts, both in colour and design, and Perugia is not rich in coloured glass. The subject represented is S. Bernardino of Siena preaching to the people of Perugia in the church of S. Maria del Popolo. The Saint is in the background—he, and the people and the architecture round him, are brown and quiet in colour. The figures in the foreground are far more brightly coloured, notably that of the old merchant in a blue cloak. The small naked boy who is leading him is perhaps the most charming point of the whole composition. The child's figure is like a little S. John, but he is probably meant to represent the Spirit of the Merchants' Guild, for he has a bundle bound about his shoulders, over which his yellow curls fall down, and a bundle or "*pacco*" is the sign of the Merchants' Guild.

The stalls in the chapel are very fine work of the sixteenth century. A whole book might easily be written about the stalls of the Perugian churches. Their wealth of beauty and of real excellency is inexhaustible, but it would be hopeless in so short a space to attempt any full description of the individual ones. The choir of the cathedral is in itself a fine example and worthy of a very careful study.

Immediately opposite the chapel of S. Bernardino is that of the Virgin's Ring. To the mere lover of art the interest of this chapel is dead indeed. Perugino's "Sposalizio": that wonderful design which Pietro created for his Duomo, and which Raphael a few years later copied, went, as so many of the very best Perugian paintings went, to swell the galleries of Napoleon. The poor picture has never travelled back across the Alps as many of its contemporaries have done. It hangs on the walls of the Gallery at Caen, and an inferior copy fills the frame which first was made to hold it.

To the pious, a treasure of infinitely greater price than Perugino's altar-piece is still shut safe and sure within the railings of the chapel, and this is the wedding-ring of the blessed Virgin Mary. It was brought to Perugia by a certain Winterio di Magonza, who "piously stole it" from Chiusi in 1472. The Ring is kept in a wonderful and exquisitely worked silver casket,[58] but so extraordinary is its value, that it can only be seen five times a year, and during the rest of the time a monstrous silver cloud covers the spot where it is stowed away.

We were privileged to see the Ring on one of Mary's greatest feast days (December 8th), and to examine it closely, even to handle it. We shall not ever forget the sight, which was impressive, and savoured almost of a pagan rite. The Ring was exposed from 7 A.M. to 6 P.M. We went to see it in the evening. In the square outside it was dark and pouring with cold rain, the great church too was dark and cold, a candle or two in the organ loft, and the organ sending a stream of mysterious music across the aisle, for the benediction. In the chapel of the Relic there was light—a blaze of innumerable candles, and underneath, the priests and an immense throng of people at their prayers. A staircase hung with crimson damask had been built for the day up the side of the wall to the little platform where the Ring is kept. We climbed the stairs to the platform and entered the chapel up above. There were only a few of the privileged Perugians there: some ladies, two smiths with the bolt and keys, the custodian, one or two members of the municipality, and the *Ring* which, in the light of all its candles, had an extraordinary, nay an even uncanny effect, and seemed cut out of some large opal.[59] When the service below was ended, the priest of the Ring arrived up the ladder. He took the relic out of its shrine, and a strange, half hysterical prayer went up from the tiny crowd. With the excessive courtesy peculiar to the Perugians we were asked to come forward: "You people of Perugia can always see your Ring, and these ladies are strangers," said the priest, who bade us examine it closely. Then the locking up began, and it was a mighty business. The relic is kept in a wonderful variety of cases. It is first locked into a little leathern case with a golden key kept by the bishop. Fifteen other different locks, their keys kept by fifteen different persons of importance in the city, follow. The weight of the last iron chest which covers the other boxes is stupendous. Two locksmiths and a custodian could scarcely manage to close it. As the locking up proceeded the candles went gradually out in the cathedral, and only one or two small tapers remained to light the mysterious burial. We passed from the chapel into the rain-swept square, and some of Ciatti's strange, unlikely fables ran in our head as we splashed through the desolate wind-swept streets. He tells us of the marvellous properties of the Ring—how the power possessed by it was so potent that people's ills were cured by merely looking at it, and how when a Tuscan lady had the audacity to wear it, her hand became withered, even as a dead leaf in autumn. And then he gives the story of the finding of the Ring:—

"Now Judith Marchesana of Tuscany, having a great love of jewellery (a thing not contrary to the nature of woman), despatched a certain Raneiro of Chiusi to Rome to make diligent search for jewels in that city. There he chanced to meet with a jeweller who had just returned from Jerusalem, and from him he bought many gems which he thought would be to the liking of his mistress. After abiding three days with the jeweller he decided to return to his home, and the Levantine, hearing of this, offered again to show him more gems till at last Raneiro grew angered and spoke bitter words to his host. 'Nay,' said the jeweller, 'I have treated thee in all good faith, but now I know not whether by a spirit I am moved, or by the love I bear to thee, but certain it is that I feel driven to give thee this Ring;' and he drew a small hoop from out the urn where the jewels lay. Raneiro, thinking it was an amethyst, an onyx or white agate, which stones are of but very slight importance in the history of gems, laughingly told his friend to keep his precious gift—'Do not esteem my offering so vile,' said the Levantine, 'but, believe me, it is the most priceless treasure I possess; for be it known to you that this is the wedding-ring of the blessed Virgin Mary. Receive it therefore with all reverence, and see that the sacred relic fall not into the hands of the profane.' "

* * * * * * *

The Story of Perugia

There is a fine "miraculous"[60] picture on the third column to the right as one passes up the aisle of the cathedral. A great many myths centre around it both as a work of art and as a healing relic. Some say that it is the earliest painting in Perugia, transferred to its present place from the column of a Pagan temple where an early Christian painted it, others that it is the work of Giannicola Manni. Concerning the miracles performed by it, the strings of silver hearts and offerings bear ample testimony. The painting is very charming, and we hear that Perugino loved it as a boy and drew his earliest inspirations from it(?). Our Lady stands against a crimson arras, her hands are opened out as though to bless, her gown is of a faded pink, her mantle blue and lined with the green of early spring. She is so calm, so young, and smiling, that one does not wonder at the crowds of worshippers which linger always round her shrine.

The chapel of the baptistery has some good Lombard stone work; and there are one or two interesting things in the sacristy; splendid *intarsia* over the presses where the priests of Perugia store their gorgeous gowns of cloth of gold and silver, and a wonderful bit of early *gesso* work in the inner chapel.

There is a big altar-piece by Signorelli in the chapel of S. Onofrio, which is interesting as being the only comparatively good piece of the master's work in the whole of Perugia. The picture has suffered much from restoration, but the restorer contented himself with mauling the principal points; he neglected the detail, which is admirable throughout. The garlands of pink and white convolvulus behind the chair of our Lady are true to life; the Infant Christ carries a stem of lilies in his baby hand, and beside the long limbed angel who plays his lute at the Virgin's feet stands a tumbler full of the freshest jasmine, whilst below him on the steps another glass is filled with fading violets. One marvels that a man who could so superbly draw every line and muscle of the human body, should care to linger over these frail details of the flowers.

In the left transept of the cathedral three of the popes are buried, and to anyone who has studied the history of the town and realised its connection with the power of Rome this otherwise rather dreary and uninteresting corner of the church will conjure up a host of half fantastic visions.[61]

The little porphyry urn on the right wall of the transept holds all the earthly remains of the three popes, Innocent III., Urban IV., and Martin IV., who all died at Perugia. A delightful legend is told concerning the death of Innocent. With his usual surprising seriousness the ingenuous Ciatti tells us that the following remarkable vision occurred to a certain Abbot of the Cistercian order who was living in the neighbourhood at the time of Innocent's death:

"Now one hot summer day, overcome by heavy sleep, the Abbot withdrew himself under the shade of certain plants and there lay down to rest upon the soft green grass. No sooner had he closed his eyes in sleep than the eyes of his mind were opened and he saw Christ appearing in the east accompanied by His angelic court and seated on a throne. Looking to the west the Abbot then perceived a naked man, hurrying all out of breath towards the throne, and not even the weight of his pontifical mitre impeded him in this most rapid progress, for a fierce and terrifying dragon followed close behind him, and he was frightened and cried out: 'Have mercy on me, oh thou most merciful God.' Wherefore the dragon too lifted up his voice and cried: 'Judge with justice, most high judge.' Then the good Abbot awoke trembling with fear and much mystified by all that he had seen, and arriving at the gates of Perugia, he heard the heavy tolling of the bells and was met by the citizens who all were wailing with loud voices, crying out: Pope Innocent, Pope Innocent is dead.' Then the worthy Abbot understood that it was Pope Innocent III. that he had seen, and he marvelled at the mercy of Almighty God who treats the humble and the powerful with equal law and mercy."

Innocent was, of course, a very powerful Pope, and the historians of Perugia gloat over the fact that he did their city the honour to die in it, devoting whole pages of their books to this important subject.

Urban IV. is another remarkable figure in the Church of Rome, and it was during his stay at Perugia that he threw his mighty bomb which was to explode with such disastrous results upon the land of Italy. He was probably staying in the monastery of S. Pietro with his friend S. Thomas Aquinas when he sent the fatal letter which summoned Charles of Anjou down to Rome. "A terrible comet preceded Urban's death which occurred in 1264," says Mariotti. There was a report that Urban had been done to death by eating poisoned figs, but this is unfounded. The Pope lived in constant terror of poison, and by his incessant talk and letters on the subject had infected the minds of those around him.

Martin IV. is the last Pope buried in the Duomo. He often came to Perugia, and in 1285 he returned with the full intention of making a considerable stay there. But he died on Easter morning, having eaten a surfeit of eels; (it appears that Martin IV. was greedy of this particular delicacy). Dante records the fact in the "Purgatorio" (canto xxiv.), where Forese points the Pope out seated among the gluttons:

" … e quella faccia
Di là da lui, più che l'altre trapunta,
Ebbe la Santa Chiesa in le sue braccia:
Dal Torso fu: e purga per digiuno
L'anguille di Bolsena e la vernaccia."

The following inscription is said to have been written over Martin's tomb:

"Gaudent anguillae quod mortuus hic jacet ille,
Qui quasi morte reas excruciabat eas."

Perhaps it was with a view to expiate this very insulting epitaph that the Perugians, in spite of the canons of S. Lorenzo, who refused to contribute to the fund, erected a magnificent tomb for Martin later on. They employed G. Pisano for the purpose, but only a few fragments of his work remain. Mommaggiore pulled it down, as he pulled so many other things, and used its priceless ornaments to adorn his own palace at Porta Sole. The two small pulpits on either side of the high altar screen were made, it is said, from the fragments of the tomb, and also, perhaps, the marble *Pietà* with the blue background which hangs on the right as you pass back down the church.[62]

The bones of the three Popes have been terribly pulled about: buried and then unearthed, buried again, and changed. Innocent, according to most authorities, was buried in the cathedral. About 1376, when Martin's tomb was destroyed by Mommaggiore, the bones of Innocent III. were taken from their resting-place and laid along with those of the other two popes in a sort of chest, on the top of a cupboard, in the sacristy of the new cathedral. Thence, in 1605, the chest was removed to another chapel by order of Bishop Comitoli. When it was opened the bodies of Martin and of Urban were found intact, with their mitres and their chasubles; but of the powerful Innocent III. only a few broken bones remained, wrapped up in a little packet. It is probable that when the three Popes were removed from their different tombs in 1376 and stuffed into the chest, the memory of Innocent III. in connection with the temporal dominion of the popes in Perugia which he was the first to found, induced some persons present to violate his tomb. Be this as it may, all the bones of the Popes now rest together in the dull little porphyry urn, crowned with a brass tiara.[63]

In leaving the cathedral it would be well to glance at the tomb of Bishop Giovanni Andrea Baglioni, a beautiful bit of low relief in marble. Very lovely are the three small angels with the ribbons in their heavy hair, guarding the Baglioni arms, very alien from the spirit of that bloody race of men, the gentle figures of the women in the panels.

The Canonica.

One great building in the square remains to be described, namely, the Canonica, or, as Bonazzi calls it, the "Vatican of Perugia." Although a mere wreck of its former splendid self, this building is still one of the finest relics of the mediæval times that the city boasts of. It stands to the left of the Duomo—a great mass of bricks, with huge cavernous rooms inside, and walls some six to eight feet thick in places. The cloister is comparatively modern, but the beautiful open-air staircase which leads from it down into the Piazza Morlacchi is probably very much the same as it was in the days when the popes arrived to take a holiday in their loved Umbrian city.

In old days the magistrates and the *Podestà* shared the abode of the clergy, but, as may easily be imagined, this arrangement did not answer, and was, as Bonazzi tells us, the cause of most extreme contention between the canons of the Church and the councillors of State. The canons had a very comfortable time in the Canonica. "Professing to follow the rule of St Augustine," says Bonazzi, "they had much to fear from the manifold terrors of conscience." Their cellars must have been excessively well stocked, for on one occasion when the *Podestà's* property was burning, the flames were quenched by wine: "To extinguish the flames, nothing would do save the immense cellars of the colossally rich Canonica."

IN THE CLOISTERS OF THE CANONICA (OR SEMINARY)

Of the visits of the popes to Perugia we have dealt elsewhere (see chapter ii.). It is enough to say that they often came to the Canonica; three of them died there, and there were five conclaves in the mysterious halls where the new popes were elected.

One beautiful story is told in the "Fioretti" about Gregory IX., who doubted of the miracles of S. Francis till the saint appeared in person and revealed the truth to him. There is little doubt that the vision occurred to the Pope as he slept or dreamed in his grand rooms at the back of the cathedral:—

" ...Now let it be known that to Pope Gregory IX., who was a little doubtful concerning the wound in the side of St Francis, and according to what he himself relates, that the saint appeared one night, and lifting his right arm on high he showed the wound in his side, and asked to have a little phial fetched; and the Pope had it fetched and St Francis bade them place it under the wound in his side; and it seemed to the Pope as though truly the phial became filled even unto the brim with blood mixed up with water which issued from the wound, and from that time forward all doubt forsook him, and he, with the consent of all his cardinals, approved the holy miracles of St Francis."

Thus the power of the Umbrian Saint penetrated this grim Umbrian building, and, appearing to the haughty Roman Pontiff, overcame him by the power of pure holiness, even as it had overcome so many furious passions in a century that was evil.

S. FRANCIS FROM THE STATUE OF DELLA ROBBIA
AT S. MARIA DEGLI ANGELI, ASSISI

CHAPTER VI

Fortress of Paul III.—S. Ercolano—S. Domenico—S. Pietro—S. Costanzo

FROM an historical point of view the crowning interest of the buildings of Perugia was to be found in the great fortress which Paul III. built in the middle of the sixteenth century in order to amaze the citizens, and to subjugate the rebellious passions of the nobles. For three centuries this huge building performed its office admirably and Perugia lay silent and subdued under the oppressive shadow of its walls. But no sooner did other influences appear, no sooner did the imperial French power open a way to a freer method of government than that allowed by Rome, than Perugia shook herself free of a yoke which had been odious from the first, and on the 23rd December 1848, in the sight of a great crowd of people, and with a pomp and ceremony dear to the Perugians from the very darkest ages of their history, the first stones of the splendid building were torn from their places. By a strange coincidence or, perhaps, agreement, the man to give the first blow was a certain Benedetto Baglioni, and as he let the hammer fall it split the cornerstone on the very spot where the palaces of his ancestors had stood in former years! The masons followed suit, and soon the bricks and stones were tumbling from their places. The whole town joined in the work of devastation, but so splendid was the mortar used by the builders of the indomitable Paul that at times nothing but blasting would destroy the masonry. In one of the great explosions several people were killed, "and thus," says Bonazzi, "did the Farnese Pope once more avenge himself on us, even after a period of three hundred and eight years!"

No sooner was the Papal fortress gone than the Perugians began to make new buildings on its site. All the modern architecture of the town has sprung, like fresh mushrooms spring, on the site of the old wood, and it is not easy in the present day to reconstruct Paul's mighty citadel, hampered as our vision is by the open squares and houses which now have taken possession of its site. It was divided into two parts. The top part covered nearly the whole of the level space which the Prefetura, the Hotel Brufani, and the Piazza Emanuele now occupy. The fire of the Pope's guns could therefore be turned on recalcitrant citizens or nobles, either up the Corso and the Piazza Sopramuro, or down the main approach to the city from the road to Rome. A strong branch or buttress of the fort ran down from this high level to a second fort which, in the shape of a fan, extended itself along the level ground which is now occupied by municipal buildings and the Piazza d'Armi; a large part of the lower building was devoted to a great walled square for games, called the Piazza del Pallone.

Adolphus Trollope was one of the last people to see and to describe the great Farnese citadel. He saw it both before and during its destruction, and the description which he gives of the building and of the hatred which it excited is so vivid that we quote it here at length.[64]

"Few buildings," he says, "have been laden with a heavier amount of long-accumulated popular hatred than this; and few have more richly merited it. The Perugians were for many ages—nay, it may pretty well be said that they never ceased to be—a hard nut for the grinding teeth of papal tyranny to crack, and this huge Bastille was, at the time of its erection, a symbol of the final destruction of liberty in Perugia.

"When I had last been in Perugia the entire building was open to the curiosity and free examination of the public. There was no crowd when I wandered over the labyrinths of its stairs and passages, guard-rooms, barracks, casemates, and prisons of every sort and size. I had the foul place then all to myself, with the exception of a few workmen, who were beginning to take the roof off one of the upper buildings; for the public of Perugia had already satiated their curiosity. I saw the large dungeons, accessible only by a circular opening in the pavement of the less dreadful dungeons above them; I saw the fearful cells, constructed in the thickness of the colossal masonry, in such devilish sort, that the wretches who had dared to question the deeds of Christ's Vicar on earth, once introduced into the cavity through apertures barely sufficient to admit a crawling figure, could neither stand nor sit in them. I paced the lofty battlements, which commanded such a panoramic view as can hardly be matched, over the beautiful country and the many cities within its circuit, all priest-trampled and poisoned; and I marked the narrow light-holes in some of the less dreadful prisons, through which a miserable, tantalising strip of far distant sunlit horizon was dimly visible to the immured victim, who knew too well, that he should never, never return to the light of day."

On Trollope's second visit, that is to say, in 1862, the work of demolition was progressing, and an inscription had been placed on the wall of the piazza fronting the former main entrance to the fortress, which struck him as ironically satirical in its simplicity. It stated that the magistrates of Perugia were removing the fortress raised for the oppression of the citizens *"for the improvement of the prospect from the Piazza"*! Some time later Trollope returned to Perugia. The fortress was then being quickly pulled to pieces.

"There were a number of people," he says, "on the occasion of my second visit gloating over the progressing destruction of the detested walls, as crowbar and pickaxe did their work. I saw one remarkable looking old man, with a long flowing white beard, sitting on a fallen fragment of wall in the sunshine, and never taking his eyes from the workmen who were tumbling down the great masses of concrete as fast as their excessive hardness would permit of their being detached. A gentleman I was with noticed the direction of my look, and said: 'That old man comes here at break of day, and remains till the workmen knock off at night. He was many years a prisoner in the fortress, and was liberated at the fall of the Papal Government.'

"I felt that his presence there was fully accounted for, and that I could guess without any difficulty 'of what was the old man thinking?' as he watched the demolition of his prison home."

But however great the damage done both to the people and their buildings by the fortress of the great Farnese, it must be admitted that the Pope at least employed a man of taste to carry out his vast designs. In building the new walls and knocking down the old, San Gallo left unharmed some of the finer characteristics of the city. He pulled down all the Baglioni strongholds, he battered down ten churches, and as many as four hundred houses—indeed, he destroyed a little corner of the mediæval town—but he preserved, with a tender carefulness, the church of the patron saint, S. Ercolano, and one of the first Etruscan gates: the Porta Marzia. As it was not possible to keep the latter in the form of a city gate San Gallo used it as a decoration, building it into the west wall of the fortress where, as Dennis rightly says, it still remains, "imprisoned in the brickwork, to be liberated by the shot of the next besiegers of Perugia, and looking as much out of place as an ancient Etruscan himself would look in the streets of the modern city." The Porta Marzia is surmounted by the usual frieze of short pillars, but the statues of four mysterious persons are inserted in the niches. A tradition in Perugia says that these statues are the portraits of a Perugian family who died from eating a large quantity of poisonous *funghi* (mushrooms). How this myth originated it is not possible to say, but the figures with their inscrutable history add a phantom touch to the already phantom portal. They are probably Roman divinities.[65] It is worth getting the doors of the Porta Marzia opened to see the funny world inside: a whole small town of battered streets, even the fragments of a chapel, and many house-walls still intact.

PORTA MARZIA

S. Ercolano.

The church of S. Ercolano is built straight against a part of the first Etruscan walls on the spot where the saint is supposed to have been decapitated by Totila. It is a strange little church, octagonal and very tall and narrow. The first church is said to have been built as early as 1200 and out of the remains of an old amphitheatre, or, as some say, the temple to Mars, which originally stood on the site. Its early history is, however, somewhat hazy. In 1600 the church was finally rebuilt by Bishop Comitoli, who at once looked about him for some suitable tomb in which to place the body of S. Ercolano, which had hitherto had such a very unquiet history. It happened that just at that time a splendid sarcophagus was dug up under the little chapel of S. Orfito at the foot of Monte Pacciano. Six skulls and a wooden cross, together with certain legends connected with some early Christian martyrs and a chapel in the woods, seemed to prove that the sarcophagus had formerly held their "holy bones." The pious bishop Comitoli very reasonably concluded that "Heaven was ministering to his need," so he took the sarcophagus and put it on the altar of his new church, and in it he laid the body of the saint. The translation of the body from its old abode in the Duomo was marked by a magnificent ceremony. The Bishop got up into the pulpit in the square, which had never been used since the days of S. Bernardino, and thence preached a sermon on the merits of their patron Saint to the people of Perugia, who came in thousands to attend him.

S. Ercolano, who is purely a local saint like S. Costanzo, plays an important part in the history of Perugia; he may, indeed, be called the presiding genius of the city. His history is often confused with that of a most obscure and highly mythical personof the same name who was martyred at Perugia in very early days and devoured by wild beasts in the amphitheatre. The shining point in the life of the second S. Ercolano is the part that he played in the defence of his city during the siege of Totila. This has endeared him to the hearts of the citizens, and his name is as familiar to the street boys of Perugia as that of S. Ubaldo to the children of Gubbio. Unlike the saint of Gubbio, however, S. Ercolano failed in his diplomacy. Barbarossa listened to the prayers of Ubaldo and departed from Gubbio; Totila took Perugia and beheaded its Bishop, and the Gothic soldiers cut off his head on a ledge of the Etruscan walls where the present church now stands to commemorate his martyrdom.

CHURCH OF S. ERCOLANO AND ARCHWAY IN THE ETRUSCAN WALL

All sorts of strange ceremonies and religious festivities grew up round the worship of this beloved saint, for the Perugians were as religious as they were warlike, and they delighted in pious displays. Indeed, one old proverb describes the *credo* of the city as consisting of three P's: *Processione, Persecuzione, Protezione*. There were countless rules and regulations concerning the processions of the various saints.

Some had a double procession, or one which extended itself over two days. On the first of these, the procession started from the house of the Saint and proceeded to the Duomo, and on the second the order was reversed. In the case of S. Ercolano his statue was carried on the first day from his house with a wooden head upon its shoulders. On the second day it returned to its abode with a silver head in commemoration of his martyrdom. So when anybody in Perugia lied or was deceitful, he was described as having two faces like the blessed Ercolano!

In Monaci's collection of the Uffizi Dramatici dei Disciplinati dell' Umbria we find many of the great tragic songs or plays sung by the Flagellants of Perugia, and some of the finest of these are addressed to S. Ercolano, who, as we have said, exercised a peculiar influence over the minds and consciences of the Perugians. The outside world made great sport of this almost infantine side to the character of the Perugians, and on one occasion the Florentine painter, Buffalmacco, made use of it in combination with their other worship, namely, their love of fishes, to play a rather hazardous practical joke upon them. Vasari recounts the history at length:—

"Now the Perugians," he says, "gave Buffalmacco an order to paint in the Piazza of S. Ercolano a portrait of that saint, who is the patron and was the bishop of their city. The price being arranged, a scaffolding of wood covered with matting was put up for him in order that none might watch him at his painting; and this being done he set to work upon it. But ten days had not passed by before everyone who happened to walk that way began to ask when the picture would be finished, as though such things as this could be cast in a mould, and at last the thing became a nuisance to Buffalmacco. Therefore, having finished his work and being wearied of so much importunity, he decided within himself to be quietly avenged on the impatience of these people, and he succeeded; for the work being finished, he showed it to them before uncovering it, and they expressed themselves absolutely satisfied. But when the Perugians expressed their desire at once to pull down the scaffolding, Buffalmacco told them to let it stand for another two days because he desired it to retouch certain points for his own satisfaction, and thus it was settled. Then Buffalmacco went back to that spot where round the head of his saint he had painted a large golden aureole, and as was the custom in those times, with a high relief of plaster he made him a crown, or more properly speaking, a garland, and wound it round and round his head, and all of *lasche*. And this being done he one day paid his landlord and returned to Florence. Then as the days passed by, and the Perugians failed to see the painter moving about as was his custom, they asked the landlord what might have become of him, and hearing that he had returned to Florence, they immediately hurried to uncover the picture, and finding their saint crowned only with a wreath of fishes, they immediately carried the news to the governor of their city and then, with hottest haste, sent horsemen in pursuit of Buffalmacco; but in vain, for he had returned to Florence with the best speed he might. Therefore they decided to have the crown of fishes removed from the head of the saint and the aureole replaced by one of their own painters, and in future to speak as much evil as they could, both of Buffalmacco himself and of the Florentines in general."[66]

The story of Buffalmacco, the saint, and the crown of fishes is comic enough, but the square in which the scene described above was acted witnessed the deepest human tragedy that the annals of Perugia have preserved for us. It was just outside the church of S. Ercolano that Grifonetto Baglioni got his death-wound. Driven back from Porta S. Pietro with only a few men, he prepared to keep the gate of "Sancto Ercolano" and there, hopeless of anything save death, he awaited the assault of Gianpaolo. It was here in this place that he fell. Did Raphael come down the street along with the other terror-stricken people after the fight was over? Did he, with the quiet eyes of the artist, look on this passionate scene of love and death? Was it Grifonetto that he painted later in his picture—"Grifonetto gracious in his person." We cannot tell; we only know as a fact that the "Entombment," now in the Borghese villa at Rome, was ordered by Atalanta Baglioni, and in a letter from Raphael concerning it we see that he was acquainted with her personally. It has been suggested to us by a Perugian who is wise in art and history, that Raphael painted a portrait of Grifonetto not in the figure of Christ as one might naturally suppose, but in the more prominent figure of the vigorous young man who supports the feet of the dead Saviour. The whole attitude of this figure is one of dauntless energy and courage such as one would expect to see in the son of two such cousins as Atalanta and Grifone Baglioni.

* * * * * * *

From the steps of S. Ercolano one of the only broad and comparatively even streets of the town—the Corso Cavour—leads to the main road through the Porta Romana, down the steep hill to the Tiber and across the plain to join the road to Rome. Most of the history of Perugia has come and gone along this road; it was here that the popes made their triumphal entries, here probably that the barbarians forced a passage, and here, even in our own days, that Perugia suffered a final and a painful siege from Rome. It was on the of 20th of June 1859 that the Swiss guard fought its way along it, burning down the houses and beating back as they advanced the ill-organised body of inhabitants. Strange thrilling details of that day have been told to us by people who were present. One inhabitant, a mere boy then, was up with his parents at the top of their house in the Corso Cavour, but smelling smoke in the shop below they crept downstairs to see what might be happening, and found the Pope's guard foraging amongst their medicine bottles. The mother and boy fled back up the stairs, but the father was caught and carried out into the street to be shot. Then the small boy leaned from the window, covering his face with a scarf, and pleaded so passionately for his father's life that the Swiss soldiers spared him and passed to more profitable pursuits further up in the town. (We hear that they were filled with so great a lust for blood that they even wrung the neck of a tame falcon in the Piazza Sopramuro!) Another gentleman who had come in with the Pope's guard gave us some details of the siege, and amongst them he told us of a certain priest at S. Pietro, who, thinking to kill the leader of the troops, shot at the drum-major, whose magnificent appearance would no doubt make him remarkable to a quiet monk. The unfortunate priest was shot for his pains up in the square on the following morning.[67]

The Corso Cavour has a very modern look about it. Most of its big buildings are used as barracks, but some few of the old are left. The Palazzo Bracceschi has a fine old outside staircase and a good collection of pictures, amongst them an exquisite Madonna and child attributed to Filippo

Lippi, but more like a Neri di Bicci, also some fine original drawings.

S. Domenico.

The gigantic church of S. Domenico towers above the street to the left. It is one of those desolate unfinished Gothic buildings which one finds so often in Italian cities—a great idea dwarfed, not by want of inspiration, but by the need of money to complete it. The church as we now see it is merely a patchwork of the first architect's original conception. It was begun early in the fourteenth century from designs by Giovanni Pisano, but it was not finished till 1459. The building owed much of its splendour to a young man of Perugia, Cristiano Armanni, who, whilst studying at Bologna, had been converted to the faith by the preaching of S. Domenico. Cristiano returned from the university in the society of a certain S. Niccolò of Calabria, and induced his parents and his friends to give him money for the new church which was about to be built to honour S. Domenico. The magistrates of Perugia contributed a banner to the cause, and they decided that wherever S. Niccolò might place this banner, there the new church should be built. He planted it near the church of S. Stefano, and on that site the present church of S. Domenico now stands. Through the fault of inferior masons, part of the choir and the middle nave fell through in 1614, but Bishop Comitoli determined to rebuild it on the original design. He spent more than 4000 *scudi* on this generous act and was as ill-rewarded as the most patient builder of card-castles ever was, for the whole of his work collapsed for the second time. It was finally rebuilt on the designs of Carlo Maderno, in 1632. But all this tinkering has left very sorry scars, and even the tower outside has not been spared. It was begun later than the rest of the church and was not finished till about the end of the fourteenth century, when Paul III. at once had the top of it knocked off because he declared that the monks of S. Domenico could, from their campanile, look down and spy upon the building of his fortress!

One or two relics alone remain of the many beautiful bits of art with which the church was rich in early days. Of these the tomb of Pope Benedict XI. is the most fascinating.

Of the life of Benedict there is not much to say; his reign covered a period of only eight months, and perhaps his greatest glory is in his tomb. He was a native of Treviso and belonged to the Dominican order. In 1304 he, like other popes and tired people, came to Perugia in search of the peace he could not find in Rome, and there, in that same year, he died. When in Perugia his mother came to see him—a thing which had only once happened to a pope before.

"Moved by a desire to see her son," says Mariotti, "Filomarina came to Perugia, and here having had herself nobly dressed by the people of Perugia, as befitted the mother of the Pope, she presented herself to her son. But he, seeing her so beautifully clad, pretended that he did not know her, saying that this was not his mother, because *she* was a poor old woman and not a lady like this one. And his mother hearing this thing, and being a good and holy woman, took off those rich adornments, and putting on her own again, she returned to the Pope, who recognising her as his mother, received her with all tenderness."

Pope Benedict was anxious to make peace between the Bianchi and Neri of Florence, and received from some of the heads of the Guelph factions a visit of state in his residence at Perugia. Twelve of them, headed by Corso Donato, came with all their suite behind them: one hundred and fifty horses we hear, and many friends and relatives. No satisfactory agreement was arranged, and shortly afterwards this holy but powerless Pope passed into his rest.

It was supposed that Benedict died of poison, and the older stories run, like the modern one of Zola, on the subject of a basket of poisoned figs.

"In the year of Christ 1304, on the 27th of the month of June," says Villani, "Pope Benedict died in the city of Perugia, and it was said that he died of poison. As the Pope sat eating at his table a young man came to him dressed and veiled in the guise of a woman, and as a servant of S. Petronilla, with a basin of silver in which were many beautiful figs and flowers which he presented to the Pope in the name of the faithful Abbess of the convent. The Pope received the figs with very great delight, and because he loved them, he made no enquiry concerning them, seeing moreover that they came from a woman, and he ate a great quantity, whereupon he immediately fell ill, and after a few days he died, and was buried with great honours by the Preaching Friars who belonged to the Dominican order at Perugia. Benedict was a good and an honest man, but it is said that because of the envy of certain of his cardinals, they had him poisoned in this fashion."

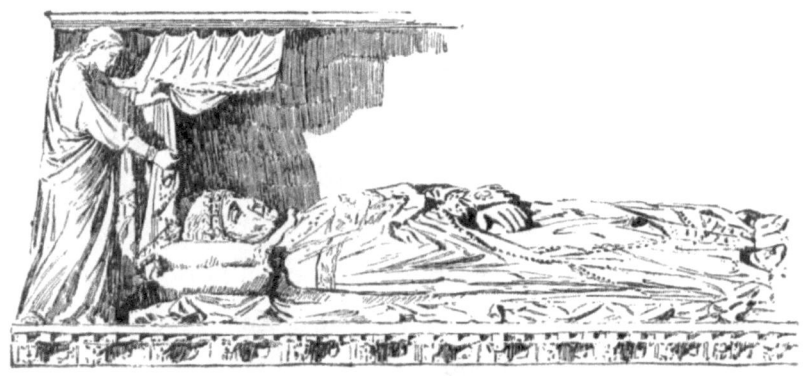

DETAIL OF THE TOMB OF POPE BENEDICT XI. IN THE CHURCH OF S. DOMENICO

Some say that Benedict was poisoned because of the ill-feeling of the Florentines towards him, and others that he died by the jealous hand of Philippe le Bel of France. The historians of the present day deny the fact of poison at all. Be these matters as they may, the fact of the dead pope's tomb remains—an entrancing bit of human workmanship. It was made by Giovanni Pisano, son of the great Niccola, "who first breathed life, with the breath of genius, into the dead forms of plastic art." Pope Benedict lies asleep; stretched out quite flat and thin in his exquisitely folded robes; there is a canopy over him with curtains strung across it and two angels have drawn the curtain back to gaze at the figure of the dead man. The columns of the tomb were filled up once with precious mosaics, but during Napoleon's occupation of Perugia, a regiment of men and horse were quartered in the church of S. Domenico, and the French soldiers are said to have employed their leisure hours in picking out these treasures with their pen-knives. Perhaps it was these same thoughtless beings who wilfully mutilated the exquisite figures of children, fragments of which are still left clinging to the spiral curves.

The terra-cotta decorations in the chapel of the Rosario are the work of Agostino Ducci—the Florentine sculptor who made the lovely front of S. Bernardino, (see chapter viii.), and they would be interesting if only for that reason. Though mutilated in parts, and spoilt by careless white-wash, much of the detail is still charming; notably the three little angels over the central arch. As for the rest of the church it has but little interest now-a-days. The immense Gothic window of the choir is said to be the largest in Italy, but the original glass is entirely gone from its frame. The whole has been carefully restored by Signor Moretti of Perugia. The stalls are covered with good intarsia work, but they have been greatly spoiled by careless restoration, and have a naked and forsaken look about them. S. Domenico is one of those pathetic buildings which leave upon one's mind the feeling of arrested decay, and one hurries gladly from it and out into the sunlight of the street.

S. Pietro.

Very different in every way is the church of S. Pietro, which one reaches after passing through the gate of Porta Romana. "The Basilica of S. Pietro is so adorned with beauties," says its faithful, but perhaps too fond, biographer, "that it would suffer and be overburdened were others added to it." The praise is certainly high, but it has a certain grain of truth, and the church of S. Pietro, is, amongst the churches of Perugia, a jewel of inestimable price, for unlike all the others it has been left with all its treasures and its pictures in it (see note, p. 163).

The church and monastery of S. Pietro are built on the hill of Capraio or Calvary, which stretches away to the south of the town. They form the first object which catches the eye as one approaches the city on the line from Rome; they serve as a sure landmark from many distant points of Umbria, and one cannot stay long in the city without becoming sincerely attached to the beautiful group of pale brick buildings, crowned by their graceful campanile, which catch the sunrise and the sunset lights, and fascinate one's fancy at every time and season.

It is difficult to decide the date of the first church of S. Pietro. Tradition says that it is built on the site of an old Etruscan temple, and that it was the first Christian building of Perugia, certainly it was the first cathedral. We hear that the earliest Christians of Perugia used to meet in subterranean passages under the present church of S. Costanzo, which stands on the same spur of hill as that of S. Pietro, and that there S. Costanzo, the second Bishop of Perugia, gathered his little flock together to "feed them with the milk of the holy word of God." We know that the present basilica was built by a certain Abbot, Pietro Vincioli, a monk of the Benedictine order, who lived in the tenth century, and was a great friend of the Emperor Otto III. Bonazzi gives a delightful description of this Abbot and of his method of building and the miracles he employed for the purpose. It seems that Pietro was famous for his great sanctity and learning, and that he lived at a time when everybody imagined that the world was about to come to an end:

"He had rich friends, the Emperor among them, and the latter, who entertained the general superstition about the end of the world, gave him a great deal of money, with which the Abbot determined to build for himself the present church of S. Pietro. The Pope, the Emperor, and many other persons showered down donations and privileges for the purpose, and the new Benedictine monastery soon became celebrated, and its monks took an active and important part in the affairs of Perugia.... Although S. Pietro was of a somewhat surly temper," continues Bonazzi, "he had the gift of miracles, and once when the Tiber was in heavy flood, and a mill belonging to the convent was threatened with destruction, the saint caused the waters to subside. On another occasion during the building of S. Pietro, the ropes which were raising one of the columns snapped in two, and the Saint caused the column to remain suspended in mid air until new ropes were brought, so that nobody was hurt. This particular column is the second on the left as you enter.... It is impossible to imagine," Bonazzi continues, "how great was the sensation caused by these miracles, and for the time being, nobody thought any more about the end of the world—perhaps they hoped that our Saint had exorcised that, as well as the lesser catastrophes."

Just as the Abbot had built his church in 963—a beautiful bare basilica, with colonnades, and naked raftered roof—so she remained till well down into the fifteenth century, waiting, as it were, for the raiment of the Renaissance to clothe her with fresh glories. Then gradually, first by the roofing of the ceiling, then by pictures, chapels, the enlargement of the sacristy and choir, and such things of rare and exquisite beauty as the stalls and the altar-piece of Perugino, S. Pietro grew into a thing of marvellous taste and finish. But it was an evil day in which some person ruined the original façade by adding the courtyard and the cloisters. In old times the campanile stood free of the church, and the front of the church had strange figures and frescoes on it, parts of which can still be seen by penetrating a dark passage under the bell-tower at the back of the little sacristy. (See Bonfigli's fresco, p. 243.)

The history of the campanile of S. Pietro is a study in itself. This most lovely and unfortunate tower was for ever suffering at the hands of man or else the elements. Its chronicler is unable to discover the date of its first erection, but he tells us that it was probably built on the site of an old Etruscan tomb, which even now forms its basement. The earliest written record of the campanile is dated 1347, at which time we are told that it was so elegant, and so very richly adorned, that an early historian thought it to be the "loveliest in Tuscany," yet a certain war-like Abbot, Fra Guidalotti, a man "who rather inclined to the affairs of war than the discipline of religion, with a view maybe to convert his campanile into a fortress, that it might thus better serve his war-like spirit," began to claw it down. He got as far as the first obelisk, and in his evil operations he tumbled down the metal statue of the Saint which once adorned the summit. The engaging work of the Abbot was taken up and continued by Pope Boniface IX., who, in 1393, spent 180 florins in turning the gracious tower into a strong fortress!

In 1468 the campanile was rebuilt by the monks at the great cost of 4000 florins, but some years later it was struck by lightning and much injured. "From this point onward," writes its historian, "the history of the tower can only be traced through one continuous series of repairs, which injury from lightning necessitated." These injuries were of such a sort and so continuous that finally the building showed signs of approaching ruin. Iron clamps were added, but the lightning continued to attack it. At last someone had the wisdom to put up lightning conductors, since when the tower is safe, and one of the loveliest points in the landscape is secured for us.

A door festooned with splendid garlands of fruit, carved deep in creamy marbles, leads from the courtyard into the church. The interior is heavily decorated, but though some of the pictures are far from good, the impression given by the whole is beautiful and pleasing; and the choir, which was added in 1400, is one of the loveliest things of its kind in Italy. The columns of the nave are some of the remains of the only pagan temple which was left in Perugia after the siege of Augustus (see S. Angelo, chapter vii.). With the exception of Perugino's great altar-piece, S. Pietro has preserved nearly all the pictures which were painted for it. Amongst these is a good *Pietà* by Perugino (perhaps one of the panels out of the big picture at S. Agostino). There are three large canvases by Vasari in the chapel of the Holy Sacrament, a painting by

Eusebio di S. Giorgio of the Adoration of the Magi on the wall outside and a picture by Guido Reni in the chapel of the Annunciation.[68] At the end of the left transept is a *Pietà* by Bonfigli. "Cette Piété incorrecte et pieuse," as M. Broussole describes it. The picture hangs in a bad light between the Vibi chapel and the door, and at first only the white naked figure of Christ shines out on the dark blue gown of the virgin; but looking a little longer we find ourselves in the study of S. Jerome: one of those enchanting rooms which this particular saint inevitably inhabits, neat and exquisite in the arrangement of its benches and its lectern. Our Lady of Pity is sitting there, holding the dead figure of her son and kissing his head upon her shoulder. To her right is a figure of S. Leonard, to the left, and wholly unconscious of the tragedy, S. Jerome sits, smiling a little slyly. There is beautiful intarsia work (older than that in the choir) on the walls of the sacristy, and some fine illuminated books; lower down the church in the right transept, a beautiful bit of work by Salimbene of Siena, and on the last wall a fine picture of the school of Perugino, very rich and bright in colour. The two Alfanis have left ample specimens of their art in S. Pietro, and there are several of Sassoferrato's copies of great masterpieces. But the greatest treasure of the church, like those of S. Lorenzo and S. Agostino, did not escape the terrible eye of Napoleon Bonaparte. Perugino's great Assumption, which formed the glory of the high altar, is gone to France. Only six of the saints, battered and cut from their frames, linger like unhappy ghosts on the walls of the sacristy.

The altar in the chapel of the Vibi and Baglioni families is a lovely bit of Mino da Fiesole's work. Vasari accuses this sweet-souled sculptor of a lack of originality—of a desire to copy the sentiment of his master (Desiderio da Settignano) rather than to draw straight for himself from the sources of nature. Be this as it may in the case of Mino's portraits of people, those of his flowers in this particular piece of work are strangely realistic. We think he must himself have gathered and bound the garlands which hang from the narrow frieze, and in doing so he took for models the sharpest and the prickliest fruits and leaves of autumn: hazel nuts and tiny fir cones, their points just tipped with gold. The halos, too, on the angels' heads, their wings, and the details of the architecture are all picked out with gold. White, clean, and flat and fair is Mino's altar-piece in the Baglioni chapel. How different from the blood-stained hands and hearts of those same men who came to tell their beads here and be buried.

Long after other details in the church have been forgotten, its choir will remain a haunting vision of excessive beauty. Every inch of it is worked with exquisite care and finish, for the monks spared no pains or money, either in its construction or its decoration. Although a piece of the purest Renaissance fancy, it does not clash with the lines of the older basilica, and the two little pulpits of pietra serena, with their rich gilding, the organ lofts and the rather rococo frescoes on the ceiling, seem only to harmonise the meeting of the different styles of building. Raphael is said to have designed the stalls, but there is no sort of document to prove this. "Because our choir is the work of a genius, it does not follow that that genius should be Raphael ... genius is not the possession of one sole person," pleads M. Cassinese. Raphael died in 1520, the present stalls were not finished till 1535, and they are probably almost entirely the work of Stefano da Bergamo and the men and boys whom the Bergamasque employed. Some few may be of an earlier date, for we know that the choir was begun in 1524, and that the work was interrupted by the same terrible pestilence as that which killed Perugino. In 1532, Stefano da Bergamo undertook the work of the choir. He worked steadily, and the monks of S. Pietro kept the most accurate account of what they paid him, and of how many measures of flour and pence they gave the men and boys whom he employed. Little is known of the life of Stefano da Bergamo; we do not even know from whom he learned his art, but M. Cassinese rightly concludes that he drew his inspiration from the divine Raphael, since his designs are purely Raphaelesque. The carving is unequal, and some of the stalls are infinitely lovelier than others. Note the ninth on the right of the choir: a mother and three children encircled by a heavy garland of fruit and flowers, and under them a child, with flying hair, playing with snakes. Note, too, the extraordinary rows of mythical beasts which lie upon the arms of the lower row of stalls; catch them in perspective one evening in the dusk—they will give you food for most fantastic dreaming. What minds, half childlike and half mad, these early carvers had!

The doors of the choir are the work of Fra Damiano of Bergamo. They are intarsia work, and show a most delightful fancy. They have unfortunately been much polished and restored; still what a jewel this panel is, which is said to represent the finding of Moses! Compare the banks of the Nile with this palace and this pleasaunce of the purest Renaissance. Its bulrushes are turned to pergolas, its pyramids to a maze of pillars and of marble terraces, and there is a bear in the foreground eating honey, a crane, a rabbit, a long-eared goat, and other beasts of singular delight. It is strange to think of Fra Damiano sitting in his rooms at Bologna and preparing these same decorative panels for a place which, maybe, he had never seen. Above the doors is a fresco attributed to Giannicola Manni(?), and when the doors open you step out straight upon a little balcony, and down below lies the Umbrian plain, without a break of building, and straight in front of you Assisi lies upon its broad, calm hillside.

The work for the stalls of S. Pietro was finished, it seems, in 1535, but the pieces were not put together till 1591. In that year, on the 4th of August, a native architect undertook to put the carvings in their places. He worked so steadily that on Christmas Eve of that same year, "at the first vespers of the feast, the choir was solemnly inaugurated in a musical mass sung by the friars."

What a picture we have—the dull light of the candles on the winter morning and the monks singing together, in the midst of all their beautiful new woodwork!

A curious incident is told in connection with the choir of S. Pietro and three citizens of Perugia. When on the 20th of June 1859, the papal troops entered Perugia, a detachment of them were quartered in the church and monastery of S. Pietro, after the town had been seized, and three gentlemen of Perugia who had been fighting for her liberty at the gates found themselves cut off from the town and surrounded by the Swiss guard, who, however, were not conscious of their presence, in the monastery of S. Pietro. It will be remembered that the monks of S. Pietro, on this occasion, sided with the citizens, and one of them, Fra Santo, hustled the three gentlemen up into a little cupboard in the organ-loft where he kept them concealed for three whole days, feeding them, as best he could, with a little bread and water. One other gentleman, who was concealed in another part of the church, managed to escape under cover of certain dust-pans belonging to the friars, with which he passed himself off on the guard at the gates as a sacristan. Either he, or someone else, let the cat out of the bag about the gentlemen in the organ, and a most diligent search was set on foot. However, the little cupboard escaped notice for the time, and on the morning of the fourth day of their confinement, whilst the Papal guard were getting their pay, Fra Santo and another monk took from the stalls the ropes which they had cut from their bells on the preceding evening, and tying these to the balcony of the choir, they hastily let out the three gentlemen from the organ, who clambered down the ropes, and waving adieu to their benefactors, scampered off as quickly as they could across the open country. Five hours later the Pope's guard went up into the organ, but even then they failed to discover the cupboard whence their enemies had so lately flown!

When, some time later, the monks of S. Pietro went to Rome to beg the Pope's pardon for the part they had played against him in the siege of Perugia, the heaviest blame fell, of course, on Fra Santo; but his Holiness with extreme good sense thus put an end to the question: "If Fra Santo has done what you tell me he has, God has willed that he should do so, and we must ever respect the will of God."

There are one or two lovely bits of della Robbia work in the refectory of the monastery, a fresco by Tiberio d'Assisi(?) in the chapel, and a fine well in one of the cloisters. The garden, too, is very charming, but it is not easy to get permission to wander in these pleasant places where popes and monks and men of learning spent such pleasant and such profitable hours. The place is now occupied by students as the whole convent was turned last year (1896) into a great agricultural college. (See Note, p. 163.)

S. Costanzo.

A little lower down the hill is the small church dedicated to S. Costanzo. For some obscure reason this saint, who is purely local, has become the patron saint of lovers, and on his feast day all the lovers of the neighbourhood assemble at the shrine. If the eye of S. Costanzo blinks at the young man or the girl who kneel before his image, they feel a happy certainty that the course of their affection will run smooth, and that the year will end in happy union.

S. Costanzo was converted to the Christian faith by S. Ercolano I., whom he succeeded as bishop of Perugia, and Ciatti gives us a long list of his virtues and his miracles. The blind of the city received their sight from him, we hear, and the lame were made to walk. But all his miracles and his conversions made him an object of hatred to the pagans, and one day he was seized together with his followers, and thrown into prison. They were then put into scalding baths, "but," says Ciatti, "the Holy Ghost, who filled their souls with fire, tempered the external heat, and they sang hymns to signify their great tranquillity." Their only discomfort lay in the darkness all around them, but soon "a wonderful brightness appeared unto them from heaven which comforted them exceedingly." Then the pagans continued their tortures and forced the Saint to walk on burning embers, but as these did him no harm he was stripped and covered with red hot coals; and all the time he went on singing much to the annoyance of his tormentors. Finally he and his followers made their escape and fled to Spello, where fresh conversions, followed by fresh tortures, are recounted. At last, in 154 A.D., he met his death at Spoleto. His body was taken back to Perugia by a certain Serviano da Foligno, who found it "surrounded by a choir of rejoicing angels, and in a shroud of heavenly light. The holy burden was too heavy for Serviano to carry alone, and he called on two men who were passing by to help him. At first they refused and scoffed at the miracles he related, whereupon they were both struck blind, and trembling, they prayed for mercy to the God of the Christians. On touching the body of the Saint they received their sight, whereat they gladly helped to carry it into Perugia. They entered by Porta S. Pietro, and were met by many of the faithful." The body of S. Costanzo is buried in the little church outside the Porta S. Pietro, rebuilt by the present Pope, and the beautiful byzantine doorway seems a fit entrance to the tomb of this suffering and much tormented martyr of Perugia.

CHAPTER VII

Piazza del Papa, S. Severo, Porta Sole, S. Agostino, and S. Francesco al Monte

THE Piazza del Papa[69] lies a little to the right of the entrance door to the Duomo. In former times the straw market was held in this square, which was then called the Piazza di Paglia, and at that period the statue of Pope Julius occupied a splendid position on the steps of the cathedral. But during the great revolt against the Papacy in 1780 the Pope's statue was taken away from its prominent place by some wise persons who foresaw its destruction should they allow it to remain there, and it was bundled into the cellar of a tavern in the town, where it remained, not, it must be confessed, entirely incognito, till people's nerves had calmed a little.[70] Not so very long ago the Pope was once more brought to the light of day and set in his present position.

Pope Julius III. is a great figure in Perugian history. He is in a sense a lay figure, for he never set foot in the city after his student days, and he was worshipped almost in the manner of an unseen deity by the Perugians. Julius succeeded Paul III., and though he by no means did away with the supreme power of the Church in the city, still he mitigated many of the hardships and the ignominies which that power had entailed in the hands of the great Farnese. When Paul III. died in 1549 his fortress remained as a legacy to the city, with a Castellano to watch over its (Papal) interests. This man proceeded to rule as his master had taught him, and he defended the castle vigilantly against the Pope's nephew, who made some efforts to gain possession of so rich a prize.

HOUSE IN THE VIA PERNICE

The policy of Julius III. was of a much milder order. "Julius had always loved our city with a peculiar partiality," says Mariotti, "and he sent his relation Cardinal della Corgna hither, endowing him with full authority, and hardly had the Cardinal arrived than he restored to the city the arms of which she had been deprived so long; and in February of that same year Julius III. sent a brief to the holders of ecclesiastical liberty, which was addressed to the *Priori delle Arte* (heads of City Guilds), a title which had not been heard of in Perugia since 1539; and to this grace the same Pope added considerable sums of money for the maintenance of those same magistrates...."

It will be easy to anyone who has formed even a dim conception of what the strength of the spirit of liberty was like in the minds of the Perugians to understand the pure sensation of delight which the Pope's open acknowledgment of their old municipal rule, followed as it was by a message couched in such friendly terms, was likely to produce. Fretting as the citizens had been for many years under the rule of the despotic Paul, they hailed his more temperate successor as a sort of saviour, and they determined to express their sentiments of joy in what Bonazzi fitly terms "a day of political bacchanalia."[71]

"So on the morning of the first day in May the heads of the principal guilds of the Mercanzia and the Cambio met in the piazza, and there having put aside their black apparel (Paul III. had Insisted on the *Priori* wearing a form of mourning, in order, and probably with perfect wisdom, to insist on his own authority in Perugia), they reassumed the crimson of the former *Priori*, and thrusting their heads through the golden chains which the Pope's Vice-Legate himself insisted upon hanging round them in token of their reinstatement, they took their seats upon the damask benches and listened to the Mass of the Holy Ghost, sung by the Vice-Legate. Then, upon leaving the church, all the religious orders, the *Confraternitàs*, the guilds, the gentlemen, the troops, and the excited populace seeing the transfigured magistrates, lifted a frenzied cry, and forming into a monstrous procession to the sound of pipes, of drums, of trumpets, bells, and much artillery, the whole crowd followed the *Priori* to the Church of S. Agostino and there, having heard another musical mass, the new magistrates, followed by an ever increasing and clamorous cortège, went on to take up quarters on the first floor of the Palazzo Pubblico."

Not satisfied with this demonstration of their delight and loyalty toward the new Pope, the Perugians determined to commemorate the occasion through the medium of art. They commissioned Adone Doni to paint the above described scene of the reinstatement of the magistrates (see the picture in the Palazzo Pubblico), whilst Vincenzo Danti, then a mere boy, was employed to make the big bronze statue of Julius III., which is one of the most remarkable points in the present town.

But to us who know the almost purely democratic, or at least municipal, tendencies of past Perugia, this great bronze figure of a Pope eternally blessing the city always excites a sense of something false and contradictory, and had we been permitted to visit the benevolent Julius in the caverns of the wine shop, we should have felt him in that place to be a truer symbol of the spirit of the town throughout her troubled history.

S. Severo.

From the Piazza del Papa several roads branch off to different points of the town. To the right the Via Bontempi leads down past some beautiful old palaces into a network of typical Perugian streets. The churches of S. Fiorenzo, the Carmine, and S. Maria Nuova, all of which have *gonfaloni* or banners by Bonfigli, lie in this direction, and are very well worth visiting. Indeed, the *gonfalone* in S. Maria Nuova is extraordinarily interesting: a typical specimen of that tragic and almost passionate form of art which arose out of, and answered to, the needs of a people convinced of its own moral depravity (see p. 232). To the left of the Via Bontempi a narrow street winds steeply up the hill to the church of S. Severo, which stands high up above the church of S. Maria Nuova, and commands a splendid view to the east of the city, and away across the valley of the Tiber to Assisi. "It is asserted by some persons," says Siepi, "that in the year 1007 a little colony of Camaldolese monks was transferred to the city of Perugia, who, during the lifetime of their holy founder, took up their abode on the hill of S. Severo, and here, upon the ruins of an ancient temple, which some believe was dedicated to the sun god, and upon a spot which might be termed the Acropolis of Perugia, they built their church, and dedicated it to S. Severo, Bishop of Ravenna, probably because they came into Perugia from that same city." As to whether the church of S. Severo was really built on the site of an old pagan temple dedicated to the sun god we cannot say; it is certain that this whole quarter of the town is called Porta Sole, but, however it be, the church of the Camaldolese monks has been quite altered in the course of centuries, and, except for its position and its fresco, it has not much to charm the casual tourist. During later restorations the outer porch with Raphael's and Perugino's fresco was preserved, and built into a little chapel, where we see it now. The fresco is signed 1505, so Raphael was no longer a boy when he painted it. Some years later he painted his great pictures in the Stanze of the Vatican, and, perhaps, he was feeling his way to these grand compositions when he drew his semi-circle of saints on the walls of the little old church of S. Severo. Did the master Perugino watch his brilliant pupil as he painted? There is a touch of pathos in the facts which follow:—Raphael the mighty genius dies, and Rome goes into mourning for him; fourteen or fifteen years go by, and Perugino, who, be it remembered, was not a young man when the slim youth from Urbino came one day into his studio and asked to learn the art of painting from him, comes back to the spot where Raphael's fresco shines upon the wall, and paints, in his most faded style, the six pale saints which we now see below it....

Porta Sole.

But to return once more to the piazza. Another road leads up immediately behind the statue of Pope Julius to one of the most surprising points in the city, namely, the bastions of Porta Sole. It was to this high point, which commands an extraordinary view over the north of the town, that Dante alluded when writing of Perugia:

"Intra Tupino e l'acqua che discende
Del colle eletto del beato Ubaldo
Fertile costa d'alto monte pende,
Onde Perugia sente freddo e caldo
Da Porta Sole, e diretro le piange
Per grave giogo Nocera con Gualdo."

Porta Sole is mixed up with a strange and a most typical bit of Perugian history. We have seen how much this city was influenced by the popes, and how, in the many fluctuations of her history, she nearly always returned to the nominal rule of the Church of Rome. Early in the fourteenth century she broke away for a time from Papal power, but in 1370 again swore allegiance to Pope Urban IV., who sent his brother, Cardinal Albano, to receive the act of submission from her people. The following year the Cardinal of Jerusalem came to Perugia to establish peace between the nobles and the *Raspanti*. He was escorted by about 500 horsemen and 300 infantry, and the people received him with enthusiasm, coming out to meet him with palms in their hands, and cries of "Viva Santa Madre Chiesa, eviva il Signore!" Unfortunately his wise rule lasted but a year, and he was succeeded by a very different sort of person, namely, the Abbot of Mommaggiore from Cluny (see p. 30), who arrived in Perugia in a most hostile frame of mind, and quite prepared for war and for revolts of every kind. The Abbot at once set to work to build for himself fortresses, the like of which, as one proud chronicler relates, had never before been seen in Italy. He erected a massive citadel at Porta Sole, and in order to be in connection with the Palazzo dei Priori he made a covered passage with high machicolated walls to join the two together. In doing this he did not scruple to knock down a large part of the cathedral which happened to come in his way. At Porta S. Antonio, too, the Abbot built some large and splendid houses, part of which may still be seen, and these he joined by means of a covered passage to the other citadel on Porta Sole. Thus Mommaggiore may be said to have had a run over half the city of Perugia. So beautiful and luxurious were his palaces at S. Antonio, that we are told they seemed a veritable paradise. In them he stored enough wine and flour and other things to last him and his French companions for at least ten years, and not content with all these preparations for a possible revolt of the citizens, he even called in the help of an English *condottiere*, Sir John Hawkwood, who was at that time in the service of the Church, to come and ravage all the country round Perugia.

The Perugians looked on in silence, and in silence they planned a desperate plan of revolution, for they were determined to resist this abominable French Abbot and to assert their former authority. Silently, and with bowed heads, they watched the Abbot's troops scouring the streets on the evening of the 12th December 1375; and not till night had fallen on the town did a hum arise. Then deep growling sounds rang through the darkness of the night, and the tyrant, sitting in his palace, knew that the men of the town were up, and that a mighty mischief was preparing. Down in the Porta S. Angelo the cry of "Viva il Popolo" was heard, and with one accord, little and great, nobles and people, forgetting private injuries and discords, and moved by a single purpose, clasping hands and crying, "Viva il Popolo, and death to the Abbot and the pastors of the Church," rushed into the piazza just as the sun had risen. The terrified Abbot, seeing that the people were about to storm the Palazzo Pubblico, fled with his friends and soldiers along the covered passages to his palace at S. Antonio. The furious citizens were quick to follow and arrived before the fortress with all sorts of infernal machines, amongst others a large catapult which hurled forth stones of such a size and with such excellent effect that it received the name of *Cacciaprete* (Kick out the priests). We hear of a great battle which took place when the Abbot, being besieged in his citadel, was forced to implore the help of Sir John Hawkwood; but the latter, having been well bribed by the Perugians, abandoned his unfortunate patron, leaving him, surrounded night and day by a crowd of angry citizens, to meditate upon the various fortunes of war. At last, however, a peace was concluded, and Sir John Hawkwood arrived at the head of 300 lancers[72] to escort the Abbot, his French friends, and his 1500 horse and soldiers safe beyond the city. The Perugians, seeing their enemy the Abbot arrayed in heavy armour and hardly able to lift his feet, slipping moreover at every turn upon the muddy ground, saluted him with shrill whistles, which even the mighty Hawkwood was unable to suppress, and a chronicler devoutly tells us that "thus in the name of God, of His holy Mother Mary, and of the blessed Saints: Ercolano, Lorenzo, and Costanzo, was the city of Perugia delivered from the hands of those accursed pastors of the Church." The happy event was celebrated by grand religious functions, although the revolt had been entirely against the temporal power of the Pope. Even Milan and

Florence rejoiced at the news, and ambassadors from Siena and from Arezzo came to Perugia to grace the feasts and the rejoicings with their presence. "*Priori* and treasurers of the Republic, doctors, nobles, *Raspanti*, and *Beccherini*, danced for a whole week, day and night, in friendly concord, and there were fireworks and much sound of music."

These things were done at Porta Sole in the past. The Abbot's palaces and covered passages were well-nigh battered to bits by the revengeful citizens, but the charm of the small piazza has not vanished with them. Looking from the bastions one still can trace a portion of the covered passage by which the terror-stricken Abbot fled at sunrise to his palaces at Porta Sant' Antonio; and on winter evenings we have often stood there, watching, with an ever fresh delight, the brown roofs of the slumbering town below—the brown woods of the browner Apennines beyond; and seen them fade and gather into one harmonious whole just as they did five hundred years ago, when Mommaggiore sat at supper and heard the first low hum of revolution.

From the piazza of Porta Sole a steep paved road or staircase leads down to the Piazza Grimani, and here one is confronted by what is perhaps the most remarkable point in the whole city, namely, the Arch of Augustus.[73]

Arch of Augustus.

In Dennis' admirable account of Perugia he gives a full description of this arch:—

"The best preserved and grandest of all the gates of Perugia," he says, "is the *Arco d'Augusto*, so called from the inscription, *Augusta Perusia*, over the arch. It is formed of regular masonry of travertine, uncemented, in courses of 18 inches high; some of the blocks being 3 or 4 feet in length. The masonry of the arch hardly corresponds with that below it and is probably of subsequent date and Roman, as the inscription seems to testify, though the letters are not necessarily coeval with the structure. The arch is skew or oblique; and the gate is double, like those of Volterra and Cosa. Above the arch is a frieze of six Ionic colonnettes, fluted, alternating with shields; and from this springs another arch, now blocked up, surmounted by a second frieze of Ionic pilasters, not fluted. All the work above the lower arch is evidently of later date than the original construction of the gateway.... This gate stands recessed from the line of the city wall, and is flanked on either hand by a tower, projecting about 20 feet, and rising, narrowing upwards, to a level with the top of the wall above the gate. The masonry of these towers, to the height of the imposts of the arch, corresponds with that of the gate itself, and seems to be the original structure, all above that height is of a later period.... The gate still forms one of the entrances to the city, though there is a populous suburb without its walls. Its appearance is most imposing. The lofty towers, like ponderous obelisks, truncated—the tall archway recessed between them—the frieze of shields and colonnettes above it—the second arch soaring over all, a gallery, it may be, whence to annoy the foe—the venerable masonry overgrown with moss, or dark with the breath of ages—form a whole which carries the mind most forcibly into the past."

The history of the arch of Augustus, or *Porta urbica etrusca*, has been given again and again by local and by foreign guide-books and historians, but we know of no better account than the above by Dennis, and little is left to say on the subject here. In speaking of Etruscan walls in another part of his book, Dennis remarks that one of their most striking features is the apparent newness of the stone. The big blocks of travertine on the Arco d'Augusto are as sharp almost as on the day when the Etruscans brought them up the hill, something like three thousand years ago, the marks of the individual masons are perfectly clear upon their faces, and time has mellowed the light and graceful colonnade of the Renaissance and Roman architecture, as much or more than that of the vanished people.

For a vivid first impression of the city one should certainly enter it from its northern side, and pass at once into its grim, dark, mediæval streets, through these splendid early portals. The usual approach from the station, which is certainly no quicker and much more tedious, gives nothing like the same impression of the real Perugia, which we love to read about and study.

ARCO D'AUGUSTO

S. Agostino.

Many roads meet in the Piazza Grimani, and joining as it were together, pass back to the heart of the town through the arch of Augustus. The whole of the Borgo S. Angelo, which spreads away to the north of the piazza, though enclosed by very early walls, is not part of the first city of Perugia, and is indeed a little city of its own with one main street, the Via Longara, and houses closely packed on either side.[74] To the right as one passes up it is the church of

S. Agostino, with its wonderful choir—one of those choirs which, by its exquisite variety of design and transformation of the wood to beasts, delights and fascinates one.

The choir was made in 1502, and, as Mariotti, who describes it at length, remarks, it is "indeed worthy of praise." Perugino himself supplied the designs, which were carried out by his Florentine friend Baccio d'Agnolo, and Perugino saw that the payment of the work was good: 1120 florins down at the end of the year when the work was done.[75]

S. Agostino, like other churches of the town, has long since been despoiled of its best treasures. We read a long list of its early pictures; the crowning glory of these, the large and many-sided altar-piece by Perugino, was pulled to bits and scattered during the Napoleonic raids. The history of this great altar-piece has been traced with extraordinary precision, and as it throws some light on the ways of the painter we give a sketch of it here. It seems that in the autumn of 1502 the indefatigable Pietro signed a contract in which he promised to paint his "Sposalizio" for the Duomo, three other smaller pictures, designs for the stalls of S. Agostino, and finally an immense two-sided altar-piece for that same church. As may easily be imagined the carrying out of this colossal contract was no light matter, and it dragged on for years during which time Perugino did not hesitate to embark on several other works; and, not at all abashed by his own lack of faith in promises, we find him writing to the friars of S. Agostino from Pieve di Castello, where he was for the time engaged on other work, begging them in a large round hand and most marvellous spelling, to give some corn to one of his protégés, bearer of the letter (see Pinacoteca). The letter is dated March 30, 1512. The next we hear of the picture is in the autumn of 1521 when there is a question about payment which proves that the work was finished. It is not an easy matter to reconstruct this picture, but we have seen the plan of it in a very early manuscript which shows a grand pile of frame and canvasses much in the style of Pinturicchio's altar-piece in the Pinacoteca. Of all its many parts Perugia has only kept a few of the saints, the Baptism, the Nativity and the *Pietà*(?). We read of scattered fragments in such different towns as Grenoble, Toulouse, Lyons, and Nantes. The Madonna herself, we hear, was pierced by a German ball at Strasburg.

S. AGOSTINO AND PORTA BULAGAJO

There is in a side chapel of S. Agostino a rather beautiful old fresco, probably by some scholar of Perugino, of a Madonna and some saints with a white rabbit in the foreground. Looking one day at the picture we wondered vaguely why the rabbit had been painted there: "Ma, per bellezza," hazarded the small son of the sacristan with the delightful intuition peculiar to the children of his nation.

No doubt he was perfectly right. Another good fresco by Perugino or his scholars may be found, strangely enough, in the back passage of a baker's shop a little farther up the Via Longara; but before leaving the church of S. Agostino it would be well to look at the splendid meeting-room of the Confraternità next door to it. This room, like that at S. Francesco, is a magnificent specimen of rather heavy and sumptuous Renaissance wood-carving.

S. Angelo.

At the very end of the Borgo, just before turning into the open country, is the little old temple of S. Angelo. One of the earliest facts we find in the history of Perugia is that this temple was the only building which escaped the fire kindled by Caius Cestius (see p. 10). The church is probably built on the site of some old Etruscan temple, but in its present state it bears only a phantom resemblance to the form of its first architecture. Some say that the early temple was dedicated to Pan, more likely it was a temple to Venus or Vulcan. Conestabile declares that three distinct periods of building can be traced in it, and he suggests that the original temple was pulled down and rebuilt by ignorant early Christians with the ruins of another temple dedicated to Flora. The pillars are certainly of different sizes and very different qualities of stone. Some few are of Greek marble, and one has an Etruscan capital; yet in Fergusson's description of S. Angelo he says that "the materials are apparently original and made for the place they occupy;" he also suggests that the church was originally used as a baptistery, or may have been dedicated to some martyr, "but in the heart of Etruria," he adds, "this form may have been adopted for other reasons, the force of which we are hardly able at present to appreciate; though in all cases locality is one of the strongest influencing powers as far as architectural forms are concerned." In the first form of the Christian building it was surrounded by a third row of columns which were taken by the Abbot of S. Pietro to adorn his new basilica, and in those times the third circle stood open to the air with vestibules and atrium. The altar of sacrifice, now a side altar, stood in the centre of the church where the hideous rococo baldachino stands today. The small square pillar with the Latin inscription was probably moved from its place, and turned to the north at the time when, as a local writer fitly says, "the architecture of S. Angelo was burdened by so many bagatelles and such a profusion of false ornament." Among other late Christian "ornaments" in S. Angelo we must mention the body of a young Saint which lies embalmed under one of the side altars. It is one of those odd pathetic bits of bad taste which somehow charm us. The Saint is dressed in tawdry armour, but his face and limbs are exquisitely fine, his expression pure and very peaceful. His hair is long, the skin of his face waxen, he seems to be merely sleeping. One of the very earliest Umbrian frescoes of Perugia, "La Madonna del Verde," is painted in a chapel to the right. The whole building is a remarkable mixture of early pagan, of Roman, and of Christian art, and we can only regret that the last should have been added later, and in its worst and most degraded era.

CHURCH OF S. ANGELO

The temple stands on a quiet plot of ground within the city walls, which, a little to the left of it, end in a great mediæval tower or portcullis put up in time of war by a *condottiere*! It needed the Umbrian sky, it required the Umbrian landscape to make of such strange contrasts an harmonious whole. Yet S. Angelo is one of those things which at once possesses men's fancy, and we read that even in the middle ages fantastic legends centred round it, and that the early writers believed it to be the "pavilion of Orlando."

Having, in this chapter, run through some few historical facts relating to a Pope, an Abbot, two Umbrian painters and a pagan temple, we may as well complete the medley with one or two calm records of the Umbrian saints. Leaving the church of S. Angelo one passes back to the street and out through the Porta S. Angelo into the open country. The gate is half a castle, and was built by Fortebraccio when he was strengthening the city with new walls. There is a charming detail in the life of S. Francis connected with it. We hear that when Pope Honorius III. was staying at Perugia, the enthusiasm for saint Francis of Assisi was at its height, and the Pope with all his court went down across the plain to visit the quiet dwelling-place of the gentle Christ-like teacher: "And the friars of S. Francis," says Mariotti, "beheld many counts and cavaliers and other noble gentlemen, and a great number of Cardinals, Bishops, Abbots and different clergy, who all came down to see the large but humble congregation of S. Francis." And then the Saint returned the visit, and coming in person to call upon the Pope in order to obtain indulgences for his new church of the Angeli, it happened that as he passed through the Porta S. Angelo he met with S. Domenico who himself was hurrying in the same direction. They met each other in the archway—these two founders of great religious orders—"and with their usual charity they embraced each other." The picture is beautiful and striking indeed: maybe a hot May morning, and the two men, who more than most on earth had overcome themselves and elevated the souls of other men, staying to embrace in a quiet, homely fashion before passing further on into the presence of the acknowledged Pontiff of the Church.

S. Francesco al Monte.

A little further down the road on the left hand side, is the monastery of S. Francesco al Monte. We hear that the place was endowed in the following manner: "It happened that a rich gentleman, Giacomo di Buonconti de' Coppoli, who, in his houses of Monteripido," (the hill on which the present convent stands) "was wont most tenderly to entertain the blessed brother Egidio, delighted beyond power of description in the ecstatic trances of that Saint; and having become a widower, by the death of Donna Vita, who died childless, Messer Giacomo took holy orders, and in his will he ordered that his houses should be turned into the convent of S. Francesco al Monte which was therefore built in 1276 by the Minori Osservanti." We may conclude that Fra Egidio, who was one of the most fascinating followers of S. Francis, long outlived his ardent worshipper, for we hear that he spent a great deal of his time in the convent that was built to do honour to the Franciscan order.

Poor Fra Egidio! when he knew that death was near he begged to be taken back to Assisi to die and be buried in the home of his loved leader; but the Perugians, although they simply idolized him, refused him this last comfort. They forced him to die in their midst so that they might have his corpse and profit by the miracles that they expected would be worked by it. They gave him a beautiful tomb at last, which may now be seen in the church of the University. His staff, his book, his poor brown gown, are kept in a crystal case tied up with roses and silk ribbons.

The monastery of S. Francesco al Monte rises bare but beautifully proportioned on its hill top. Tall lines of slender cypress trees guard either side of the steep ascent or "sacro monte" which leads to it. We cannot explore the cells; the little church is bare, its Perugino altar-piece and other pictures gone, like the rest, to the Pinacoteca; but sitting on the grass-grown steps we may read one of the most delightful and ingenuous stories ever told about either Perugia or the followers of S. Francis:—

"So S. Louis, King of France, went upon a pilgrimage to visit all the sanctuaries upon the earth, and hearing great fame of the holiness of Brother Egidio, who had been one of the first companions of S. Francis, he set his heart on visiting him in person, wherefore he came to Perugia where Fra Egidio then was living. And coming to the door of the convent dressed as a poor and unknown pilgrim with but a few companions, he enquired with great insistence after Fra Egidio, saying nothing to the porter of who it was that asked. So the porter went to Fra Egidio, and told him that a pilgrim was asking for him at the door, and to Fra Egidio it was revealed by God that he who waited for him was the King of France, whereat he immediately and with the utmost fervour left his cell and hurried to the gate; and without further questioning and although they had never met before, with the most deep devotion those two kneeled down together kissing each other with such a sweet familiarity it seemed that they had held long fellowship together: but in spite of all these things neither the one nor the other spoke a word; they merely held each other in that close embrace, with every sign of charitable love, in silence. And having stayed together thus for a long space of time without exchange of words they parted from each other; and S. Louis went forth upon his journey and Fra Egidio returned unto his cell." ...

Then we hear that the monks in the convent arose and murmured together, and questioned Fra Egidio about the mysterious guest with whom he had stayed so long in close embrace, and Fra Egidio told them very simply that it had been the King of France. Then they upbraided him for his discourtesy towards so great a man: "O Fra Egidio, wherefore hast thou been so rude as never to have spoken even one syllable to so devout a King who came all the way from France that he might see thee, and hear from thee some holy words?" And Fra Egidio answers them with the childlike and unruffled candour peculiar to his order, and begs them not to marvel at the mutual silence of that meeting,

"Because," he says, "as soon as we had embraced each other the light of wisdom revealed and showed to me his heart, and likewise mine to him; and thus by a divine concurrence seeing into each other's hearts, we understood far better, he, what I desired to say to him, and I, what he desired to say to me, than if we had spoken together with our mouths; and we found far greater consolation than if we had attempted to explain with our voice that which we felt in our hearts: for, had we spoken with our mouths, such is the faultiness of human speech, we should more likely have had discomfort in the place of comfort: now therefore understand, that the King went from me marvellously contented, and his whole soul refreshed."

So King Louis of France went out across the Umbrian hills, the Umbrian Saint returned to his cell, and Perugia added a new and splendid number to her list of royal visitors.

Probably this story, be it a myth or be it truth, has caused the confusion between the French King and the French bishop, one of whom is certainly a patron of the city to this day. The lilies of France are scattered everywhere at the feet of the Umbrian griffin. But the true patron of Perugia is S. Louis Bishop of Toulouse, and as far as we know the visit of King Louis of France was only recorded by the author of the *Fioretti*.

CHAPTER VIII

Via dei Priori—Perugino's House,—Madonna della Luce—S. Bernardino and S. Francesco al Prato

JUST under the bell tower of the Palazzo Pubblico a narrow street, called the Via dei Priori, well-paved, and preserving many characteristics of the mediæval city, runs steeply down through the Porta S. Susanna and into the open country by the station. Once when the nobles were fighting in the square above, or more probably in the Corso, the blood flowed so freely that it is said to have come running down the street in a crimson stream at night—hence the name of Via del Piscinello which is given to the street a little lower down. The houses are very old, very grim, and closely packed in the Via dei Priori. The *lumieri*, where the heads of enemies were hung, stand out maliciously upon the walls of the Palazzo Pubblico to the right, and many of the palaces have still their narrow doors for the dead or *porte del mortuccio*.[76]

From the Chiesa Nuova (built in 1218 but entirely remodelled and spoilt by bad decoration) a narrow street leads off to the left and down past some charming red brick palaces into a narrower street where what is known as Perugino's house still stands.

THE OLD COLLEGIO DEI NOTARI, SAID TO BE THE STUDIO OF PERUGINO

The Story of Perugia

Though there seems to be but very slight evidence about the real abode of the painter, his studio has been fixed in the beautiful old corner palace with the red marble windows in the Via del Commercio off the Corso. But one place does as well as another to pin a legend to, and this little house of mean appearance tucked away in a dark and somewhat dingy street, with only a marble slab to mark it, serves the purpose well enough. Indeed, if one believed Vasari, one could with ease imagine Perugino choosing such a spot as this to hide his wife, his crimes (?) and all his money in, and see him hurrying thither in the dusk of a December evening from some big church or city where he had been to paint an altar-piece for prince or pontiff. One can even picture the long dark cloak he wore to cover up his money bag, his little cap pressed low upon his rather cloudy forehead, and one can almost hear him chuckle as he eats his maccaroni and strokes the fair hair of the woman he so loved, thinking with the joy of malice of all the other women who would come to pray and weep before his saints and his *Pietàs*.

The Story of Perugia

TORRE DEGLI SCIRRI

But this is nothing better than a dream. Blankly one looks at the slab above the door, at the wall from which even the frescoe of S. Christopher has vanished, and from the utter silence of the place one hurries away and further on down the Via dei Priori. The street ends, and one passes into the open country through the Porta S. Susanna. Just above is the *Torre degli Scirri*—one of the only specimens remaining of all the wealth of towers in the past. A tree has grown upon its very top as though to seal the peace which follows after strife. A little further on is the small church of the Madonna della Luce. The front of this church is a very dainty bit of architecture and was designed by Cesarino Roscetto, a Perugian goldsmith, who also made the silver shrine in the cathedral which holds the Virgin's ring. It has inside a beautiful altar piece by some scholar of Perugino. The picture is exquisite in colour and in sentiment. Siepi gives a long history about it, which, although it does not altogether fit in with the facts of dates, we cannot refrain from mentioning here. (Perhaps he was alluding to some older fresco which has disappeared.) He says that on the 12th of September 1513 some youths were playing at cards under the wall of a butcher's shop which in old days stood outside the church of S. Francesco. One of them, a young barber, called Fallerio, lost heavily at the game, whereat he swore a terrible oath, hearing which blasphemy the Madonna in her shrine by the wayside closed her eyes, and kept them closed for the space of four whole days. On the 16th she opened them again. So great was the fame of this miracle, and the sensation it caused, that processions and great multitudes of people came to worship before her shrine, and on the 7th of April 1513 her picture was carried to its present place in the new church which the people built for her, and she was no longer called the Madonna di S. Luca, but the Madonna of Light to commemorate this wonderful occurrence.

ETRUSCAN ARCH OF S. LUCA

From the church one road leads out into the country through the old Etruscan gate of S. Luca and another to the right into the Piazza della Giustizia: that fair open green which holds one of the loveliest flowers of Renaissance art—the façade of the Oratory of S. Bernardino.

S. Bernardino.

The Oratory was built in 1450 by the magistrates of Perugia, who were anxious to leave to their city some enduring mark of the man whose influence in times of extreme moral depravity and perpetual party strife had been so purely one of good to the citizens of Perugia. The life of S. Bernardino of Siena is familiar to most people. He, like S. Francis, exercised an extraordinary power over the minds of men in the middle ages by the mere example of pure living and sweetness of character, but perhaps his power lay a little more in preaching and in stirring men to action than that of the saint of Assisi, whose influence was more absolutely that of peace.

S. Bernardino of Siena was born at Massa, near Siena, in 1380. His mother died early, leaving the child to the care of an aunt. By this lady, Diana degli Albizeschi, he was educated with extreme care and tenderness, and he grew up beautiful, gracious, and very pure of heart. At seventeen he joined a confraternity at Siena, and by the early age of twenty-four he had already shaken an always weak constitution by his great labours for the sick in the time of plague. He died at Aquila in the Abruzzi, and was canonized in 1450 by Pope Nicholas V. S. Bernardino's life was one perpetual strain towards the light in an age which was dark, and one of its greatest objects had been to reconcile the mutual hatred of the Guelphs and Ghibellines. He was full of child-like faith and wise philanthropy; and tradition says that it was he who started the first *Monte di Pietà* or pawnshop, and Perugia claims the privilege of having seen the first of these institutions.[77]

The figure of S. Bernardino is always unmistakable in art, and it becomes familiar to us in Perugia, where he exercised an extraordinary power, and where he would preach from his pulpit in the public square to an almost maddened crowd of penitents. The saint is always represented holding a square tablet with the initials of Christ set round with rays upon it, because he was accustomed to hold one of these whilst preaching. His face is emaciated, but beautiful both in line and in expression; it is a face which the spirit illumines with an unmistakable glory. Mrs Jameson, in her life of the saint, says that the finest sculptured portrait of him is that on the façade of his Oratory at Perugia; and certainly, if taken merely as a graceful bit of art, few things could do more honour to the man whose best tribute, however, will always be his extraordinary hold on the hearts of men throughout the whole of Italy.

In 1461 the people of Perugia called in a Florentine sculptor, Agostino Ducci or Gucci, to ornament the façade of their new oratory. This sculptor is described by both Vasari and Mariotti as Agostino *della Robbia*, and connected, either as a son or a brother, with that well-known family. The connection is, however, not proved, neither does his work seem to corroborate it in any way.[78]

The façade of S. Bernardino is a marvellous and perhaps a unique thing in art. The work on it is light and airy like the winds of spring. The figures of the angels, the garlands, and the saint himself, are full of that elegant and subtle charm which now and then surprises one in sculpture. Ducci made wonderful use of the pale pink marble of the country, mixing it with terra-cotta figures, bits of blue sky, and marble, creamy white, for all his garlands. Perhaps the loveliest figures, where all are lovely, are those of the six virtues, Mercy,[79] Holiness, and Purity, Religion, Mortification, and Patience, on either side of the entrance doors. But the different angels playing on different instruments, and the flying angels round the figure of the saint, are each delightful in their separate ways. Even the inevitable griffin seems softened by the hand of the Florentine sculptor, and he has admirably caught the purely spiritual nature of the saint, both in the large central portrait, and in the smaller plaques where some of his miracles are represented. Siepi gives a full description of the different scenes:

MERCY. DETAIL ON FAÇADE OF THE ORATORY OF S. BERNARDINO

"Under the two higher niches," he says, "are two squares, and on the right one of these we see the Saint, who, whilst preaching on the Isola Maggiore of our Lake of Trasimene received into his order the blessed Giacomo of the Marches…. To the left," he continues, "the Saint is discovered preaching, and illuminated by a star, which in the full light of day shines over his head, a miracle which happened in the city of Aquila five years before his death, while preaching the praises of Mary.... Three other miracles of the Saint are given on the frieze below. In the middle one of these we see the Saint preaching to the people of Perugia, and the bonfire which he made them light on the piazza of our Duomo, where books of superstition, of necromancy and the law of astrology were burned in public, together with fashionable follies of the period: packs of cards, obscene pictures, forbidden weapons and ornaments of female luxury—instruments all of iniquity and of delight. Therefore it is that from the flames demons are seen to rise. In the miracle to the right we see two children saved by the intercession of the Saint from the furious waters of a millstream in which, having been caught, they were miraculously saved by the Saint from death...."

It is not very clear why this particular spot was chosen from all others on which to build the Oratory of S. Bernardino, but it was probably because it stood so close to the convent of S. Francesco al Prato, where the Saint, who himself was a Franciscan, would naturally stay when he paid his visits to Perugia. We hear that he was deeply attached to a certain bell which hung in the campanile of the convent, and which bore the name of Viola and was noted for the peculiar sweetness of its voice. It happened once, when all the bells of the town were ringing, that Viola fell. S. Bernardino was preaching at the minute up in the square of the cathedral, but by a miracle he heard her fall and stopped his sermon for an instant, saying to the people: "My children, Viola has fallen, but she is not harmed!" and he was right. Viola was set up in her place again and rings with a clear strong voice, dear to the heart of the Perugians, even in the present century.[80]

* * * * * * *

Long even before the birth of S. Bernardino a much older order or *Confraternità* held its meetings in the small church at the back of the present oratory. This was the *Confraternità di S. Andrea della Giustizia,* and it was one of the earliest of those remarkable societies—one may almost describe them as religious guilds—which rose up out of that great devotional movement at the end of the middle ages which resulted in the extraordinary processions and displays of the "Flagellants." "The movement," says Doctor Creighton, "passed away; but it has left its dress as a distinctive badge to the confraternities of mercy which are familiar to the traveller in the streets of many cities of Italy."

The Story of Perugia

Morals, as we have seen, were very low in the thirteenth and the fourteenth century; blood flowed freely in party feuds and towns were devastated and corrupted by the strife of church and people. All these things, and the great pestilence which ravaged the country and the cities, were taken, and probably with perfect justice, to be the signs of an offended deity. "It was then," says Bonazzi, "when men had grown familiar with death, that those strange songs arose which the people sang in the moonlight, wrapped in white sheets, whilst they danced the dances of the dead about the streets, clanging the bones together in weird accompaniment to their songs." Doctor Creighton[81] dates this movement to the end of the fourteenth century. He says also that it originated in Provence. Perugia, however, lays strong claim to having herself sown the first seed, and this as early as the middle of the thirteenth century, of the displays of the Flagellants.

In 1265 we read the strange tale of a monk who describes himself as "*Fra Raniero Fasano de Peroscia Comenzatore della Regola dei Battuti di Bologna.*" Raniero tells us that he was accustomed, as a young monk at Perugia, to lead a life of excessive privation and abnegation, and one day, when scourging himself as was his custom, he was joined in a vision by certain saints who accompanied him to the church of S. Fiorenzo, and there they all beat themselves together in front of the high altar. This vision occurred day after day to

Raniero, but at last one of the saints spoke to him and told him that it was the will of heaven that men should purge their sins in this same fashion. Raniero carried his tale to the Bishop, who expounded it in a sermon to the inhabitants of Perugia, and this, according to some historians, was the origin of all the fantastic demonstrations of public repentance which soon spread over Italy, and from which, as years went by, there arose the calmer and more practical institutions of Confraternities in the several cities. One of the earliest of these at Perugia itself was the company of S. Andrea, and it is interesting to read its laws and statutes. Through its own annals we find that it was started in 1374, during the reign of Pope Gregory XI. "for the furtherance of the worship of God and of His Mother the blessed Virgin Mary, and of the glorious martyrs and protectors of the city—Messers Sancto Ercolano, Sancto Laurenzo, Sancto Costanzo, and Sancto Andrea the apostle; and for the honour and estate of the Holy Mother Church and her protectors; and further for the maintenance, the governing, the magnificence, and the peaceful state of the people and the city of Peroscia."

Infinite and careful laws of civil and religious duties follow—laws for the maintenance of peace and the Christian comfort of souls: the day of the saint was to be most strictly kept, fasting if possible, or by him who could not fast, a feast was to be given to a beggar or twenty-five paternosters told, "and all must be at mass that day or pay a fine of twenty soldi." But the great work of the society of S. Andrea was the help and protection of criminals. Its members got permission from the city government to meet those who were going to execution, and to accompany them to the scene of death, comforting them by the way, and sustaining them with prayers and even sweetmeats to the very last. In early times criminals were beheaded far from the city walls; and in Perugia the place of doom was down in the open country on the site of an old Etruscan tomb, the Torre di S. Manno. "Wherefore," writes one historian, "in the fatal passing of these miserable people, the pious *disciplinati* met them on the threshold, comforted them, assisted them, and went with them even unto the gallows." Hence probably the name of "Giustizia" given to this particular square, and not, as is usually said, because justice was carried out on the spot itself.

The *Confraternità* of S. Andrea continued to increase both in power and in size. Other societies of the same charitable sort sprang up all through the city, and after the death of S. Bernardino of Siena a new one was started in his name at Porta Eburnea. But in one of the great fights between the nobles, their buildings were so knocked about and mutilated that the members of the society had to seek out different quarters, and they then joined themselves to the older confraternity of S. Andrea down at S. Francesco and thenceforth "worked together, extending their labour of charity to the inspection of prisons, and to the Christian comfort of prisoners."[82]

S. Francesco al Prato.

To the right of the Oratory of S. Bernardino is the immense, but quite ruined, church and convent of S. Francesco al Prato. S. Francesco, more even than S. Domenico and so many of the churches of Perugia, is only the skeleton of a once beautiful body from which the silken robes, the jewels, even the flesh, have been torn rudely off by men and time. The church was built in 1230, in the form of a Latin cross with a single nave. But from the moment it was built, owing to the crumbling nature of the soil, and the heavy and overweighted style of its architecture, it was threatened with immediate destruction, so that in 1737 it fell in almost completely.

Throughout the history of Perugia we read of great events which centred in S. Francesco, of great men who were buried there, artists who painted, and popes who blessed and prayed. Of all these former splendours, nothing remains beyond a carcase of stone walls. The pictures—the Raphael, the Pinturicchios and the Peruginos, with the exception of Bonfigli's banner in the chapel of the Gonfalone,[83] and one interesting early fresco down in the crypt,—have been removed to the Pinacoteca and to other towns. Fortebraccio's bones have gone to the museum, Fra Egidio's tomb is in the church near the museum, and the roof has fallen in upon a rubbish heap of beams, and bricks, and mortar.

S. Martino.

There are several ways of returning to the Duomo from the Piazza della Giustizia. One of the pleasantest runs through a bit of cultivated land outside the town walls: the Via di San Francesco, and, joining the Via della Conca, passes up under the Arco d'Augusta and back by the Via Vecchia. But another way, which few could find who did not know of it, winds back into the heart of the old town, actually crossing the Etruscan walls in one place, and comes out opposite the Canonica, having passed the little old church of S. Martino.

S. Martino is so old, and so much overshadowed by the big palace opposite, it is sunk so low upon the street, that passing by it hurriedly one scarcely recognises it as a church at all.[84] The high altar has a very beautiful altarpiece by Giannicola Manni—one of the loveliest bits of Umbrian colouring that we remember in Perugia, and there is a rather faulty fresco by some scholar of Perugino on the west wall, redeemed by that subtle and sweet charm peculiar to the work of the master. The little church is guarded by a true friend, who not only honours its pictures, but has even copied them with faithful care, and the whole place is filled with something of the quiet and religious fervour which lingers only after centuries of prayer and incense, and which is lacking in so many of the more frequented churches of the town.

CHAPTER IX

Pietro Perugino and the Cambio[85]

THE name of Perugia is naturally connected with that of Pietro Vannucci *detto il Perugino*, or, as he preferred to sign himself, *Petrus de Castro Plebis*, who stamped the peculiar personality of his painting upon a whole school of Renaissance Italian art. Vannucci was by no means the first artist of the Umbrian school, but he was the man who brought it into general notice, and it was in the city of Perugia that he lived and worked, and had his school of painting.

The best of Perugino's work, however, with the exception of his frescoes in the Cambio, is not to be found in his native town. The indefatigable Napoleon had a profound admiration for Pietro's altar-pieces. He sought them out, he insisted on getting every inch of them, down to their smallest predellas, and the splendid pictures of S. Pietro, S. Lorenzo, and S. Agostino went over the Alps to swell his galleries in the Tuileries. The frescoes of the Cambio could not go, and they at least remain exactly as the master painted them. To understand the man Pietro as well as the artist, we must study in the Cambio, for there his portrait hangs face to face with a whole set of his frescoes, and the contrast of the painter's face and the faces he invariably gave to his saints is almost as strange as that between the Umbrian saints and the history of the times in which they lived and worked.

To understand the painters of Perugia one must understand the period in which they were produced. One wonders whether Vasari reckoned at all with this when he wrote his life of Perugino. The Florentine was not particularly just to Umbrian painters in general, and of Pietro Vannucci he paints a very unsympathetic portrait. He accuses him of two great faults: avarice and irreligion, and these have become so inevitably connected with Pietro's name that it is not easy to dispute them. Yet, if not absolutely false, the facts have been grossly exaggerated. Concerning the first—avarice—Vasari maintains that Pietro painted exclusively for the sake of gain, and never for that of art or faith. This accusation has been disproved by later writers in so far as the early life of Perugino is concerned. We hear, for instance, that he painted several banners for his native city in the time of plague and war, that he asked no money for them, and when the time of need was past he took them back and kept them in his studio. Also, merely as an amusing anecdote, Vasari himself tells us that Pietro could open his purse for the woman he loved, and dress her in the fairest and the costliest clothes, setting the pins and folds himself upon her headgear. In the latter part of his life, which was not without some shadow, he did paint for money, allowing soulless pictures to pass from his studio to the altars of believing monks and ladies;

but his best work belongs to his earliest period, and there is no reason to believe that it was uninspired save by the inspiration of gold.

Concerning the second accusation—lack of faith—we have dealt with it at the end of Pietro's life, and we can only add here that the man must have been of super-human gentleness who could live through the scenes that Vannucci lived through, and maintain the faith of childhood.

The portrait in the Cambio is a stumbling block. The expression is heavy and unspiritual. This fact jars, and we resent it. (See frontispiece.)

But whatever Pietro's appearance, whatever his personal character may have been, he did two things: he left behind him an enduring mark in the history of art, and he gave the soul to that considerable school of painting from which young Raphael went forth into the wondering world, together with a host of other painters whose tendency was entirely in the direction of the spiritual and purifying elements in human life.

* * * * * * *

Away to the southwest of Perugia, above the lakes of Trasimene and Chiusi, with a wide view southwards towards

Rome, and northwards to Cortona, is the little Umbrian hill-town of Città della Pieve. It is so deeply buried in its oak woods that one can barely see it from the hills and plains around it. The town is very old and very sleepy, built of red bricks with hardly any stones, and scarcely any buildings of importance. The streets seem fallen dead asleep. "Why do you come here? The place is dead. Nothing ever happens in our city," said the melancholy daughter of the landlord, and the girl, by her unconscious words, explained the very reason of our visit.

Nothing ever happens in Città della Pieve. The town has fallen on sleep in its delightful landscape—on sleep as silent and profound as that of all the fossil shells in the banks along the roads which lead to it. But the place is strangely and marvellously beautiful; it holds the very essence of that intense religious charm peculiar to the landscapes of Umbria, and to the painters who have painted them; without exaggeration, we may say that the city looks to-day just exactly as it looked over four hundred years ago, at the time when, to the lovers of art, its history began and ended. [86]

Pietro Vannucci de Castro Plebis *detto il Perugino*, was born at Città della Pieve in the year 1446. His parents were very poor, but they were of a good family and position. There were many children, and life was a struggle for bread

The Story of Perugia

in the small boy's home. When he was about eight, his father, Christoforo Vannucci, decided to educate him as a painter, and so he brought him to the city of Perugia, and there, as Vasari says, "this child, who had been reared in penury and want, was given as a shop drudge to a painter who was not particularly distinguished in his calling, but who held the art in great veneration, and highly honoured the men who excelled therein." The painter was probably Bonfigli, one of the most delightful artists of the Umbrian school, but Pietro must have gathered instruction from other sources too, from Fiorenzo di Lorenzo and Piero della Francesca, who we know were painting at that time. Maybe the boy met them at their work in churches, maybe he even travelled with them as a sort of journeyman. But it was probably Bonfigli who early inspired him with an ambitious desire to spread his wings in higher spheres of art than the little Umbrian town afforded him, and who gave him the worldly-wise advice retailed to us at some length by Vasari: Perugino must go to Florence,

"for the air of that city generates a desire for glory and honour, and gives a natural quickness to the perceptions of men. Yet it is true that when a man has acquired sufficient for his purposes in Florence, if he wishes to effect more than merely to live from day to day, as do the beasts that perish, and desires to become rich, he must depart from its boundaries and seek another market for the excellence of his works and for the reputation conferred on artists by that city. For the city of Florence treats her painters as Time treats her works, which, having perfected, he destroys, and by little and little gradually consumes."

Pietro listened to these naïve counsels; he drank them in and he followed them out to the letter. When quite a young man he started across the hills to Florence. He probably travelled as a journeyman, begging or earning his bread along the way. He reached Florence, entered the studio of Andrea Verrocchio, buried himself in a passionate study of his art, and, barely ten years after the date when, as an almost unknown artist, he had entered Florence with the secret of his genius in his soul, he left it again to go to Rome and paint a portion of the Sistine Chapel at the command of the reigning pope. Pietro studied in good schools and in excellently good society. In Florence he probably met with men like Botticelli, Credi, and certainly Leonardo da Vinci. Raphael's father, Giovanni Santi, is said to have written the following lines about the two young painters:

"Due giovan par d'etate e par d'amore
Lionardo da Vinci, e 'l Perusino
Pier della Pieve, ch'è un divin pittore."

Divine in truth were the two young men, for they were to be the fathers of the Lombard and the Umbrian schools of painting.

The Story of Perugia

Perugino's earliest commissions for pictures were received in Florence, but nearly all the work of that period is lost. We cannot exaggerate the loss, but it is useless now to dwell on it and to describe the vanished frescoes of the Gesuati convent. Pietro was called to Rome about the year 1483. There he painted several pictures on the walls of the Sistine chapel. Only two of them remain, and the figures of Michelangelo's Last Judgment have long obliterated the sweet-faced Umbrian saints and landscapes which used to cover the east wall.[87] Having spent a little time in Rome, Perugino returned to his native land, and the best of his paintings belong to that period—namely to the years 1490-1502.

This is no place in which to describe the works of Perugino's prime. The world knows them and the capitals of Europe possess them, but from the city of Perugia, for which some of the very best were painted, they have been taken away by "*quel stupendo ladro*—Napoleone Bonaparte."[88] Perugino's fame spread like wildfire over the cities of Italy. "This *maestro Pietro*," says a very old chronicler, "was distinguished (*singolare*) in his art throughout the universal world." So intense was his fame and popularity, and his work in such demand, that it was impossible for him, for one single man, to supply all the work which men demanded of him. We should not therefore feel surprised at the number of second-rate pictures, planned by the master and carried out by his scholars, which have come down to us bearing his name.

PERUGINO: MADONNA AND PATRON SAINTS OF PERUGIA PAINTED FOR THE MAGISTRATES' CHAPEL AT PERUGIA, NOW IN THE VATICAN AT ROME

From the period of his prime, Perugino perhaps went wrong—that is to say, he realised his own charms, specified, docketted them, stereotyped the smile of his saints and set his scholars working, so to speak, on the reproduction of the labels he himself had painted. His personality extended itself into a school, where, at times, it became mere caricature. Other stars had risen on the horizon, great and shining; some of them straight from the master's own workshop, some from other cities. There is a pitiful story told of the jealousy of the old Umbrian master for the growing fame of Michelangelo. It ended in a lawsuit from which Pietro withdrew his claims; but the tale may be unfounded, and we know that Vannucci praised the David when called to pass a judgment on it, we also know that he named one of his own children after the Tuscan sculptor.

But if we can recognise the later weakness of Perugino, the men who lived in his days and who openly declared him to be the master of masters never apparently recognised it. They seem to have worshipped his decadence as they had worshipped his dawn. They paid large sums for the feeble saints which rose like ghosts beneath his brush. They desired no better man to save them in the time of plague and bloodshed by the creation of a S. Sebastian which they might carry in procession, or a Madonna that they might kneel to. And truly to the end an ineffable sweetness, a religious amiability, is the undercurrent of the master's painting.

Pietro Vannucci died of the plague in the year 1523 at Fontignano, a small village near Perugia, where he had been called to paint a S. Sebastian in the time of pestilence. He was hurried into some desolate grave under an oak by the wayside, and he died, as they say, without faith of immortality, denying to the last that Saviour, whose face and figure, whose Mother and surroundings, he, of all men on earth, had striven through life to idealize.

So writes Vasari, but on this accusation we would pause. There may have been some sickness in Pietro's soul, we feel and see it in his work and portrait; but he had lived in terrible times and seen much evil and striven to paint much good. The fact that he was buried in unconsecrated ground proves literally nothing, for an old chronicler, describing the wretchedness of the times, combined with the terrors of the plague, tells us, "that such was the state of affairs, that the dead were paid as little attention to in those times as in our day we might give to goats or sheep; and that especially in the country where no one attended to anything, all died, almost without exception, not like men but almost like beasts; and as the consecrated ground did not suffice for burial they put the bodies into ditches, covering them up with a very little earth." Furthermore, "it was prohibited to visit the sick, and to attend the funerals of the dead." This being the case, how was it possible to find the corpse of one old man in order to lay it in consecrated ground? Pietro's sons tried hard to find it. We read of them: of Giambatisto, Francesco and Michaelangelo, searching diligently but in vain for their father's bones, that they might lay them in the Church of S. Agostino.[89]

Mariotti the chronicler of Perugino, whose loving and infinitely careful search has soothed, if it could not obliterate Vasari's spiteful words, ends his notes on Perugino with the following quotation from a Latin poet:—

"Se pictus moreris, non moriturus obis."

* * * * * * *

It was just at the end of the period of Pietro's prime, namely, about the years 1499 to 1507, that he was commissioned to paint the walls of the Cambio. It is interesting to remember that at this time Perugino was in correspondence with the monks of Orvieto, who wished him to paint the frescoes in their Duomo. He had long dallied with his answer, he had certain other large works on hand, but when his fellow-citizens sent in their request that he should undertake this very considerable work for them he did not hesitate; he threw over his previous engagement, which, as we know, was magnificently taken up by Signorelli, and he at once set to work upon the walls of the Cambio.

Perugino was perhaps out of his element in this new undertaking. He had no choice of subjects, for they had been selected for him by the members of the Guild, who throughout show a most naïve interest and concern in the decoration of their rooms. These men were determined to secure the very best work they could; their seats, their panels, their doors were of the finest wood, worked by the most skilful carpenters and artists of the day. They were not wise in literature themselves, so they applied to the best scholar of their city, Francesco Matarazzo, for instructions, and it was he who most probably arranged the curious mixture of classic subjects and inscriptions which Perugino, with a certain child-like and ingenuous persistence, painted as he had painted all the familiar subjects of the Bible. For the ceiling of the audience chamber, which deals entirely with mythological figures, he may have consulted certain old illustrated missals in the Perugian archives; one of these, a Cicero (unhappily stolen from the library some years ago), very probably suggested some of the figures and beasts of the Zodiac which decorate the ceiling.

The impression made upon one by the painting in the Cambio is very calm and pleasing. The whole is a harmony—a harmony of subjects sacred and profane such as the classic-loving minds of scholars in the days of the Renaissance delighted to create, and give to one of their purely religious artists to carry out successfully. The left wall is covered by two frescoes—two lines of figures—eight Romans and four

Greeks. Behind these figures stretches the fair, calm, Umbrian landscape, dear to the heart of the Umbrian painter. In the sky above them are four female figures, Prudence and Justice, Fortitude and Temperance, and below them small angels hold the long inscription which is written over every group. Very soft and tender is Perugino's conception of Roman Emperors and Greek philosophers. They have the hands of women, their faces are sweet like the faces of saints. They look a little sad, and very gentle as they bend towards each other—not one of these men could have proved a ruler of nations. What did Perugino mean when he painted in the second group this visionary host of warriors? Surely he dreamed of some fair Umbrian girls that he had met in May along the lanes, but not of heroes. These youths, with their wonderful headgear and their long, limp bodies would have fallen as field flowers fall before the scythe or even a summer shower. That they are fair no one denies, and in the face of Cincinnatus there is a mysterious sweetness which disarms our criticism; but they are merely spiritual or imaginative portraits of the men whose names are carefully inscribed beneath them. The opposite wall is covered by a group of Prophets and of Sibyls—a combination which was not uncommon in later Christian art. To the left Isaiah, Moses, Daniel, David and Jeremiah, and opposite them the Persian, Cumaean, Lybian, Tyburtine and Delphic sibyls. Perugino crowned this most singular mixture of pagan and of Hebrew figures with a portrait of God the Father in glory. Many of the faces in this group are very beautiful, notably that of Daniel, which is said to be a portrait of young Raphael, and is a truly exquisite thing. Jeremiah is represented as a young and very melancholy man, and his face is said to be a portrait of Pinturicchio, but if this fact is true the likeness is much idealized.

In the two frescoes at the end of the room, namely, the Nativity and the Transfiguration, Pietro was in his old and dearer element. The former of these is a beautiful bit of his best religious work, but it has been terribly damaged by smoke, as the lamp of the Cambio used to hang beneath it.

There is some dispute as to whether Pietro worked alone at these frescoes. It appears almost certain that he did do so, with the exception, perhaps, of one of his scholars, l'Ingegno, who is said to have painted the face of Christ in the Transfiguration.[90] The ceiling, where the planets are painted in medallions, is perhaps the work of his school, although the drawings were entirely supplied by Perugino. Pinturicchio is said to have helped in the painting, and Raphael doubtless watched it with delight, and from it drew suggestions which he carried later to the Vatican. Delightful animals, dragons, and different birds pull the chariots of the various planets. The arabesques are infinitely varied, and form a study in themselves. Small boys and cherubs ride astride of dragons or of goats, and strange fantastic animals turn and twist themselves through flower stalks and bowls of fruits and flowers. Squirrels, peacocks, snakes, and many other known and unknown creatures, cover the arches like enamelled gems.

It is curious to pass from Perugino's frescoes in the audience chamber of the Cambio to those of his pupil Giannicola Manni in the chapel of the same guild. Manni's work is very rare, and indeed it is barely seen outside Perugia. [91] He was a scholar of Perugino, and in his earlier years he followed in the steps of his master, but in later life he went to Florence and there acquired a love for the style of Andrea del Sarto. The influence of the two distinct schools of painting is strongly marked in the chapel of the Cambio, the ceiling of which was painted early in Manni's life, the walls after his return from Florence. Manni is a genial and attractive painter. He paints exactly as he pleases, regardless of religion or of history, and in his series of scenes from the life of S. John he gives us a set of luxurious human beings leading a very human cinque-cento life. The colour is bright, the figures portraits of the time. The ladies are very decolletées, fat, and dressed in comfortable gowns of the most beautiful stuffs and the simplest cut. One lady in the Nativity is particularly attractive. She wears a gorgeous gown of red; her fluffy yellow hair is neatly gathered in a net, embossed with bobs of the purest gold. S. Elizabeth, too, may be envied the splendour of her bed, and the looping of its heavy damask curtains. There is a sense of luxury, a sort of wanton abundance which is almost Venetian, throughout Manni's frescoes of the life of S. John. In the banquet scene, a dog and cat are preparing for a playful battle in the foreground of the picture. Had the Umbrian painter seen some canvasses of Veronese? Certainly he had wandered far afield from the early teaching which shows so clear upon the ceiling. He died in 1544, and most of his work, which we know to have consisted chiefly of banners, is lost to us, lost too, the painting of the city clock which Mariotti records for us with such minute precision. [92]

On leaving the Cambio it would be well to look in at the Magistrate's audience chamber which opens on to the Corso two doors further on. It is a magnificent piece of Renaissance woodwork where every inch is exquisitely carved and finished. Perugia is rich in rare and lovely carvings, but nowhere more than in this single hall.

CHAPTER X

The Pinacoteca[93]

" ...Parmi de pareilles mœurs, les âmes se maintiennent vivantes, et le sol est tout labouré pour faire germer les arts.

Mais quel contraste entre ces arts et ces mœurs!"

H. Taine, "Pérouse et Assise," *Voyage en Italie.*

THERE is perhaps no gallery in Europe as single-minded—as devoted to one set of men—as the gallery at Perugia. In passing through its separate rooms one feels none of that painful sense of clash and strain produced by a mixture of different schools, which haunts one in so many collections of statues or of pictures; and the most tired and indifferent traveller will feel something soothed and softened in his brain before he turns his back upon the quiet sacred pictures of the Umbrian masters.

In no land perhaps, and in no school of art, was the feeling of the painters more purely and more absolutely *religious* than in the land of Umbria. The saints were painted for places where saints were worshipped; the Christs have the love of the Father in their faces; the Marys are Mothers of pity and of grace; the bishops have renounced the ways of earth—their faces are calm and grey beneath their mitres. And the Umbrian angels are crowned with roses, but they are the roses of Paradise, and not the flowers of earth and of her banquets. Think of the galleries of Venice, of Bonifazio's Dives, and the glorious women of Titian; think of the Roman collections, of Bologna and Guercino; nay, even think of the later art of Florence, and then come back to these calm Umbrian masters. The gap is wide; the one is full of the passion and splendour of earth, the other of the sentiment of heaven.

In M. Rio's chapters on the Umbrian school (*l'Art Chrétien*, vol. ii.), he dwells at length on the purely spiritual tendency of the Umbrian school, and to enforce this he points out two of its most remarkable characteristics; firstly he remarks that the Umbrian painters rarely painted portraits, and secondly, he gives an account of one of their chief products, namely, the painting of the *gonfalone* or banner.

We have seen in the history how the inhabitants of Perugia, driven to desperation by their own wickedness, would take fits of the most passionate religious revolt, and, casting aside the vanities of the flesh, half kill themselves with cords and stripes and lamentations. This excess of repentance took different forms. Sometimes, as we know, it resulted in an appeal to the saints through wild, mad litanies; at others in an appeal to Christ's mercy through art; and it was at such times that the Umbrian school, beginning with Bonfigli and ending in works like Raphael's Sistine Madonna and

Baroccio's much later designs, painted the *gonfalone*, a style of picture which is very typical of Umbria, and which should be looked at with a knowledge of the events from which it first originated. These banners were carried about the city, the priests walking in front, the populace behind, a wail and shriek of lamentation falling on the air as the procession passed. Sometimes, as in the banner of Bonfigli at S. Fiorenzo, a poem of supplication to God would be painted, upheld by angels, on the banner itself, with passionate words of prayer upon it. It is difficult to render into English the palpitating style of the original verses, but we quote some passages to illustrate the sentiment which inspired the painting of the *gonfalone* of S. Fiorenzo (the date of the banner is about 1476):

"Oh, most obstinate and wicked people—cruel, proud, and full of all iniquity, who hast placed thy faith and thy desires on things which are full of a mortal misery, I, the angel of Heaven, am sent unto you from God to tell you that he will put an end to all your wounds and weeping, your ruin and your curse, through the mediation of Mary.... Turn, turn your eyes, most miserable mortals, to the great examples of the past and present, to the utter miseries and heavy evils which Heaven sends to you because of all your sins: your homicide and your adultery, your avarice and luxury.... O, miserable beings, the justice of heaven works not in a hurry, but it punishes always, even as men deserve.... Nineveh was a city florid and magnificent, and Babylon was likewise, but now they are as nothing; and Sodom and Gomorrah, behold them now—a morass of sulphur and of fetid waters.... Oh, therefore be grateful, and acknowledge the benefits and graces of Our Saviour, and let your souls burn hotly with the fire of faith and charity, of hope and faithful love.... But, and if you should again grow slothful and unwilling to renounce your errors, I foretell a second judgment upon you, and I reckon that it will prove more terrible, more cruel than the first...."

The *gonfalone* on which this menacing appeal of the angel of God is painted is by Bonfigli, and was made at the time of a terrible pestilence which raged through Perugia at the end of the fifteenth century.

In Umbria therefore, more than in most countries, the history of her art should be studied side by side with the history of the times in which it was produced, for the one was, as it were, the spiritual escape or reaction from the other. The art of Umbria was perhaps only another form of that spirit which produced the teaching of S. Francis. The first pictures of Perugia are full of man's best prayers, the earliest of them bear his stripes, in very few can we detect his wantonness or humour; and when we say that the later ones are imbued with man's weakness, or at least his sentimentality, we make a most apparent platitude. It is sufficient in this place to note that whatever the final faults of the school, it originated in a purpose that was pure—the purpose of men who strove to represent the very opposite of all that fury, blood, and passion peculiar to the time and place in which they lived and painted.

To most people, therefore, who once have grasped these facts, there will be something sad, nay, even offensive, in the Pinacoteca at Perugia. Why, and for whom, were these purely religious paintings torn from their niches in the quiet churches, and hung up, side by side, in a glare of light on the walls of a gallery? How pale, and how sad they look, after all, the saints and the Marys, the angels and the holy Child, here on the bare grey walls. The thing has been said a hundred times before, but a friend at Perugia said it to us in a way we have never forgotten. He was a priest, and he loved his church. We were discussing together the present system of local picture galleries. His eyes grew dark. "Yes," he said, "it is as though they would tear a child from the breasts of its mother. The mother withers and dies, and the child dies too, without her care in the wilderness where they laid it."

It is the student of art who profits by the present arrangement, for the pictures at Perugia are not difficult to find. With the exception of the Duomo and S. Pietro, most of the churches have been ransacked, and their canvasses and panels neatly stored in perfect order of dates and names on the walls of the Pinacoteca, and it is an easy matter, even in a quiet morning's stroll, to follow here the rise and fall of Umbrian art. In the limited space before us it will not be possible to give anything but a skeleton sketch of the school of Perugino. Larger works contain abundant store of facts about this particular centre of Italian art; but if one only shuts one's eyes and dreams of it, the three great names start up before one: Pietro Vannucci, Raphael, and Pinturicchio. Close upon these follow other names; some, and these perhaps the fairest and most charming, rise like the dawn behind them: Ottaviano Nelli, Bonfigli, and Fiorenzo di Lorenzo. The pupils follow after Manni, Lo Spagna, Eusebio di S. Giorgio, l'Ingegno, Sinibaldo Ibi, Tiberio d'Assisi and a host of others, who die at last, feeble, but not utterly degraded, in the works of the two Alfanis.

An easy-going historian of Perugia summed up the earliest stages of her art in the following sentence: "I have not been able to discover that Perugia had any painters before the time of Bonfigli, but even if she had them, they will not have been worthy of mention." The assertion was sweeping, and later writers have taken pains to contradict it, but for those who have only time for a superficial and general study of Perugian pictures it yet holds a good deal of truth. No great original work (with the exception of the missal workers, in which style of art Perugia is very rich) is left to us from the hand of a Perugian artist before the time of Bonfigli, and the early history of her art may be said to have been a great deal that of outside influences, for from very early times the best and greatest masters appear, like foreign tribes before them, to have climbed the hill and left some subtle marks upon her churches and her palaces.[94]

As the School of Siena died, that of Umbria awoke to life. Close upon the heels of Taddeo Bartoli, those men followed who were born to precede the School of Perugino. Before them there were around Perugia only phantoms: stiff saints on panels and on parchment, without dates, ghosts of unattained, though dimly felt, ideals—a scattered flock of "primitives," left here and there on chapel walls or psalters. Then gradually, all through Umbria and her border lands, in a steady circle of glory, like the stars on a summer night, the lights arose and burned. At Gubbio, Camerino, Foligno, Gualdo, Fabriano, and Urbino we trace their steady progress through the work of men like Nelli, Piero della Francesca, Gentile da Fabriano, Niccolò Alunno, and many others. And as these stars arose great comets travelled through them—Giotto, Fra Angelico, Benozzo Gozzoli, Filippo Lippi, and others, till the whole sky was full. Then from the centre, straight from the hill of Città della Pieve—there rose Pietro Perugino, and to his school came one with the halo of pure art upon his forehead,—Raphael Sanzio of Urbino.

The Story of Perugia

The following notes on the Pinacoteca and its pictures may be of use to anyone who requires a few more details than a guide-book can supply. They pretend to be nothing like a serious criticism, for the history of art is long and the books about it full; in most of them the art of Umbria is freely treated. We have gleaned our notes about the painters of Perugia from such sources as Vasari (who, however, is often prejudiced), Crowe and Cavalcaselle, and several local works. Any personal gossip has been drawn from the ever delightful works of Mariotti, whose words, if they be now and then a little antiquated, are as trustworthy as those of a faithful student's only can be. We have dealt chiefly with the work of the Umbrian painters, and indeed, with the exception of Fra Angelico's panels and those of some of the Sienese masters, there is little else to study in this small and charming gallery.

The Umbrian School followed close upon that of Siena, and the Gallery of Perugia has some fine bits of Sienese work, notably some panels by Taddeo Bartoli (1363-1422) in Sala IV. This room has some other good panels of early masters—of masters who probably influenced the Perugians, but whose names are lost to us.[95]

Room I.

Sala dei Cimelii.

The first room in the gallery is devoted to the very earliest art of Siena and Umbria, and is one of those rather painful collections of pictures which we find in every local Italian gallery—a room of the primitive painters—which are, as the narrow path of art, beset with many thorns, where only those who passionately love the goal need try to push the briars back and tread the damp and pebbles. But we never forget, though we may even dislike, the pitiful pale figures of the crucified Christ, and the staring wooden saints in triptychs, for in them is shown the strain of technical ignorance, but of ignorance which strives with passionate pain to get beyond itself and soar towards the expression of some deep emotion. This strain and impotent desire is amply shown in the monstrous figure of our Saviour by Magaritone d'Arezzo (see No. 26), which used to hang inside the chapel of S. Bernardino. Such as it is that figure had the seed of art in it, and of an art which, perhaps, had a greater power of appeal to the souls of men and women in pain than all the finished figures of the later painters. No. 28 is an interesting picture, inasmuch as the Bishop whom it represents holds tight to his breast a picture of the old town of Perugia. No. 16 is one of the earliest paintings known in Perugia. It is terribly damaged, and it is difficult to trace the story of the Saint in the battered little panels. These same panels were the first coffin of Beato Egidio. Sometime after his death a splendid tomb was made for the Saint, which can still be seen in the church of the University, and when the humbler coffin was pulled to pieces, some unknown local painter took the strange fancy to paint on it the history of the man whose bones it had first covered, together with an accurate portrait of his new and lovelier tomb. There are many other pictures in this room, among them (No. 11) an exquisite fragment of some old predella with two small angels on it; and one or two remains of early Sienese work.

Bonfigli.

The room which follows that devoted to the early schools, namely, the Cappella del Bonfigli, is to a student of history one of the most interesting points in the whole gallery, for here, through the frescoes of a most childlike and delightful painter, we live again the life of old Perugia; and here too we stand, face to face, with the authentic work of a man whose celebrity formerly centred round the fact that he was the first master of Perugino, but who, as the years go by, will, doubtless, ever more and more stand on his own feet, and shine because of some strange, subtle and ever-living charm, that of the individual, which clings to all his work.

The Pinacoteca has many of Bonfigli's works, and no one who once has realised the fashion in which this early Umbrian master crowned his women and his angels will ever be able to forget it. How thin and exquisite the veils upon the pale, calm heads of his Madonnas; how fair and neat the wreaths of roses on the yellow hair of his young angels! Bonfigli was, indeed, a pleasant painter, and it is strange to think that his home relations were of a tempestuous order: "Certainly he had a wife," says Mariotti, "and he had her of such a sort that she caused him nothing but anxiety; moreover, he was in constant strife with her." But Bonfigli was not always calm in his painting. He could be humorous, he could have a touch of Carpaccio in him, as will be seen in his frescoes for the Magistrates' Chapel; but he could also be passionate and dramatic. To understand him fully one must study him in his *gonfaloni*, or banners. Perugia has five of these—one of S. Bernardino, now in the Pinacoteca, another in the sacristy of S. Francesco al Prato; another in S. Fiorenzo; the fourth in S. Maria Nuova; and the fifth in S. Lorenzo.[96] All have suffered from exposure and from restoration, but they are unique and individual forms of art. The Christ in them is inexorable and revengeful, Death strives with man, saints and the Madonna try to interfere, and sad and supplicating groups of citizens kneel by their city walls and pray for grace.

Nothing is definitely known about the early life of Bonfigli. There seems to be no record of his birth. He was probably born about 1420, and died about 1496. The first authentic mention of his work is in 1454, when he undertook a commission from the priors and their chaplain to paint the walls of the Magistrates' Chapel in the Palazzo Pubblico. That Bonfigli was well known and very highly appreciated in his native city before that date is evident. Mariotti tells us that he was called in by the citizens as one of the judges to pronounce judgment on Agostino Duccio's façade at S. Bernardino. It is probable that he even had a school of painting—that school to which Vasari somewhat slightingly alludes in his life of Perugino.

Sala II.

Cappella di Bonfigli

(*formerly the chapel of the Magistrates' Guild*).

Mariotti gives a long and humorous account of the contract between Bonfigli and the magistrates about the painting of their chapel. Undertaken in 1454 the work was still unfinished at the time of the painter's death in 1496, and Mariotti is unable to discover any sufficient reason for such undignified delay. "I do not easily think ill of anyone," he writes, "and least of all of painters, but certainly in those years we have no record even of any influenza raging in the city of Perugia." When the chapel was half painted, Fra Filippo Lippi was called in to judge about its excellence. He found the pictures good, and voted a sum of four hundred florins in payment to Bonfigli, who once more, and with infinite slowness, went to work upon them. Only the skeleton of this work remains. At the end of the last century, Mariotti thus bewails it: "But the pictures of Bonfigli—oh, my God—how have they been ravaged by the little care bestowed upon them, how devastated by the course of time." Half ruined by a form of restoration which perhaps is worse than none, ill-lighted, and without their former colour, the frescoes yet remain a delightful and engaging study. They represent the lives of the two bishops, St Louis of Toulouse, and S. Ercolano, patron saints of Perugia. To the right as you enter, and in a dark corner by the window is the Consecration of S. Louis; next to it the miracle of the fish performed by that Saint. This picture is admirably preserved. The landscape is one of those half real and half fantastic follies of a wise man which always charm one. Bonfigli knew that he must paint a town by the seashore; he painted the sea, but he put his own fair Umbrian city straight down upon its shores. There stands the church of S. Domenico with its celebrated windows, and up behind it, tier on tier, there rise the towers and the brown roofs of the city that we read about, the Perugia of the middle ages, against a dark blue sky. The miracle is a naïve one. A merchant lost his bag of gold during a storm at sea. He prayed to S. Louis to reveal to him what had become of it. S. Louis appeared in heaven and showed that a certain large fish had swallowed the purse. The fish was caught, cut open, and inside it was the merchant's bag of gold. We see the fisherman toiling up from his boat with the heavy fish upon his shoulders, and then we see the monks cutting open the fish, and the merchant and his wife receiving their money.

So realistically is the scene presented, that we even see the blood of the fish upon the bag.

The next picture has been terribly damaged, and it is difficult to understand the subject; but a learned gentleman of Perugia, to whom we are indebted for various most ingenious suggestions, fancies that it is simply the representation of some miracle of healing performed by the Saint in Rome; certainly Bonfigli has striven to combine in his background a marvellous mixture of Roman and Etruscan architecture, the arch of Constantine mingling with Porta Susanna and the Colosseum!

The following fresco is perhaps the most delightful of the series. It represents the burial of the Bishop of Toulouse. Now S. Louis is known to have died in his father's castle of Brignolles in Provence at the early age of twenty-four, but all this was of very secondary importance to the ingenuous Bonfigli. It was sufficient for him to know that a dead Bishop had to be painted. He selected the architecture that he loved best—his own Perugian church of S. Pietro—he sliced it in half so that all might look inside it, and on a bier in the centre of the aisle he laid the corpse of a quite middle-aged Bishop. With infinite care and faithful precision he copied the lines of his church. The true basilica is here, not touched at all by decoration. There was no choir in those days; a dark blue sky looks in at the windows, the roof is bare with all its rafters showing. But the central figure is out of all proportion. The feet and the head of S. Louis of Toulouse almost touch the columns in the aisle. His robe, with the golden fleur de lis, is neatly folded round him, his mitre glistens in the light; his face is grey and calm, and full of dignity and of repose. Bonfigli had a sense of humour and could not refrain from a touch of caricature. It is impossible to look at the group of monks and prelates round S. Louis, and not to feel at once convinced of this. A fat and pompous Bishop, in golden cope and mitre, is saying the mass for the dead. His large red book is supported by the head of a kneeling friar, and the very thumbs of this friar express his disgust and discomfort. To the left of the Bishop a group of roaring monks take up his words and repeat them in dolorous voices. Only to look at their faces one knows that their litany is absolutely out of tune. At the head of the Saint another priest is reading in a book, his acolytes swing incense, one holds the Bishop's staff. The rest of the church is filled with quiet groups of men and women; and the most charming figure of the whole is that of a young man in a red gown with a shock of yellow curls, who kneels, lost in prayer, at the knees of the dead Saint, his back turned to us.

The next picture represents the siege of Perugia by Totila. No doubt this siege—that most memorable event in the annals of Perugia—was rather a chaos to the mind of Bonfigli as it is to many people nowadays; but the following history, taken from old chronicles, will explain the whole fantastic pageant. It will be remembered that Totila besieged Perugia in 549, and that the little town held out valiantly, but finally fell into the power of the Goths. During a terrible siege the Bishop of Perugia, S. Ercolano, attempted certain childlike and vain subterfuges of war, which unhappily ended in failure and in his own martyrdom. Ciatti, in his somewhat weariful and dreamy style, records the events of the siege as follows:—

FIRST TRANSLATION OF THE BODY OF S. ERCOLA-
NO (FRESCO IN THE PINACOTECA OF PERUGIA)

"It is said that the saintly Bishop S. Ercolano, receiving much heavenly aid and holy counsels, and perhaps led by God, turned his soul to an act of human prudence. It happened that the city was reduced to extreme misery by reason of the scarcity of victuals, so that the citizens decided to surrender or to die fighting. S. Ercolano counselled them to bring him any grain which should still be found in the granaries, and they, knowing his great sanctity, obeyed and brought to him, after most diligent search, one small measure of corn. Then the Saint took the sole surviving lamb" (Bonfigli in his frescoes has painted an ox) "and, to the wonder and silent indignation of the people, he gave it to eat of the grain; it ate abundantly and the Bishop then threw the lamb with great force down from the ramparts, when, by reason of its great fulness and the height of its fall, the innocent beast was at once killed. When the captains of the enemy beheld this thing they were angry, saying: 'These Perugians have so much grain that they can give it to their beasts to eat, and so much meat that they cast it carelessly away, how can we, therefore, hope to subdue them by famine?' But it chanced that a young acolyte spoke from off the ramparts to some Goths and unwittingly revealed to them the distress and the mortality reigning in the city by reason of the want of food; and the stratagem of S. Ercolano becoming known in the camp, the infuriated Goths, hot with anger, returned to the attack and with impetuous fury assailed the deserted walls.

Greeks and Perugians rushed to arms, but what could they, poor starvelings, do against the Gothic host?"

Thus fell Perugia. Our learned author goes on to describe how S. Ercolano was conducted to the ramparts and after his skin had been torn off in strips from the neck downwards, he was beheaded and his body thrown into the ditch. Some faithful adherents gave it secret burial, and finding the body of the foolish young acolyte near by, laid it in the same grave. Later, Uliphus, governor of the city, allowed the Perugians to give their beloved pastor proper burial. To the astonishment of all beholders the Saint's head was found joined to his body, which seemed like that of a man asleep. This miracle converted many of the Arian Goths to the Roman faith, and "with rejoicings and hymns of praise the body of S. Ercolano was borne through the streets to the church of S. Lorenzo."

The next picture gives the burial of S. Ercolano. It is only a fragment, and we can hardly piece the scattered groups together. There is a lovely little group of ladies to the left—a set of typical Bonfigli women with exquisite white headgear. The curving front of the Palazzo Pubblico upon the Corso is painted with accurate care, the loggia of Fortebraccio too, is clearly seen and understood. But the picture is only a shadow; the part we most wish to see, namely, the north front of the Palazzo, is wholly obliterated, and the restoration spoils it terribly.

In the next fresco the body of S. Ercolano is being carried from S. Pietro to S. Lorenzo, and Bonfigli has seized this excellent opportunity to paint a fresh portrait of his native city. In the foreground the basilica of S. Pietro with a colonnaded front and unfinished campanile is faithfully depicted, and behind the funeral procession (which by the way is moving in quite the wrong direction) the town towers up into the sky like a pack of yellow cards, broken only by its towers and campaniles.[97]

Rooms VI. and VII.

Sala di Bonfigli and Sala di Bernardino di Mariotto.

Before leaving the subject of Bonfigli it will be well to look at some other pieces of his work which are painted in quite a different manner. Amongst these is a Madonna and Child (No. 13). It is a beautiful specimen of the master's purely pietistic painting.[98] Tradition says that Fra Filippo Lippi ordered this picture. It has suffered terribly, for in old days it was hung in the lavatory of S. Domenico, and as the friars washed their hands they must have splashed the water up against the panels. No. 10, the Adoration of the Magi, is also by Bonfigli. The picture as a whole is perhaps more interesting than beautiful, inasmuch as it is one of the very few religious pictures of the Umbrian School where the portraits of living people have been introduced. Orsini tells us that the Madonna is a portrait of Bonfigli's sister, the Child a picture of his nephew, and the youngest of the three kings that of his brother. The loveliest point in the picture is the group of angels up in the roof. Bonfigli must, we think, have seen the swallows flitting at springtime in and out of some low breezy barn, and put their movements into angels' forms. The predella, too, is a perfect gem in itself, notably the panel of the Baptism where the wilderness is painted dark and brown, but the sunrise is full upon the figures of three angels who stand with crowns of roses on their heads and watch the scene among the rocks. There is an Annunciation in the same room by Bonfigli; and it again is chiefly charming because of the treatment of the angels. They come fluttering up behind a group of cypress trees, all in the flush of dawn. But the foreground figure is strange indeed. What did Bonfigli mean when he painted S. Luke and his ox, and planted them there in the midst of the picture so as quite to distract one's attention from the principal figures of the piece? In the next room (Sala VII.) Bonfigli's angels can be studied with ease. There are in all eight panels of them, and it is interesting to see how the early painter strove between realism and idealism in the faces. He loved his smiling angels best; what care he took to crown them with pink roses; what baskets too of roses he gave to them to carry! yet to his angels of the Passion he gave no roses, only the symbols of the Crucifixion, its anguish and its thorns.

We have lingered long over the work of a man whose figure is such an attractive one in the Umbrian school. Before passing on to the work of his contemporaries we must mention the name of another artist four of whose pictures are hung in the room of the Bonfigli angels: namely, Bernardino di Mariotto. Bernardino is an interesting figure in the gallery, and one is struck at first sight by the quality of his work, which differs from everything round it. He seems like some strange missing link in the history of the Umbrian and the Roman school; and so little is known about him that up to a quite recent date his work was confused with that, first of much earlier painters, and then of Pinturicchio. His treatment of detail: the Virgin's gown, the garlands of fruit and flowers, the angels' wings and the saints' dresses, is beautiful though his colour is cold and hard. His peculiar use of a very stiff baldachin made people say that he was a master of Raphael. As a matter of fact he lived at S. Severino in the Marches and worked about the years 1502 to 1521.

In the same room there are two big pictures by Bartolomeo Caporali, who was a pupil of Perugino. His great flying angels in No. 12 are like the angels of Bonfigli gone mad, there is something grand in the rush of their wings, and whatever the faults of the somewhat exaggerated composition, it forces one's immediate attention.

*GONFALONE OF THE ANNUNCIATION
BY NICCOLÒ ALUNNO*

To return to the order of the earlier painters, we come to one or two names which are probably more familiar to most people than that of Bonfigli: these are Fiorenzo di Lorenzo, Boccati da Camerino and Niccolò Alunno. There is a fine bit of Alunno's work in Sala VII. (No 14). It is about the only thing of his which is now attributed to him in Perugia. Such a host of angels singing and playing to God in the heavens, and a charming garden scene round the young Virgin! She kneels very quietly at her desk. Neat pots of flowers stand on the marble wall behind her and three stiff cypress trees against the sky; round a corner of the garden wall two very engaging angels stand gossiping together, their heads thrown back, their mouths a little pouting. In the immediate foreground two patron saints are kneeling to introduce a group of lawyers who commissioned the painting of the banner.

Boccati da Camerino's work is rare. There is a charming thing of his in Sala VI. (No. 13): a Madonna and a fascinating choir of angels. His largest picture (No. 16) is in the same room and represents the same subject. The Madonna sits enthroned under a heavy pergola of roses, and all around her is a stiff little choir of angels: a most delightful and original conception. The picture was painted for the monks of S. Domenico, and so the emblem of the saint, his dog, had to figure in it. What Boccati was about we cannot judge, but he certainly painted an ermine instead of a dog, and the little Christ receives the strange beast with delight. The predella of the picture is full of stories almost in the style of Carpaccio. Boccati had a rare and charming fancy. In his scene of the procession to Calvary, he shows how a rude soldier attempts to strike the fainting figure of Christ; and one of the horses of the guard, with ears bent back, stoops forward to bite the hand of him who would distress the Saviour.

Rooms VIII. and IX.

Sala di Fiorenzo di Lorenzo, Gabinetto di Fiorenzo di Lorenzo.

We now come to Fiorenzo di Lorenzo, to whose name two rooms in the Pinacoteca have been dedicated. Very little is known about his life. We can only gather that he studied in the school of Bonfigli, and that he competed with Bonfigli in the painting of banners. He may have been a rather younger man, but he was earlier than Perugino and his scholars, and so he forms a sort of link between the masters and the pupils of a great school.

Fiorenzo may be said to have begun the school which now is called the school of Perugino. It was he who distinctly and for ever broke away from that Greek or Byzantine influence which we feel in much of Bonfigli's work. In his own day he was eclipsed by the greater lights which rose up round him, and it is only to us, who try to trace the school, that he is such a really important and delightful figure. Throughout his work one feels a great effort towards light—towards fresh issues. His drawing and his colour are often very beautiful, but there is a great difference in the style of the various works ascribed to him. Compare No. 53 (Sala VIII.) and its surrounding panels, with Nos. 30, 6, and 5. (The three latter probably all formed part of one large altar-piece.)

The Adoration, attributed to Fiorenzo, is a crowded but a beautiful composition. The Virgin, S. Joseph, and a group of shepherds kneel in the foreground, and exquisite flowers, grape-hyacinths, even some fluffy heads of dandelion seed grow at their feet. Behind them is the stable—an Umbrian stable in an Umbrian landscape—filled with a host of angels. In the dim distance the shepherds feed their flocks upon the hills. The figures are mere sketches of some Umbrian goat-herds whom Fiorenzo must have met outside the Umbrian farms at dawn. Nos. 10 and 16 (in Sala IX.) are beautiful specimens of the master's later work. Note the hand and the crimson sleeves of the Virgin.

The Story of Perugia

*ADORATION OF THE SHEPHERDS
BY FIORENZO DI LORENZO*

But if Fiorenzo could apply himself with the religious ardour of his school to sacred subjects, to the Bible of his art, he could also sometimes take a holiday and write a fantastic and entrancing *scherzo* on his own account. It is his series of pictures on the life of San Bernardino of Siena which at once attracts us in the gallery. Here we find one of those wonderful visions of the past—a record of men's manners, of their costumes and architecture, as seen through the eyes of some intelligent yet child-like artist.[99] To describe the miracles is not an easy matter. In seeking the subject one is carried away by the charm of the models, just as the painter was who painted them. A company of entrancing youths with long thin legs, their marvellous crimson tunics trimmed with fur, their small caps barely clinging to their shocks of golden curls, strut up and down the panels, but barely conscious of the Saint and all his patient care of them. No 3, represents the miracle of a girl who has fallen into a well, and whom the Saint has saved from drowning; we see a lovely and impassive creature sitting upon the marble floor, her yellow hair has not been wetted, the small red fillet binds it gracefully; her relations and her lovers pray and pose all round her, but little ruffled by the memory of the late catastrophe. Just the same is the accident of the mason, treated in No. 7. His comrades stand about the wounded man, exquisite and undisturbed. "Ah," they seem to say, "thus and thus it happened, thus, maybe, he fell"; but all the time they are thinking of their well-set tunics and of their long and lovely legs; and who can be surprised at this, seeing that their *toilette* is carried to perfection? No. 5 shows the capture and escape of a prisoner. It has a pleasant landscape in the background, a sort of park, with a lake and trees about it. In No. 6 the Saint appears in a cloud under a beautiful marble palace and heals the blindness of a fellow friar. The doctors do seem somewhat interested, but everything is too beautiful and finished for much pity or, anyhow, for pain; and as for the hair of the young men in this panel, it is more excellently curled than in any of the series. The remaining miracles are by another hand. Some pupil or imitator of Fiorenzo tried to finish them, but the treatment is coarser, the charm of the first is gone.

Room V.

Sala dell' Angelico.

Before passing on to the work of Perugino and his school, which one must confess, with the exception of Sala XI., is but a disappointing show of canvasses and panels, one passes through the little room of Fra Angelico.

In Taine's slight but exquisite sketch of Perugia and its pictures we read the following words about the work of Fra Angelico at Perugia: "He was happier here than in his pagan Florence, and it is he who first attracts us (in the gallery). Looking at his work there, one seems to be reading in the 'Imitatio Christi,' for on the golden background the pure sweet faces breathe a quiet stillness, like the immaculate roses in the gardens of Paradise." Taine is right; everyone is at once attracted to the work of the Florentine monk when they come to the gallery of Perugia. We have searched for some record of the friar's visit to Perugia, but have not been successful. It is certain that the Florentine painter came to stay in Umbria, leaving behind him as a legacy to later painters the influence of his pious gentle art. He became a monk in 1408 at Fiesole, but his convent got mixed up in painful religious disputes, and the monks had to fly and wander into other lands, hoping to return when times should be more peaceful. Fra Angelico came to Cortona, and there did some of his very earliest work. Thence, very probably, he travelled to Foligno, staying on his way to rest at Perugia, and leaving there, in the church of S. Domenico, that wonderful picture, all the parts of which now hang together in the Pinacoteca. They are jewels, these small panels—jewels fresh as dewdrops on the first May wreaths of girls. Angelico never lost this bloom of utter purity, and here we find it at its very dawn. The Madonna and Child are in the centre; round them stand four angels, their baskets full of roses. "Two angels in long dresses," says Taine, "bring their roses to the feet of the small Christ with the dreaming eyes. They are so young, and yet so earnest." Again, of the Annunciation, he says: "The Virgin is candour and sweetness itself; her character is almost German, and her two hands are clasped with deep religious fervour. The angel with the curly hair who kneels before her seems almost like some young and happy girl—a little raw perhaps—and coming straight from the house of her mother.... These indeed, are the delicate touches that painters of a later date will never find again. A sentiment is an infinite and incommunicable thing; no learning and no effort will ever reproduce it absolutely. In real piety there is a certain reserve; a certain modesty is shown in the arrangement of the draperies and in the choice of little details, such as even the best masters, only a century later, will not understand at all." It is difficult to choose any particular point for description in the twelve narrow panels of saints. Angelico carefully studied to show the individual character of each. He gave to his Magdalen a new and lovely attitude—a sort of ascetic repose. Of her physical beauty he only left the yellow hair; it falls to her ankles gold as the maize in autumn, but her body is wasted beneath it. St Catherine of Siena is said to be a really authentic portrait of the Saint. The Bishop of Toulouse is unlike that of Bonfigli, younger and gentler in expression. The whole set make an ineffably sweet impression on our mind, and it is difficult to turn to the other pictures in the room. Of these the best and the most interesting is by Piero della Francesca.

Piero was one of Perugino's first masters. He was born early in the fifteenth century at Borgo San Sepolcro. He had a passion for perspective, and was one of the first men who made a real study of this branch of art. We hear that he wrote books on geometry, and grappled with Euclid and the laws of measurement. He also studied the proportion of light and shade, and all these points are admirably proved by his picture at Perugia (No. 21). Vasari gives a full account of it in his life of Piero. He describes the lower part, then adds: "Above them is a most beautiful Annunciation with an angel, which seems, in truth, to have descended from heaven; and what is more, a range of columns in perspective, which is indeed most beautiful." St Elizabeth of Hungary is a fine point in the lower composition. She wears a green gown, and in its skirt she carries the loaves which, by grace of heaven, and to defend her from the anger of her husband, were turned, as we know, to roses.

Room X.

Sala del Perugino.

An irresistible sense of sadness creeps over us as we pass through the room which bears the name of Pietro Perugino. Looking at the collection one feels much in the same frame of mind as one does in searching the wearisome domestic letters of a genius. Only one or two of the pictures attributed to Vannucci in the Pinacoteca of Perugia have the touch of the spirit in them. No. 25, which is double-sided like most of the altar-pieces of convents, where the one side faced the congregation and the other the monks or nuns, is a beautiful bit of Perugino's work, fine both in colour and in sentiment. No. 10, too, is a small gem from one of Pietro's really beautiful altar-pieces.[100] Nos. 20 and 4 are fragments of one enormous altar-piece (see p. 190), which used to hang in the church of S. Agostino and which like many others of Pietro's finest works was torn to pieces, and carried across the Alps to swell the galleries of Napoleon. One hurries shuddering past pictures like Nos. 1, 5, and 26. It seems so impossible that what the Germans call a "Schöne Seele" should have allowed such things to be.

Room XI.

Sala di Bernardino di Betto detto il Pinturicchio.

In the little room which leads out of Room X. we make an interesting study of Perugino's pictures, for it contains some of his earliest and also some of his most decadent work. Had the municipality of Perugia just a touch of humour or malice when they hung No. 25 side by side with No. 16? Whatever they had in their heads they have given to us a curious study. Here are two works by the same man, the latter probably a pot-boiler of his school but still burdened with his name. Both represent precisely the same subject, the same set of saints is in each of them; but the early work is full of thought, of reverence and feeling; the early Sebastian, calm and grave, has the arrow in his very flesh, and the later Sebastian, simpering and affected, toys with his arrow and turns with painful affectation to the Saviour. There is a lovely little set of sketches on the predella under No. 6; the Nativity, a mere hurried impression, seems full of the breeze of early spring in Umbria.

We have a splendid bit of Pinturicchio's work in this room which bears his name, and also one of the rare paintings of Lo Spagna; one or two pictures which bear at least the name of Raphael, and the much disputed "Adoration" which has been ascribed to more than one distinguished person.

Bernardino di Betto, usually known as Pinturicchio and sometimes as il Sordicchio because he was deaf, and small and of a mean appearance, studied in the school of Perugia, and indeed was one of its most distinguished painters; but having left that earliest studio he carried his talents to other parts, and painted as we know for popes and princes, painted above all things those two wonderful series of frescoes in the Duomo at Siena and in the Borgia rooms at the Vatican. He has been called sometimes the Umbrian Gozzoli; certainly he was the historical painter of the great school which grew in the times of Perugino. Vasari with a certain prejudice and ill nature insists that Pinturicchio's success was one rather of opportunity than of talent; but it is much more probable that the painter was beloved because he was faithful to his promises and carried out his orders with care and with precision. We know, too, that after all the sums he got, and all his heavy labours, he died of hunger and neglect on a winter's night at Siena, his wife having deserted him and eloped with a new lover.

Pinturicchio had a grant of land given to him in the neighbourhood of Perugia in 1495, by Alexander VI., and he determined to return to his native city and live there; but some years later, when in money difficulties, he was forced to sell it to a gentleman of Perugia.

The splendid altar-piece (No. 10), which alone remains to Perugia of this distinguished pupil of Perugino, is ill lighted and rather difficult to judge from top to bottom, but is interesting as well as beautiful; for the picture remains just as the painter painted it with all its panels in their proper order, unlike the panels of so many of Perugino's finest altarpieces. The Pietà, the angel of the Annunciation, both the figures of the Virgin and the detail of their dresses, fruit and books, are exquisitely finished.

There is in the same room an excellent specimen of the work of another of Perugino's scholars—Lo Spagna (No. 7). Giovanni di Pietro was one of the most distinguished of Vannucci's school, and Kugler indeed pronounces him to be *the* most distinguished after Raphael. It is probable that he studied with Fiorenzo di Lorenzo before going to Vannucci's studio, but it is difficult to discover any details about his private life. His whole career is shrouded in some mystery. His name would make one think he was Spanish by birth. We know that he left Perugia and went to live at Spoleto. Vasari declares that this was because the painters of Perugia were jealous of him and made life in their midst impossible; this fact is however severely denied by our gossip Mariotti, who declares that Lo Spagna was excessively well off in Spoleto, where he not only received the rights of citizenship but also secured a charming wife. Be all this as it may, of this really good artist, who combined in his work the influence of Raphael and of Perugino, only one piece is left in the place where he learned his art. The Madonna and Saints (No. 7) is a fine specimen of his work. The mother and the child are fresh and beautiful in colour and expression, and all the details of the dresses and the landscape infinitely careful. Note St Jerome, his gloves, his book, his hat and splendid gown. One other picture is ascribed to Giovanni in the same room, but it is greatly inferior in treatment.

We now come to the Adoration of the Magi, which after much dispute was some time ago ascribed to Perugino's scholar Eusebio di San Giorgio, but which is still the subject of endless local discussions, as, owing to further and more minute investigations it is at length declared by excellent judges to be the work of Raphael. One reason given for this is that the young man to the right of the Virgin has on his trousers a strange design, the arms of Raphael. Poor Eusebio must turn in his grave. His former biographers, anxious to seize on any gem of painting which should save the artist from a rather mediocre position in the history of art, always stayed to shout exultant praises when they came to this picture, and now the critic would tear even this glory from his brows and crown another man whose head is already heavy with their laurels.[101]

No. 20—a Madonna and Child—is ascribed to Raphael. The picture certainly has something of the master in it and it may be the work of the mere boy, when first he came from

Urbino to paint with Perugino, and in the Umbrian city dreamed his great Madonna of the future. Raphael Sanzio passes like a dream through Perugia, leaving no certain relic of his mighty fame save one faint faded fresco on the church wall of S. Severo, and these poor relics in the gallery.[102]

Room XII.

Sala di Giannicola e di Berto di Giovanni.

From this point forwards the interest of the gallery begins to wane. We have tracked the dawn and seen the sunrise; now we feel the dull warmth of midday, and passing through the weary hours of the afternoon, most fully and amply represented in the work of the two Alfanis, we pass to night through the fevered rooms of the Decadence. Sala XII. is devoted to the work of Perugino's scholars, but most of it is weak. Still there is a touch of the old sweetness here and there among the figures. Note No. 15 by Giannicola Manni. It has a charm though it is very imitative. The rest of Giannicola's work in this room is rather dreary. But there is charm, too, in the purely imitative, nay copied work of Berto di Giovanni. Berto was another of Perugino's scholars. He lived probably towards the end of the fifteenth century and it is evident that he felt a passionate admiration for his fellow student, Raphael. All we can gather of facts about Berto comes to us through his connection with Raphael. In 1516 he contracted to paint, in combination with his hero, a picture for the nuns of Monteluce. Bits of the predella are now in the Pinacoteca. In the flat and almost womanish sketches of Berto one traces his persistent admiration for the greater artist. It is as though an intelligent child had torn the leaves from its mother's sketch-book and filled in the lines with faithful and laborious colouring. (See Nos. 19 to 26.) But Berto's charm, such as it is, went all wrong when he tried to paint big subjects. Nos. 16 and 14 are little more than failures.

* * * * * * *

To anyone who admires the work of the two Alfani, Domenico and Orazio, a happy hunting-ground exists in the last big rooms of the Pinacoteca. How it came about that one of Perugino's really lovely frescoes got hung in this part, we cannot tell, but it is certain that the Nativity (No. 31, Room XIII.) is one of the loveliest things that remain of Pietro in the town of Perugia. It is very like our own Nativity in the National Gallery, faint and fair in colour, calm and true in composition, with a peculiar lilac colour of crushed grapes throughout the dresses and the landscape.

It would be impossible to close any account of the school of Perugino without a slight sketch of the two Alfanis whose intense admiration for the genius of painting became a fault, and who, through their very earnestness preserved the corpse from which the life long since had fled. The Alfanis, Domenico the father, and Orazio the son, had money and long life. These two happy gifts they employed in the paths of art; with these two gifts they at length degraded what they really attempted to exalt. Domenico was such a passionate admirer of Raphael that one of his historians declared him to have died in the same year as Sanzio. Mariotti denies this. "However passionate a friend and inseparable a companion," he urges, "Domenico had not for certain such a crazy folly as to accompany him to the other world." Domenico far outlived Raphael. In his long life he absorbed the teaching of many schools, and utterly obliterated his own personality in the work of other people. His son Orazio did the same. They went into partnership, started a large school or studio, and there created the innumerable, rather middle-class pictures, which cover the walls of the Pinacoteca. Grazio survived his father about thirty years, and was the first president of the Academy of Perugia founded in 1573.

* * * * * * *

One word to close these notes about the painters of the Umbrian school.

Seek out the painters in the places where they painted. Go to Spoleto for the works of Lo Spagna, to Gubbio for the masterpiece of Nelli, to Spello for Pinturicchio, to Foligno for the early men who have not even names. Go in May to Montefalco, when all the green of Umbrian angels' wings is in the lanes which lead to these. Learn by heart the Umbrian landscape if you wish to really love and understand the spirit of Umbrian art. The Pinacoteca of Perugia serves only as a backbone for the genuine study.[103]

CHAPTER XI

The Museum, [104] and Tomb of the Volumnii

HAVING traced the first Etruscan walls and seen the tomb of the Volumnii, a note of sombre and half melancholy interest will inevitably have been struck upon our mind whilst trying to realise the lives of those mysterious people who created these things and left these dumb indications—dumb, because the language is so dead—upon the country where they lived and died. This note is of course by no means confined to the mind of the passing traveller. It is the people of the place itself who feel it most, and in Perugia, thanks to their efforts, we have, in the museum at the University, a very complete, if only a small collection of the relics of Etruscan civilization as found in the immediate neighbourhood. In a small book written by Signor Lupatelli upon the growth of the museum, we read that the noble families of the place have always loved to trace their earliest ancestors by carefully collecting any sarcophagi or other relics which they found upon their lands. In this way the Museum has been formed, and a crowd of tombs, laid open by the plough or winter rains, have been preserved with all their treasures in them. [105]

The study of the Etruscans is, after all, the study of the dead, and an Etruscan Museum has about it all the mysterious atmosphere of the tomb. What barrier greater, what ocean more profound, than that between ourselves and this dead people! Their tombs, their busts, their playthings and inscriptions seem to chill the very air around them. Ordinary people, not students of archæology, must face this fact quite boldly and come prepared to plunge head foremost into a very chilly atmosphere if they wish to learn about the ancient Etruscans. The present writers are bound to confess, that, on glad spring mornings, they have turned from the sarcophagi and the bronzes and terra-cotta vases in the cases to look with undisguised delight through the windows of the museum and up beyond to the brown roofs of the wicked old mediæval city opposite. The Duomo with all the blood upon its steps, the Piazza with all its passionate and burning history, seemed to them more real, more sympathetic, than the uneventful countenances, the harmless funereal urns, of this quiet race of men, who lived and died over one thousand years before our era.

"Les Tyrènes," says M. André Lefèvre, "durant leur longue domination *sont restés des étrangers, c'est ce qui explique pourquoi leur langue et leurs dieux ont disparu avec leur puissance*, et pourquoi nous sommes réduits à fouiller leurs tombeaux pour connaître leur vie. C'est de leurs demeures funéraires que nous exhumons aujourd'hui leurs industries, leurs arts, leurs festins, leurs danses, leurs jeux, leurs pompeuses cérémonies triomphales, et leurs nuptiales, et aussi leur courte philosophie faite de fatalisme et d'insouciance."

VIA DELLA PERA UNDER THE AQUEDUCT ON THE WAY TO THE UNIVERSITY

It is probable that when the Rasenae first arrived in central Italy, they were still an almost barbarous nation, and that their arts and civilization were developed later in their northern settlements, in Tuscany and Umbria. They seem to have adopted little from the races who preceded them in Italy, though some say that they learned the art of statuary from these still more mysterious people; but, being, as we know, themselves a sea-faring nation they may have taken their first conceptions of art from the Carthaginians and Phœnicians, and in this way they might easily have come in contact with the art of Egypt and of Carthage. But by far the strongest influence was that of Greece. This they perhaps felt first in Greece itself, and later through their contact with Greek settlers in Italy.

The Etruscans were a receptive people; they easily grasped a new idea, and carried it out with careful precision, though with rounded edges, so to speak. The spirit of the inspiration of pure art is lacking in their work. They were excellent craftsmen, and Rome is said to have learned certain points in the uses of casting metal and in masonry from Etruscan artisans. They were also an agricultural people, who did much towards improving the soil wherever they settled. The Etruscans were a very religious, or at least a superstitious race, full of faith in augury, constantly consulting natural oracles, such as the flight of birds and variations of the atmosphere, and, like the Greeks, they had their household gods or *lares*. The Medusa's head is for ever recurring in their monuments and on their house-doors. Having some strong belief in the immortality of the human soul, they crowded their dead with gifts, putting their most elaborate work upon the tombs, and giving to the corpse all the necessaries for a long journey to a distant land, or for a possible reawakening. They had different modes of burial. Usually the body was burned, but sometimes—and we have admirable instances of this in the Perugian Museum—it was simply buried in a stone sarcophagus. Women were respected and held a high position in society. This fact is clearly shown by their prominence upon the tombs, where they sit side by side with their husbands, as they were probably in the habit of doing at their feasts. The toilet was also respected, and the dead took as many pots of balsam to the grave as they took tear-bottles. The richer bodies have a wonderful array of dressing-table nicknacks at their head and feet, and the loveliest and most careful work in the whole museum is that upon the hand-mirrors (see Case 12, Room vi.), which were also probably laid in the tomb of the beloved dead.

The chief interest in this museum of Perugia is the wealth of its inscriptions. The passages are lined with them, and a catalogue or dictionary has been made of them. The Etruscans lived side by side with the Romans and the Greeks, and often we find inscriptions written in both languages upon one tomb; yet, though the two latter peoples were the greatest scholars of the world, the Etruscan language is dead to us for all practical purposes; and the longest Etruscan inscription which is known—the pride of the Perugian Museum—is little better than a blank wall to all who look to it for purposes of study.[106]

The Etruscans lived luxurious lives, but their race ran long upon the soil of Italy. As far as it can be traced, their rule, or at least their occupation, lasted for about twelve centuries. By the beginning of the Christian era they were already dying out.

M. André Lefèvre gives the following final summing up of the influence of the Etruscans upon the greater nation which gradually took their place:—

"Bien que, même aux temps de leur plus grande puissance ils n'aient pu imposer ni leur langue ni leurs dieux à des peuples établis depuis mille ans sur le sol Italien, leur part n'en a pas moins été considérable dans la civilisation Latine. Leur influence a été moindre sur les hommes que sur les choses, sur l'esprit que sur les formes extérieures, cérémonielles et rituelles,—qui, à leur tour, affectent les institutions et les moeurs. Ils ont appris aux Romains à bâtir des maisons et des temples, à ordonner les festins, les processions, les pompes triomphales et les jeux sanglants du cirque. Les meubles, les sièges, les statues, les licteurs, le costume, la bulle d'or des enfants patriciens, sont aussi d'origine Étrusque. Enfin, ils ont ajouté aux superstitions déja si nombreuses des Latins et des Sabins la science, si ce n'est pas profaner un tel mot, la science augurale, élevée au rang d'institution politique, perpétuant ainsi, au sein d'une civilisation avancée, les plus niaises pratiques de la sauvagerie la plus infinie."

As it would have been impossible in the slight scope of this small book to give any detailed account of the different objects in the Perugian museum, we have thought it wiser to offer the above sketch of the Etruscans themselves, adding only some promiscuous notes about the collections for those who care to read them as they pass through the different rooms. The new Catalogue by Signor Donati, the profound works of Count Conestabile and Signor Vermiglioli, and the delightful chapter in Dennis' *Etruria* contain all the information that a genuine student will desire.

Room II.

Case A.

No. 5. A Medusa's head in terra-cotta; exquisite and of unusually careful workmanship. This head was probably one of those plaques or tablets which were put up by the Etruscans over the lintel of their house-doors to keep away the evil spirits. The Medusa is commonly used in this way, and we find her constantly in tombs and other places. Her face is usually calm, and often lovely, though in this instance it is calculated to strike terror, as well as admiration, into the mind of any witch or evil spirit. Beside it are two tablets of the same sort, but much coarser in treatment and design, and apparently worked under Egyptian influences.

No. 12. Some charming pieces of Etruscan glass; small tear and balsam bottles; also some larger bottles, square in form. These latter were probably used for medicines. Their chief interest lies in the fact that they bear the stamp of their Etruscan makers.

No. 6. A row of terra-cotta *pateræ*, such as the dead hold in their hands on tombs.

No. 9. A plateful of little glass balls, which shine like handfuls of the most lustrous emeralds and opals in the dim light of the Museum. These were used as counters by the Etruscans in their games of dice, and it is thought that they were put into the graves of habitual gamblers, so that the soul of the dead man, during its passage to eternity, should not be denied the consolation of its favourite diversion.

No. 27. Some beautiful fragments of feet, heads, and arms. It has been supposed that the Etruscans often made whole statues of wood or of some such cheap material, only giving to the extremities the careful work required by terra-cotta. Hence these apparently disconnected relics.

Cases B. and C.

Most of the objects in this case came from Chiusi and are made of the black ware called *bucchero*. Some are

Etruscan, some of an even earlier origin. All along the top of the case are some quite simple cinerary urns of a different form to the vases inside the cases, which latter were designed more for decoration in rich men's houses.

No. 5. Two beautiful trays or toilet tables belonging to the Etruscan ladies. Looking at these one seems to understand the elaborate wigs on the heads of those ladies who smile upon the tops of their sarcophagi. Several objects in Case D. explain them further.

No. 4. A lovely line of graceful vases, good illustrations of the imitative power of the Etruscans. Not only the forms, but even the shining texture of the Grecian bronze, is here copied in *bucchero*.

No. 8. These vases are the work of those people who preceded the Etruscans in Umbria. The forms are simple, the patterns purely geometrical.

Case D

Nos. 2, 3. Some quite common earthenware urns for the ashes of the poor who could neither afford tombs nor inscriptions. On one or two of these a name is scratched in rough black paint, probably with the finger, and as a last token to the dead from someone who had loved him.

No. 7. Some earthenware bottles corresponding to the beautiful glass ones in Case A: those in earthenware were used for the tombs of the poor.

Room III.

Sarcophagi.

This room has a selection of the most interesting Sarcophagi in the museum. The corridors outside, and the staircase also, are filled with other specimens of more or less interest.

There is always a certain monotony in a collection of Etruscan tombs or sarcophagi, and the ordinary person wearies easily of the recumbent figures which lie so stolidly in effigy upon the lids of their own burial urns, with an expression of comfortable contentment on their somewhat unexciting and uneventful countenances. They seem, one and all of them, like persons who have fallen asleep on peaceful days with easy consciences,—persons whose hope of heaven is as slight as their fear of hell. They are, most of them, middle-aged, the pathos of old age, the hope and the passion of youth, is lacking in their faces. Their charm is to be sought in their extreme repose.

There are several forms of tombs in the Perugian collection, that with the recumbent figures on the lid being probably the one used by the richer and more prosperous families. With few exceptions the work on the sarcophagi is rather coarse—a singular and persistent monotony of subject is displayed. The simpler forms have either a rose or a Medusa on their front panels, the more elaborate are ornamented with subjects from the Greek mythology, which seem to clash at times with the conventional figures on their lids. The story of Iphigenia is a favourite theme for the sarcophagi of women.

On those of men, battles and boar-hunts figure largely, the labours of Hercules too, and fights with the Amazons. It is probable that these cases were kept in stock, and that when one was needed, the order was simply given to add a face, a portrait face of man or woman, to the figure, and sometimes an inscription. Most of the figures hold the familiar *paterœ* in their hand, others clasp their long and heavy necklaces, some of them carry a flower—a lotus, maybe, or a rose.

There was one quite different form of burial, when the whole body was preserved in a stone sarcophagus. Sometimes the corpse must have first undergone some kind of disintegration in the earth, as, in one or two cases, we find the bones gathered together in a small urn, into which the whole body could never have been pushed. At other times it was stretched full length in its long stone case. Infinitely pathetic is the figure of an Etruscan lady in the corridor. There she lies just as they found her, exposed to the most casual observer, with all the requisites for an exquisite toilet upon the resurrection morning: her hot-water can, her *strigil*, her looking-glass, her pins, the money to pay her passage across the river to Eternity—nay, even the little metal weights she wore to keep her long straight skirts in order—all laid out carefully beside her, and nothing of the beauty left beyond her white and shining teeth.

Faint traces of colour linger on some of these sarcophagi. Note No. 8. The hair of the Medusa is painted a delicate lilac hue, and the acanthus leaves which encircle it are blue like the sky in spring time.

No. 23. An exception to the usual design of Greek mythology. The defence of a city—dare we say of Perugia—is here depicted. The men are fighting beneath the walls; and in the towers above, a row of valiant ladies are preparing to crush them with large and heavy stones.

No. 30. These much smaller sarcophagi are made of terra cotta and come from Chiusi. In many of them the dead are represented in a new way; they have fallen asleep wrapped in long thin veils which cover the entire figure.

Room IV.
Case A.
No. 9. Some good specimens of Etruscan helmets, one of them with flaps of iron to protect the ears of the warriors. We learn clearly in this room that the Etruscans

wore elaborate armour—helmets, belts, greaves, and bronze and iron spear-heads being plentifully represented.

Case B.

No. 31. *Pempobolo* or *graffio*—an instrument used for stirring the bodies of the dead as they burned, and for raking in the ashes afterwards.

No. 35. *Cottabu.* This strange looking implement was probably used for a kind of game practised at Etruscan feasts. It is supposed that at the end of a feast, when the guests grew merry, a toast was proposed, and that a glass was put on the tray at the top of the pole just under the little deity, and then carried round the room. The broader plate below was put to catch the wine as it fell with the swinging of this most ungainly instrument.

Case D.

Nos. 10 to 33, 40 to 60. A collection of small metal images, Lari, or household gods, most of them very Greek in treatment, some of them archaic.

Nos. 34 to 40. A collection of lead missiles for slings. These are inscribed with words of the most marked abuse designed for the enemy. On one of them is written: (in Latin characters) "For thy right eye"—the sort of naïve thing a schoolboy might design.

Room V.

"As beautiful pottery like that of Vulci and Tarquinii is very rarely found at Perugia, it seems probable that it was not manufactured on the spot," writes Dennis. And if one has seen the various other local Etruscan Museums in Italy, one will feel decidedly disappointed in the vase-room at Perugia. One or two interesting points may however be noted. It is strange to mark the difference between the two separate classes of vases, between the genuine Greek work, which the Etruscans had the good taste to prize, and that of their own imitations of it. Note Nos. 3, 5, 14, all of which are probably Etruscan copies from real Greek vases. They are like the imitative sketches of children, lacking in understanding and in feeling, and pathetic in their clumsy failure. Nos. 7, 8, 10, and 12, are all specimens probably of real Greek work.

No. 22. A fine terra-cotta vase—probably genuine Etruscan work—with four heads of Bacchus at the base.

Room VI.

The gems of the museum may be said to have been gathered together in this room, and the object which at once attracts one on entering is the large sarcophagus of an Etruscan gentleman and his evil genius, or Fate, which stands by the east window. Dennis has an admirable description of it: "An Etruscan of middle age," he says, "is reclining in the usual costume and attitude of the banquet, with a bossed phiala in his left hand, and his right resting on his knee. At his feet squats a hideous old woman, stunted and deformed, whose wings show her to be a demon. She seizes one of his toes with her right hand and grasps his right wrist with her left. (Some authorities say she is feeling the pulse of the dying man.) She turns her head to look at him, yet he appears quite unconscious of her presence. She doubtless represents the Moira or Fate, whose touch deprives him of life. The monument is from Chiusi, and of the fetid limestone of that district. Both heads are moveable, and the bodies hollow, proving that this, which looks like the lid of a sarcophagus, is itself a cinerary urn."

No. 18. An Etruscan helmet of the finest work.

No. 14. Two exquisite sarcophagi differing in every way from the one described above. So flowery is the work upon them that one scarcely realises to what dark ages they belong. The terra-cotta seems just baked, the paint is sticking to it. The griffins and sea horses, the portraits on the lids, all are most exquisitely treated.

No. 12. The wonderful mirrors in this case have been admirably described by Dennis (see page 428). The one with the story of Helen engraved on it (No. 11) is quite one of the loveliest pieces of work ever discovered in the soil of Etruria.

No. 3. A sarcophagus with the most delightful procession depicted upon its panels. There has been a good deal of discussion about the subject represented. Some say it is a migration, or a colony going forth to fulfil the vow of sacred spring; others that it is a procession going to a sacrifice. Dennis suggests another interpretation. "It seems to me," he says, "much more satisfactory to suppose that it is a return from a successful foray. There are captives bound, and made to carry their own property for the benefit of their victors; their women behind, not bound, but accompanying their lords, their faithful dog following them into captivity, their beasts of burden laden with their gods; their weapons and agricultural implements carried by one of the guards and their cattle driven on by the rest." The sacrifice is the most probable interpretation, for there is something solemn and sinister about the composition. Not only criminals but also human victims are being taken along by the fascinating but inexorable guards. The treatment of the figures is very archaic, and yet it is realistic. The long-eared goats, the horses and the mules step forward with an engaging regularity. Their shepherds or their leaders turn, as such people invariably do turn, to gesticulate and to explain among themselves upon the way. The two side panels represent banquet-scenes, banquets, we may imagine, which were given to commemorate whatever event the procession itself was leading to. The work on this Sarcophagus has been ascribed to the fifth century before Christ.

No. 8. Under a glass shade, a strange little figure in bronze about 14 inches high, representing Hygiea, the

Goddess of Health (daughter of Æsculapius) or, as some say, the Genius of Long Life. Smaller figure under same glass represents Telesphorus, the genius of convalescence, seated, entirely enveloped in a cloak.

Room VII.

has a rather miscellaneous collection of later Roman and Etruscan work, also some objects from Cyprus.

No. 36. A little tomb where the door is left half open, the key hung up upon a peg, perhaps to show that the spirit is free to wander in and out.

RoomS VIII. AND IX.

contain the private collection of Count Guadabassi collected by him throughout a life-time and from very different places, and left to the town at his death with the request that their original arrangement should be preserved. Thus the impression of the whole is somewhat distracting to a student. One of the greatest treasures of the Museum is in

Room VIII.

Case H.

A very beautiful Etruscan mirror with Bacchus, or a Bacchante, riding on a panther upon the cover. Two good mirrors in the same case, and a fine Etruscan gold ornament, with figures delicately traced upon it.

ETRUSCAN MIRROR IN GUADABASSI COLLECTION

To the right of the door, a white marble *oscillum* or slab, with the figure of Archimenes on one side, and on the other the portrait of a juggler taming snakes. This was probably put up outside the house or booth of a juggler, and served as his sign.

Case L.

Some good bits of Etruscan jewellery. One necklace with a large bit of glass like an opal, set in gold and precious stones; also some very delicate Etruscan earrings, with golden nets of filagree on a gold ground.

Case H.

Some specimens of Etruscan money. The pieces were valued according to their weight, and form seemed quite a secondary consideration.

Case P.

A collection of *strigils*, or brass scrapers, to be used after the bath. Some of these were evidently used as ornaments (hung from an elegant bracelet or ring), which leads one to imagine that the bath was a rarity with the Etruscans, and the *strigil* an object of luxury and decoration rather than of frequent use.

Room IX.

Case G.

A fine collection of gems. A little tomb, with pent-roof and tiles in the shape of violet leaves (unnumbered).

The following rooms of the museum, from Room X., contain various mediæval and renaissance works. The only point we would mention here is the case which holds the bones of the mighty man of Perugia: Braccio Fortebraccio di Montone.

There they lie, bare and grim before us. Poor bones, insulted by a Pope, buried and then unburied, and now laid out for any man to look at! There is a note of pathos in the sight, which the inscription does not lessen.

Hospes lege et luge.

Perusiæ natum Montonium me exulem excepit.
Mars patriam Umbriam et Capuam mihi subegit.
Roma paruit Italia theatrum spectator orbis fuit.
At Aquila cadentem risit quem patria lugens brevi hac urna tegit.
Eheu! Mars extulit, Mors substulit.
Abi.

A portrait of Braccio hangs above his coffin—a strong pugnacious countenance, differing quite from his other portrait in the Confraternità di San Francesco. On the opposite wall is a picture of Niccolò Piccinino.

To close these notes on the museum we would mention another private museum in Perugia full of extraordinary interest; that of Professore Giuseppe Bellucci, in the Via Cavour.

Prof. Bellucci has made a special study of the people who preceded the Etruscans in Umbria, and, after years of careful search and indefatigable energy, has accumulated a grand collection of objects belonging to the stone age, and to the earliest settlers on the hills. Arrow heads, battleaxes from Trasimene, pottery and ornaments of infinite variety, are carefully stored and arranged in the top rooms of one of the most charming of the old Perugian palaces; also a surprising collection of amulets against witches and the evil eye, of which Prof. Bellucci has made a special study. This museum can be visited by anyone who is interested in the subject, and its owner is always willing to show it.[107]

The Tomb of the Volumnii.

About three miles from Perugia, down at the foot of one of the last hills which fall into the valley of the Tiber, a mysterious necropolis of *Perusia Etrusca* was discovered many years ago on the property of Count Baglioni. It was a big necropolis full of innumerable urns of more or less artistic interest, and the land about the hill seemed honeycombed with small vaults holding their respective sarcophagi and ashes.

Some time later—so tradition tells us—whilst a peasant was driving his oxen over a field in this same place one of the oxen fell forward. When the man came up to see what had happened, he found that the creature had stumbled through the stones of a great arch which covered a hitherto unsuspected subterranean passage.[108]

When the hole thus made was examined it was found to be in truth a steep staircase cut in the tufa and covered over by a travertine vaulting. It led steeply down to a huge door of travertine, and when this was opened, the wonderful tomb, belonging to the private family of the Volumnii, was disclosed. Unfortunately the ox was not the first person to open up this extraordinary place. The earth and dust of centuries had, it is true, fallen in upon it, but in the Roman times it had been already ransacked for its possible treasures. Beautiful and extraordinary as the place is, haunted by the silent grandeur and mystery of the dead, it is not quite complete, and many of the urns are missing in its first compartments. Still, as Dennis says, "it is one of the most remarkable in Etruria.... To enter the tomb," he continues was to him "like enchantment, not reality, or rather it was the realization of the pictures of subterranean palaces and spell-bound men, which youthful fancy had drawn from the Arabian Nights, but which had long been cast aside into the lumber room of the memory, now to be suddenly restored.... The impressions received in this tomb first directed my attention to the antiquities of Etruria," Dennis adds, and many people will echo his words.

Leaving the dust and the sunlight, the green trees and the sunny banks of the outside Umbrian world, we plunge down a narrow staircase and through the tall doorway of travertine into the darkness of the Etruscan sepulchre, and find ourselves in a dim, low vestibule with stone seats round it, small chambers branching off to right and left, and one large chamber at the end. Strange and fascinating heads look down upon us from the ceiling, marvellous little deities, suspended by many leaden chains, hang silent, as though they dreamed, above our heads. Weird serpents' heads pierce through the walls and seem to hiss at us; and in the dim light of the candles we realize a whole new world of wonderful and deep set imagery, combining with that solid sense of comfortable respectability peculiar to the race of men who lie here.

The tomb of the Volumnii has a strong and a convincing individuality. In this fact consists its charm. The necropolis was built for one family. The clear cut inscription on the door post at the entrance points to this, the name repeated again and again upon the tomb proves it yet more forcibly. [109]

To get a first and full impression of the place it is well to sit down on one of the low stone seats which run round the walls of the vestibule. These benches were probably used by members of the family in the peculiar fashion of the Etruscans. We hear that in order to bring themselves nearer to the dead and to communicate with the Spirit of Death, they would come to the sepulchres at night-fall and sleep beside the urns of their dead friends—their brothers, wives, their children or their lovers—and there receive visions from the souls which always hovered near the place where the body was buried. Members of the Volumnii family who were courageous enough, or peaceful enough in their own souls to do this thing, must have received strong and convincing visions from surroundings so unearthly and mysterious.

A great round disk, the sun probably, guards the entrance door of the vestibule. It seems to rise up out of the sea; two dolphins plunge head foremost into the waves beneath it; and under these, above the left lintel of the door, a great wing stretches, one knows not whence or whither, into the darkness all around it.

On the opposite wall, and guarding the tomb, is another great disk covered with scales, or as some say laurel leaves, and a splendid head in its centre. The face is grandly moulded and belongs to the best period of Etruscan art, when the souls of the artists were probably steeped in the art of Greece. The expression is calm, pure, and full of strength. It is probably meant to represent the God Numa, though some imagine it to be Apollo himself. Below it are two busts which are supposed to be portraits of Apollo in his two qualities of shepherd and of poet; and guarding the disk, two great scimitars with birds perched over them. (It is imagined that the Etruscans shared the Greek belief about birds sympathising in the death of mortals. The flight and ways of birds, certainly formed a large part of their religion, but in this case nothing can be actually proved). Vermiglioli having studied various other points in the necropolis, suggests that the Volumnii were a race of warriors and that the scimitars were a symbol of their warlike ways.

Passing through this second doorway one stands in the actual presence of some members of the family of the Volumnii. There they sit together on their beautiful stuccoed urns: "each on a snow-white couch" says Dennis, "with garlanded brow, torque-decorated neck, and goblet in hand—*a petrifaction of conviviality*—in solemn mockery of the pleasures to which for ages on ages they have bidden adieu."[110]

They are surprisingly real, this family, and they sit there now, just exactly as they were sitting two thousand years or more ago.[111] The figures and the sarcophagi are made of terra-cotta covered by a dead white stucco which gives them a singularly modern look. Each sarcophagus has the head of a Medusa on it, but of a marvellously fair Medusa, a creature to adore, a woman to attract, a creature incapable of inspiring aught save admiration.[112]

The sarcophagus in the centre of the group appears to have belonged to Aruns Volumnius the head of the family. It is the most heavily decorated of the set. Aruns lies on a well-draped couch. Two mysterious figures—Furies, but attractive Furies—guard his urn. They are a splendid piece of work, and have naturally enough been compared with the work of Michelangelo; there is something muscular about them, and their pose is tragic, like that which the sculptor of the Renaissance delighted to give to his figures. Unfortunately the fresco, which was perfect when the tomb was opened, has fallen to bits in the damp air which enters through the open door. To Aruns' left his daughter sits on her urn, to his right his son, and next to his son the beautiful young wife Veilia, or Velia. One could write a romance about Veilia. The beauty of her profile haunts one like a dream. Was she an Etruscan or some woodland creature? Surely the dull and conventional gentleman to whom she was early married bored her into a decline? Certain it is that she died young, and that the sculptor who made this portrait of her, loved and understood the beauty of her human face, and drew it in as faithfully as he had drawn the dull one of her husband and his family. All the other portraits have the usual respectable Etruscan stamp upon them. Veilia alone has a touch of the divine.

TOMB OF ARUNS VOLUMNIUS

One beautiful little sarcophagus in the group differs from all around it. It is exquisite in all its detail and built in the form of a temple with doors and Corinthian columns, pent roof, and exquisite tracery upon its walls. (The inscriptions upon it are written both in Roman and Etruscan characters; but although this sounds like a delightful dictionary they do not appear to coincide.) Four exquisite sphinxes and a little frieze of lions' heads guard the roof; heavy garlands of fruit and flowers hang from the skulls of oxen on the panels;

and birds and butterflies—symbols of the immortality of the human soul—are marvellously carved about them.

The remaining cells have each some beautiful and interesting thing in them, but the main historical interest is passed after the chambers of the Volumnii urns; and the most beautiful things to note are the heads of the Gorgons or Medusas carved in the tufa of the ceilings. Some say that these heads are portraits of the family. Their eyes and teeth are painted white. They seem to stare at one with calm kind eyes which have looked into the centuries and realised the futility of human things.

To the present writers the Medusa of the Etruscan people is its greatest and its most attractive study. She is always grand, beautiful and mysterious; the material and conventional aspects of the Etruscan race vanish and fly before her steady gaze, and in the Volumnian tomb she reigns supreme.

CHAPTER XII

In Umbria

L'Apennin est franchi, et les collines modérées, les riches plaines bien encadrées commencent à se déployer et à s'ordonner comme sur l'autre versant. Cà et là une ville en tas sur une montagne, sorte de môle arrendi, est un ornement du paysage, comme on en trouve dans les tableaux de Poussin et de Claude. C'est l'Apennin, avec ses bandes de contre-forts allongés dans une péninsule étroite, qui donne à tout le paysage italien son caracterè; point de longs fleuves ni de grandes plaines: des valleés limitées, de nobles formes, beaucoup de roc et beaucoup de soleil, les aliments et les sensations correspondantes; combien de traits de l'individu et de l'histoire imprimés par ce caractère!

H. Taine, *Voyage en Italie.*

WE cannot study the history of a single town without acquiring a certain knowledge of the towns around it, for the character of one set of people was formed and influenced by that of another, and the land on which cities are built is often in itself an explanation of their past. In no country perhaps are these facts more strongly marked than in Umbria, where even the smallest hamlet is perched upon a high hill-side as though to provoke attention, and where the larger cities glare at each other from commanding eminences, seeming, even in this peaceful nineteenth century, to challenge one another by the mere aspect of their mighty walls.

We cannot stay long in Perugia without getting its surrounding landscape stamped upon our minds. That circle of small cities so distinctly seen: Assisi, Spello, Foligno to the east, Montefalco, Trevi, Bettona, and Torgiano to the south, and Città della Pieve westwards, all of them perched upon their separate hill-top around the bed of the now vanished lake (see chapter i.), excite one's fancy and one's longing, at first perhaps unconsciously, and later with an irresistible persistence. Finally we are driven to pack our trunks and wander out amongst them.

From a practical point of view, travelling in Umbria, even in its most remote villages, is made extremely easy. The inhabitants are friendly and courteous, and utterly unspoiled by tourists. The inns are clean, the main roads excellent; prices reasonable, and carriages, with few exceptions, good. From a romantic or artistic point of view, nothing can excel the charm of such travelling. We are weary of hearing the stated fact that every town in Italy is worth the visiting; but, however hackneyed the remark, we must make it once again in the case of the towns around Perugia. Each has an individual charm, a long and carefully recorded history. We exclude Assisi, for that town is a study in itself, a thing above and apart. Assisi may be called the Jerusalem of Italy; its connection with one of the greatest Saints of the Catholic world has made its churches monuments of art and history, a centre for pilgrims and for painters throughout a period of nearly seven hundred years; and quite apart from its history as a town (the walls of Assisi date back to 400 B.C.) this presence or possession of the saints has excited a whole literature of art and of devotion.

But besides the towns we have mentioned above, there are a host of other cities very near: Gubbio, Arezzo, Città di Castello, Terni, Spoleto, Narni, Orvieto, Chiusi, Cortona and many others less or better known. It is the diversity and contrast of these towns which charms one, but space forbids that we should offer anything beyond a few small travelling notes concerning one or two of them.

Gubbio.

The road to Gubbio from Perugia leads over a mountain pass as wild, and as forbidding in its aspect, as that of any in the Alps. Leaving the broad and wooded valley of the Tiber it winds in long fantastic wind-swept curves across the spines of the lower Apennines, then plunges somewhat suddenly down into the smiling fields and oak woods of the valley under Gubbio. The position of the town is most remarkable. It looks out on a smiling peaceful valley, but is backed by a terrific mountain gorge which would serve as an iron breastplate in the time of siege. Gubbio is a small brown-coloured town, compact and perfect in its parts; it has never changed since the middle ages. A fine Roman theatre, a mysterious Roman mausoleum, fallen asleep on the cornfields outside the city walls, tell of her early prime, but the character of the place, as we see it now, is purely mediæval. The people themselves have the spirit of their ancestors; the worship, which is almost like a fetish worship, of their patron Saint Ubaldo is as passionate in its intensity to-day as it was seven hundred years ago, when Barbarossa threatened to destroy the town.[113] There is scarcely a single new building in Gubbio. The great weaving-looms in the piazza are a relic of the city's commerce in the Middle Ages, and the exquisite line of the palace of her rulers, Palazzo dei Consoli, with the slim bell tower soaring up against the barren outline of the gorge, lives in one's memory long after many other points of Umbrian cities are forgotten.

Gubbio's bell tower and Gubbio's Madonna are points which we remember with delight. Almost every Umbrian city has its local painter. Nelli is the painter of Gubbio and the gem of all his works has been left on the actual wall for which it first was painted. It was icy wintry weather, although the month was May, when we arrived at Gubbio, but in the fields all round it the flax shone grey and blue like a lagune. Had Nelli seen such flax fields when he painted his Madonna's and his angels' gowns? The stuffs he gave them were as blue, as pure, as all these flowers put together.[114]

Spello.

Early one morning we left Perugia and passed along the plain to Spello. We found it in a halo of May sunlight. There was nothing grim or forbidding, nothing Etruscan about the smiling little town; the sunlight and the air crept into the heart of its streets and seemed to linger there. Yet these were narrow and steep and made for war and not for peace or comfort, just like the streets of Perugia. Their character indeed is so purely mediæval and untouched, that the chains which guarded them at nightfall are even left hanging in one place to the walls.

Right away from the town amongst the olive trees we came to the convent of S. Girolamo. There in the back of the choir is the little fresco of the Marriage of the Virgin by Pinturicchio—faint in colour and fragile in outline, but charming in its composition.

Pinturicchio is the painter of Spello; there is much of his work in the churches. He came there to paint for Troilo, one of the Baglioni, lords of Spello. Hence he was called to Siena to do his well-known series of frescoes for the Piccolomini. A whole chapel in S. Maria Maggiore is covered with his works, and he has put his own portrait amongst them with a string of beads, a brush and palette hanging from it. The artist's face is thin and melancholy, but the frescoes round it are large in line and treatment and some of the best specimens of his religious work. There they stand mouldering mysteriously in the dim light of the little old church for which this master made them four hundred years ago. We lingered long before them, then passed back into the sunlit street and drove away through the gate of the town with the Roman senators above it and out across the hot dry plain to the city of Foligno.[115]

Foligno.[116]

Sunk, as it were, in a broad basin of plain, through which the quiet waters of Clitumnus drain slowly to the Tiber, is the city of Foligno—that city which Perugia so detested, so offended in the past. The town has all the character of the towns of the plain. Driving through its straight and even streets we felt as though we were in Lombardy, in Padua or Ferrara. There were Lombard lions in the porch and Lombard beasts around the arch of the Duomo. The houses were all shut up, square, silent, cool, preparing, as it seemed, for summer heat and dust, and infinite hours of afternoon. The place was flat and drowsy, but we liked it and studied in its churches with delight.

Niccolò Alunno is the painter of Foligno. Some of his work is scattered through the churches, and more is gathered together in the small Pinacoteca together with that of other early Umbrian masters. Very gold and brown the frescoes seemed, very sober and religious in their sentiment.

Here one could study the Umbrian school, apart from the Peruginesque, and it struck us that the art of the first Umbrian painters was a natural, and (if one may say so in this age of critics) an inspired one, which sprang straight up from the soil about the feet of the painters, and was only influenced at certain purely decorative points by the teaching of the Florentines. The angels were the Umbrian children, well groomed, well fed, and wholly unaffected. Neither Paganism nor Christianity had very much to do with them. When Perugino's ripened influence came in, they weakened as garden flowers weaken, in their power of appeal through pure simplicity. The first faces of Umbrian saints and angels were simple like the Umbrian dog-rose. Perugino turned them into garden roses. Both in their way were fair, but the former flowers seemed nearer the divine than those which had been trained and cultivated.

It is not possible to mention here all the pictures of Foligno. There are two fine Alunnos in S. Niccolò; and a rather surprising Mantegna with the colour of brown wine—colour of passion and pain, which clashes with the Perugino just beside it—on the chapel of the Nunziatella. The Palazzo Communale is covered with the work of Nelli, but one feels that the painter who so loved what was gay and rich and beautiful (see his picture at Gubbio) wanted a lot more gold and ultramarine than his patron allowed him when painting the ceiling of this chapel.

Before leaving Foligno we went into the church of S. Maria infra Portas. It is so old, this little low basilica, that it has sunk quite deep into the soil around it. Inside are many faded frescoes, brown and gold, and full of almost painful early sentiment. As we stood among them in the dusk, a blackbird poured a flood of freshest song in through the door from the light of the courtyard. "How your bird sings!" we said to the custode. "Yes," said the man; "he sings all day; but whether for love or rage I cannot tell." ... And it struck us that no Umbrian of a hill town, or no Perugian anyway, would have made this profoundly melancholy statement about a tame bird's song.

Montefalco

The road from Foligno to Montefalco leads all along the flat at first, through the peaceful vale of the Clitumnus. Sometimes we crossed the water and saw the reeds and rushes growing, and felt the cool fresh breath of the enchanted stream. Then passing under a mediæval watch-tower we left the flat land and began the steep ascent to Montefalco.

The town stands on a hill in the very heart of Umbria, and hence it is called by the people the *ringhiera d'Umbria*. We saw it "on a day of many days," and it struck us that this was the site of the city of our dreams—the best, the fairest we had ever met in travel. The sun was low as we drove through the gates. Far below us and around us stretched the Umbrian landscape, the bed of the old Umbrian lake: long green waves of blue and green, seething in the heated air of the May afternoon.[117]

The town felt very quiet and deserted. The grass grew everywhere through the stones of its piazza. In silence the children played, in silence the women sat at their doors, the place had fallen asleep. But once the city knew prosperity, and many painters climbed the steep roads from the plain below, and came to Montefalco to leave some impress of their art upon the walls of chapels and of churches. Hither came Benozzo Gozzoli in 1449, and here he painted many of his early frescoes. What brought the splendid Florentine to the tiny town we wondered? He came in the very prime of his youth, and they say that he did so, simply because he was connected with the Dominicans of the place. Certainly he settled here for seven years or so, did good work, and spread the influence of Florence throughout the minds of the rising Umbrian masters. Benozzo's early work at Montefalco is fresh, raw, naïve. It lacks the finish and the gilded ornaments of the Riccardi chapel, but in exchange it holds a certain simple and religious sentiment which is lacking in his later frescoes. The best of his paintings are in the church of S. Francesco,[118] and there are several other good pictures of the Umbrian painters here—a fine Tiberio d'Assisi and some things by Melanzio. In one of the latter, a portrait of the painter by himself—a tall, slim youth with long light hair and earnest face full of quiet thought and strength.

Melanzio is the painter of Montefalco, and luckily his work is well preserved in many of the churches. The little frieze of angels playing with carnations above the left hand altar as one enters the church of the Illuminata, is one of the most fascinating bits of detail that we have ever seen.

Before leaving Montefalco we drove out to the convent of S. Fortunato, which lies to the east of the town. There were pictures there—of these we remember little; but the lanes which led to the convent we never shall forget. They were warm deep lanes and the hedges above were full of dog-roses and honeysuckle, the light inside was green and blue like the landscape down upon the plain. The lanes of Montefalco were as beautiful a vision as we have ever seen. Like the frescoes of Melanzio they had the colour of a tropic butterfly, and like the flight of butterflies they hover in our memory.

Foligno to Spoleto.

In the very height of the midday we left Foligno and took the road to Spoleto. It is a fine broad road, passing along the site of the old Flaminian Way, grand, dusty, white, with a feeling that Rome is at the end of it, and Umbria but a little land to be passed quickly by. As we trundled along in our clumsy landau dragged by a pair of miserable horses, we thought of all the popes, the emperors and legions, who, going south or northwards, had passed in this direction.

The dust flew up and almost choked us; it was the week of the wild roses, and the hedges were all aglow with their delicious blossoms, their petals bent wide back as though to catch the very essence of the sunlight on their golden stamens. We left the main road a little below Trevi, and driving through fields and oak woods, passed up the hills by a steep short cut which leads to the town above. This road cannot be recommended to travellers unless they go on foot; our poor little city horses struggled painfully over the sand and pebbles of the numerous streams it crosses. But what a stretch of country for the artist! Everywhere the poppies were in flower—a shimmer of pure cadmiums and carmines under the oaks and the olives. After about an hour's climb we came out suddenly on the broad bastions of the road which runs from Trevi to the convent of S. Martino.

Trevi.

The tiny town of Trevi is a familiar object to all who pass along the line to Rome. It stands, as one expects all Umbrian towns to stand, a crown of buildings closely packed upon a little hill-top. The city felt bare and baked when we entered it, and we left it soon to wander round its bastion-road; a thing which was fairer far than all the pictures in the churches.[119] Long we sat in the grasses, tracing out the landmarks in the heat mist far below us: Montefalco in the foreground, Perugia behind it, Assisi and Spello a little to the right, and, sunk in the broad plain of the Clitumnus, just as Raphael painted them four hundred years ago, the houses and the towers of Foligno.

The Temple of Clitumnus.

"Hinc albi, Clitumne, greges, et maxima taurus
Victima, saepe tuo perfusi flumine sacro,
Romanos ad templa Deum duxere triumphos."
Georg. ii. 146.

Barely three miles from Trevi, just off the dusty road, in the burning heat of a brewing storm, we came to the Temple of Clitumnus. This marvellously romantic spot needs no description of ours, for the tiny temple seems to hold the very essence of what is best in pagan art and worship, and its praises have been sung by classic poets throughout the course of centuries.[120]

The Story of Perugia

THE TEMPLE OF CLITUMNUS

With the following stanzas passing through one's mind, one may linger very long and pleasantly down by the water's edge, and dragging one's hands in the cool stream, and looking towards the temple up above, dream golden dreams of river gods and hamadryads as well as of "milk white steer."

"But thou, Clitumnus! in thy sweetest wave
Of the most living crystal that was e'er
The haunt of river nymph, to gaze and lave

The Story of Perugia

Her limbs where nothing hid them, thou dost rear
Thy grassy banks whereon the milk-white steer
Grazes; the purest god of gentle waters!
And most serene of aspect, and most clear;
Surely that stream was unprofaned by slaughters—
A mirror and a bath for Beauty's youngest daughters!

"And on thy happy shore a Temple still,
Of small and delicate proportion, keeps,
Upon a mild declivity of hill,
Its memory of thee; beneath it sweeps
Thy current's calmness; oft from out it leaps
The finny darter with the glittering scales,
Who dwells and revels in thy glassy deeps;
While, chance, some scattered water-lily sails
Down where the shallower wave still tells its bubbling tales.

"Pass not unblest the Genius of the place!
If through the air a zephyr more serene
Win to the brow, 'tis his; and if ye trace
Along his margin a more eloquent green,
If on the heart the freshness of the scene
Sprinkle its coolness, and from the dry dust
Of weary life a moment lave it clean

With Nature's baptism,—'tis to him ye must
Pay orisons for this suspension of disgust."

See "Childe Harold's Pilgrimage," Canto IV., stanza lxvi., etc.

Spoleto.

Late in the light of a thundery evening we drove into the town of Spoleto. As our weary horses dragged us through the city gates, and up and under the walls of the silent town, a sort of terror and of gloom possessed our spirits. Here was something new and big and strange. What did it mean? Gradually we became accustomed to the spirit of the place, and seemed to realise the reason of its grim impression.

For days we had been steeped in Umbrian landscape as one expects to know it nowadays, in gentle fields, in lanes, and hills and sunny pastures—in those same things which gave to the Umbrian saints and painters the spirit of peace. Spoleto had none of these. Spoleto is purely Umbrian, as far as geography goes, she was at one time the head of Umbrian matters, but the town was always independent, a thing apart, or rather, perhaps, influenced by the influence of larger rules and kingdoms. Hers is a stirring history,[121] and the sense of her wars and of her dukes lives on within her stones, and is stamped upon her houses and her church walls. There was a smell of dukes and cardinals, of pomposity and vastness, even in the rooms of our inn[122]; and the very landscape round seemed throttled by the passing of imperial people. It was as though a great emperor had taken a peasant girl and dressed her up in gorgeous clothes and given her a splendid palace for a home. The girl (the gentle spirit of Umbria) withered, but the palace built for her remained, and the best thing about it—its grand supply of freshest water from the hills above, brought down in great Roman aqueducts—has never been removed.

As we pondered these things we remembered the brown roofs and the square of S. Lorenzo at Perugia, and we thought them better than all the grandeur of imperial powers stuffed into a narrow creek of the Umbrian hills.

Yet Spoleto is a place which excites a strong and lasting fascination. Its situation is magnificent. The citadel of Theodoric soars above it: a mighty block of masonry; at its feet the Duomo and the town, and at its back the towering crags, covered here and there with a dense growth of ilex, box, and oak. Town and mountain are divided by a deep gorge, but this is spanned by the Roman aqueduct, 266 feet in height, and the most remarkable point of the whole town. To get a full impression of Spoleto one should cross the aqueduct and walk or ride to Monte Luco, a convent built immediately above the city, in the midst of the ilex woods. Thence, on a broad bastion, outside the cell where S. Francis came to pray, one's eye wanders over a magnificent stretch of plain and hill and river, backed by a land of barren mountain tops and gorges.

Very few treasures of art are left in the town itself, and these are as bruised, as scattered, and unsatisfactory as those of any city whose history is one of fighting and perpetual sieges rather than of artists or of fame. Lo Spagna lived at Spoleto, and worked there largely; but the gentle style of his colouring, the peace and often affectation of his figures seems out of place on the altars of half barbaric or barocco churches. Everywhere there are bits of Roman building picked up and stuck about on pavements and façades: a painful mixture, lacking care and order. Several of the churches have good Lombard fronts; the Chiesa del Crocifisso is built from the ruins of a Roman temple, but the place is only a pain to see in its dilapidation.

The Duomo is a really impressive building, with a splendid Lombard front—a broad balcony supported by columns, and eight rose windows above it. The roof of the choir is painted by Filippo Lippi.

Filippo Lippi died at Spoleto in 1489. He was poisoned, some say, this Florentine monk, because of his loves with an Umbrian lady. Lorenzo de' Medici tried to get his body back that they might bury it in Florence, but the Spoletans refused, pleading that they possessed so few objects of interest of their own that they must needs keep the bones of this great painter for an ornament. So Lorenzo caused his tomb to be built in the cathedral of Spoleto. As we turned from the long Latin inscription written above it we felt that Browning's lines would have served the purpose just as well, and much more shortly:

*"Flower o' the clove,
All the Latin I construe is, 'amo' I love!"*

Narni.

Leaving Trevi and its cataracts to the left we passed in the train to Narni. We came there for an hour, we stayed a whole day and a night, fascinated by the marvellous view which met us from the windows of the inn.[123] Part of the city of Narni is built immediately upon the steep crags which overhang the gorge of the Nar. From this side the position of the city may be practically called inaccessible, and over it our windows looked. We had seen the Umbrian plains and valleys, we had seen Spoleto; Narni again was a fresh surprise, it seemed to represent to us the Umbrian Alps. The place has a tempestuous history. There is a certain beaten look about its walls which reminded us of Perugia, and, indeed, the cities are alike in many ways. Both were practically in the power of the Popes whilst considering themselves as independent republics, both fostering perpetual feuds between the neighbouring cities.[124] But whereas Perugia has kept an ample record of her past, that of Narni is almost obliterated. Through a piece of misguided policy she laid herself open to a horrible siege in 1527 (see pamphlet by Giuseppe Terrenzi). The Bourbons entered the town, sacked the houses, butchered her inhabitants, destroyed her considerable treasures of art, and finally, made an end of nearly all her archives.

In Narni, however, we did not look for art. We came there almost unexpectedly, and unexpectedly we stayed, wandering through its streets, discovering with delight the rare and lovely bits of Lombard tracery on house and church door, and passing in and out between the Roman gateways. [125] At night we sat in the quiet rooms of the Angelo inn, and listened to the nightingales which sang with their habitual vehemence deep in the ilex woods across the river Nar. They had sung, no doubt, in just this fashion hundreds of years ago, when the Bourbons broke into the town and half destroyed her people.

Orvieto.

In the dull light of coming rain we turned our backs on Narni and took the train for Orte. We left the sun at the same time as we left the green and wooded hills and valleys. The rain came down in sheets at Orte; and we found ourselves in the deadly land—the land of grey volcanic strata, bare like a bone, in the valley of the Paglia. Dreary enough was the outlook when we came to Orvieto. The city seemed as though it had been drenched in the ink of a wounded sepia; the streets were black and foul, the houses low and closely packed; walls without towers, dwindled and decayed rather than bombarded, and people with fever-stricken faces huddled in the square.

NARNI (WITH ANGELO INN IN FOREGROUND)

Heavy drenching rain of spring. Under the darkness of the clouds, soaring high as a glorious vision above the miserable houses—a peacock in a hen-coop, a miracle of marbles and mosaics—the Duomo of Orvieto!... No one who has ever seen the building can forget it, for it is like a great surprise; it startles and astounds one in the midst of the decay around it. Here, if anywhere in Umbria, the power of the Pope or of the Church was sealed on the rebellious souls of its inhabitants; here to commemorate a dubious miracle men made a dream in stone.[126] To describe its splendours were in this small sketch a mere impertinence. But if we wish to see what is perhaps the finest bit of Gothic work in Italy, if we wish to learn the power of Signorelli's painting, it is certain that we must come hither and study at Orvieto.

As we turned our back on the cathedral we wondered what it was about her people which had allowed them to foster such a mighty piece of purest art throughout a turbulent history. Certainly the popes had power in the city. [127] They made it a mighty church, they made for it an almost mightier well! When Clement VII. fled from Rome in 1527 he took refuge in Orvieto, and, haunted by the fear of drought in case of siege, conceived the extraordinary idea of building a colossal well, for which purpose he employed the same architect as Paul III. employed to build his fortress at Perugia.

Signorelli painted a picture of the Inferno for Orvieto, Sangallo built for it an Inferno in bricks! Feathery mosses, sombre ferns have grown across the inside walls of the great *pozzo* (which was built on a scale to suit a train of ascending and descending elephants); they seemed to seethe like sulphurous smoke in the dark and fetid air and we hurried from it gladly into the rain of the street....

Chiusi.

From Orvieto we went to Chiusi. The rain went with us too, and of the town itself we saw but little, only all around us in the dense woods, in the silent soaking air of night, the nightingales were singing their piercing penetrating songs of love and May. The air was full of the strong sweet voices and of the scent of growing leaves, of privet, and wet earth. Chiusi is a centre of interest to students of Etruscan history, and although the little town exports its treasures to every museum in Europe its own is full of beauties still. We lingered long among them, fascinated by the goblin birds which are perched upon the vases and the pent roof of the tombs, fascinated by the excellence and the variety of the greater part of all the objects in the cases. The rain poured pitilessly upon the streets of Chiusi; it swept in sheets across the lake and over the towers of Montepulciano, and we abandoned all hopes of going to the tombs themselves and drove away across the marshes and up the wooded hills to Città della Pieve.[128]

Città della Pieve.

... "j'étais tout de même persuadé que Città della Pieve reste la ville la plus merveilleuse de l'Ombrie," says

M. Broussole; and we ourselves in many ways agreed with him. The charm of the town consists firstly, in its situation, and secondly, in its association. It commands wide views northwards over the lakes of Chiusi and of Trasimene, and southwards towards Rome. The hill on which it stands is densely wooded, there is perpetual peace in its streets, it is the birth-place of Pietro Perugino and contains some faint fair bits of the master's later work. All day we wandered through the town, and when the evening came we found ourselves at service in the church of Santa Maria dei Servi.

It was May, the month of Mary. The people from the town came pouring in for benediction. They were nearly all of them very poor people, the men haggard with perpetual labour in the fields,[129] quiet and eager even when very old; the girls fair, slim, colourless, their shawls too well defining the slender slope of their thin shoulders; the children brown and fascinating, and the older women lost in prayer. (We have noticed that the veriest hags in Umbria seem to pray as though they fully realised the sins of their forefathers, and felt the present generation needed all their prayers.) Peace and poverty were the two things which were stamped most clearly on the faces of the congregation. The priests themselves looked poor and worn, shorn of their fat homes and privileges. There were not many candles on the altar and these they lighted slowly one by one. Then they begun to sing a long low wailing chaunt in praise of Mary.

It had thundered and rained since morning. The day died out in an orange glow which filtered through the hedges on the road outside and fell through the door of the church, gilding, as though with the softness of a vision, the groups of tired people. It rested with a wonderful radiance on the faded fresco above the chapel where we sat.[130]

In all the country round, it would have been difficult to find a scene more steeped in the spirit of pastoral Umbria than this one: the half-ruined church, the graceful tired people, the thin priests, and the faded fresco of Perugino; the whole saved from squalor by the splendour of the sunlight on the land outside the door.

We opened a book which we had carried with us on our journey and read the following lines:

"Oh! qui nous délivrera du mal de science! N'est-ce point folie d'avoir étouffé à grand peine tous les meilleurs instincts de notre être, pour obéir à la mode du jour et nous faire une âme critique! Adieu les beaux enthousiasmes! On n'ose plus aimer la vérité d'aujourd'hui depuis qu'on ne sait jamais qu'elle sera celle de demain! Il y, a des erreurs dont on ne peut se consoler. Quelle pitié de s'être prosterné tant de fois avec toutes les tendresses de son âme croyante devant un escalier vermoulu que des moines trompeurs exhibaient depuis des siècles comme ayant abrité la sainte pénitence d'un saint Alexis qui n'a jamais existé! Ne donnons plus jamais notre cœur à la vérité! Promenons sur les choses et les hommes l'eternel sourire de notre indifférence moqueuse. C'est là qu' est le plaisir et le charme de la saine critique. Tout sera parfait quand les histoires commenceront et finiront par ce gai refrain *Chi lo sa.*"[131]

* * * * * * *

Chi lo sa.—The words brought up before our eyes a host of images: hedges and fields, woods and plains, green with the green of the May-time: white roads and poppy fields, the oak woods under Trevi, the ilex groves of Spoleto, the long low lines of shining Trasimene, the marshy shores of Chiusi; and still more fair and more romantic, the cool green stream of the Clitumnus flowing beneath the pagan temple of a Roman river god.... That was the vision we had learned to love and know, with no attempt to criticise, and it was all composed of natural things. Dimly in the past we saw another vision: our study at Perugia. Piles and piles of manuscripts were there; books and maps, and guides, pamphlets, chronicles and histories—the records of men's doings, one and all.

The Story of Perugia

What about all this history, these interminable records of building and of quarrelling, of burying and strife? What in fact about all these Perugian P's:—*Persecuzione, Protezione, Processione*; Popes, people, painters, and *Priori*? What had all these persons done to touch or trammel permanently the eternal smile of Umbrian nature through which we had been passing? Surely there were lovers who, amongst the savage bands of men who skirmished down the hill across the plains in order to insult or to offend their neighbours, stopped to snatch a white rose from the hedges where they grew in thousands? And there were women, young and pure and peaceful, ignorant of the Pope, indifferent to the Baglioni, who waited for them in their homes—women with the faces of Bonfigli's angels, Bonfigli's roses, maybe, twisted in their hair?...

With dim delight we realised that whatever the doings of the past may have been in Umbria as elsewhere, the microscopic scratches made by him through centuries upon the calm smooth breast of Nature have now all turned to a delicate adornment. The war and the strife, the hurrying and skurrying to power have vanished utterly. Man's work is there: wonderful little cities of men made one with Nature now; frescoes fading into death around the quiet altars of forgotten churches, fortresses and wells and city walls, bridges and the tombs of vanished nations; new buildings rising here and there upon the old, new people praying or parading, where the old had fought and prayed. But above them all the balm of sun and rain, of rivers, lakes and watercourses doing their work.

* * * * * * *

As the twilight fell we left the church. Early the following morning we turned our faces northward on Perugia, but took a last long look at Perugino's altar-piece in the church of the Disciplinati. Faint golds, faint greens, a quiet landscape, with low hills falling peacefully on a low stretch of valley. No harsh shadows, no high lights, the shepherds crossing down the paths behind their browsing sheep. The Virgin, a type of purest girlhood with just enough of the woman in the way she holds the Child to show it is her own; young men, for kings, with angel faces, and the smile of saints; no touch of passion, no glimmer of pain ... that was the sense of the picture.

As we looked at it the people from the town came in to see it too, the baker and the smith, the driver and the local painter. "You see," said the smith, "it is a very beautiful thing this picture of ours; and when we hear it is uncovered we come to see it too. We particularly like that white dog in the background, and the shepherds are exactly like the life. We often come to look at it—how should we do otherwise?"

The smith was tall and slim and very gentle. His face was like that of the youthful king who holds the chalice in Pietro's fresco, it merely lacked the affectation, and his perfectly simple comments seemed to us more genuine and impressive than many books of critics. We listened to them gladly, but as we turned our faces homewards, we remembered certain other subtle and delightful phrases written by Alinda Brunamonti upon a work of Perugino. With these calm words we close a book which opened with the clash of swords and the conflicts of the Umbrian people:

"Sorrow does not disturb serenity; pain is at enmity with joy but not with peace. This Christian law is incarnated within our art. Peace and not joy is in her idylls; peace in the landscapes which are so utterly our own, and so serenely beautiful. How often—even whilst my vision wandered into the infinitude of sky behind our blue green hills, and further again beyond the outposts of the Apennines, and further still away into the depths of the azure-laden air—have I not said unto myself; 'This vision surely is of an insuperable loveliness! How therefore could our artists fail to be above all things *ideal* when Nature of herself had trained them in schools of such an exquisite perfection?' "

The Story of Perugia

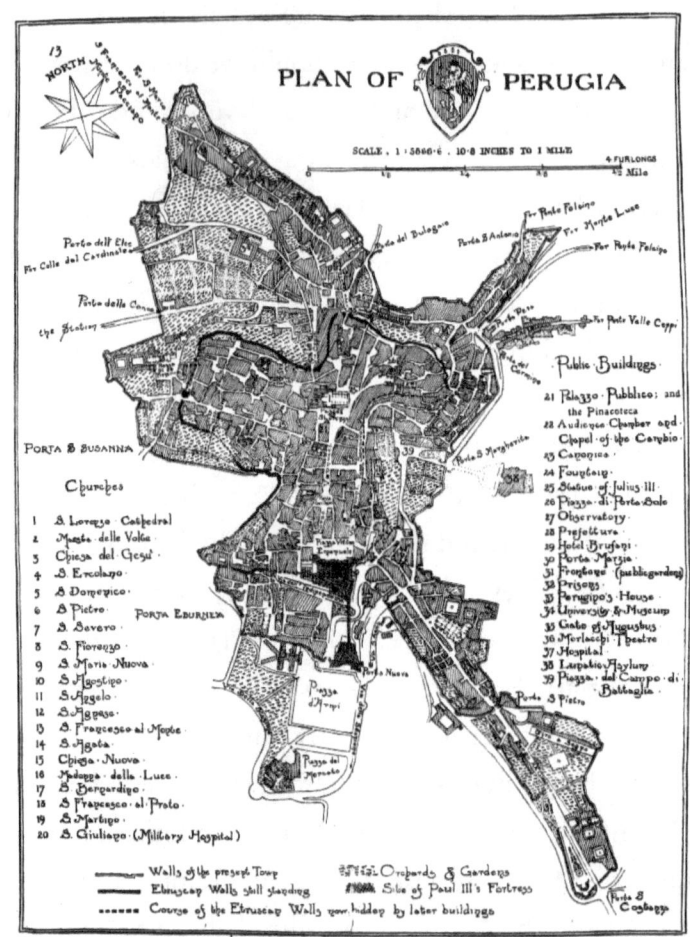

www.ingramcontent.com/pod-product-compliance
Lightning Source LLC
Chambersburg PA
CBHW030518230426
43665CB00010B/667